GESTURES OF CONCERN

A *Cultural Politics* Book
Edited by John Armitage, Ryan Bishop, and Douglas Kellner

GESTURES
OF
CONCERN

Chris Ingraham

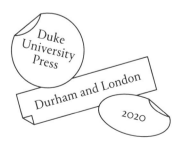

Duke
University
Press

Durham and London

2020

© 2020 Duke University Press
All rights reserved
Printed in the United States of America on acid-free paper ∞
Designed by Drew Sisk
Typeset in Portrait Text and Univers by Westchester
Publishing Services

Library of Congress Cataloging-in-Publication Data

Names: Ingraham, Christopher, [date] author.
Title: Gestures of concern / Chris Ingraham.
Description: Durham : Duke University Press, 2020. | "A cultural
  politics book." | Includes bibliographical references and index.
Identifiers: LCCN 2019051656 (print) | LCCN 2019051657 (ebook)
ISBN 9781478008583 (hardcover)
ISBN 9781478009511 (paperback)
ISBN 9781478012177 (ebook)
Subjects: LCSH: Politics and culture. | Social change—Citizen
  participation. | Political participation—Social aspects. |
  Communication and culture.
Classification: LCC JA75.7 .I54 2020 (print) | LCC JA75.7 (ebook) |
  DDC 306.2—dc23
LC record available at https://lccn.loc.gov/2019051656
LC ebook record available at https://lccn.loc.gov/2019051657

Cover art: Adam Milner, *Petals (in der Ferne locker, zu Hause unter
Druck... FOCUS 42/2015, page 6)*, 2017, interior latex paint on
magazine page. Courtesy of the artist.

THE AFFECT OF ABSTRACT EXCHANGE, THE FEELING THAT EVERYTHING IS
FUNGIBLE — WHAT IS ITS SONG?

—Ben Lerner, *The Hatred of Poetry*

CONTENTS

ACKNOWLEDGMENTS

It's fitting that a book about gestures should begin with that most gestural of all genres, the acknowledgments of those who have helped to make this book possible—many of whom may not realize that they have. The project that became *Gestures of Concern* began in Boulder, Colorado, where it benefited from the sound counsel of its first readers: Lori Emerson, John Jackson, Jens Kjeldsen, Pete Simonson, and most of all, Jerry Hauser, a true paragon whose wisdom is matched only by the delight he brings to sharing it. The project grew legs in Raleigh, North Carolina, thanks to fabulous friends at NC State University who somehow showed confidence in "my book" without my letting them read it: Grant Bollmer, Vicki Gallagher, Jean Goodwin, Katherine Guinness, Atilla Hallsby, Andrew Johnston, Carolyn Miller, Jeremy Packer, Dave Rieder, Lynsey Romo, Adriana de Souza e Silva, Sarah Stein, Nick Taylor, Steve Wiley, and Emily Winderman. Each in different (and sometimes indirect) ways influenced the direction of this book. Their support is on every page. The ever-sage Ken Zagacki did read the introduction before I sent it off, and readers should be glad that he did.

The editors of the Cultural Politics book series at Duke—John Armitage, Ryan Bishop, and Douglas Kellner—did not need to get behind this project, but I'm grateful that they have, especially to Ryan, who supported the idea despite his suspicions about affect theory. Courtney Berger at Duke University Press championed my writing start to finish and graciously indulged my questions over tea and emails as I slow-cooked through revisions and production. The manuscript's anonymous readers deserve special appreciation for their generous comments, which inspired me to be more assiduous about fashioning revisions commensurate with their insights. And in Norway, where the bulk of those revisions happened, I am indebted to the Fulbright Foundation for supporting my stay, and to my brilliant hosts in the Digital Culture research group at the University of Bergen: Scott Rettberg, Jill Walker Rettberg, Daniel

Jung, Rolf Ivo Beev, and Daniel Apollon. Their extraordinary kindnesses have made me reevaluate what real kindness looks like.

Along the way, my family, Peggy, Tim, and T. J. Ingraham, have been a source of endurance and support, as have a number of friends. Josh Reeves deserves the greatest thanks for demurring my misgivings as I bent his ear more than anyone, time and again, over several years, about the undertaking's directions and misdirections. Allie Rowland, with whom I collaborated on research adjacent to chapter 6, has always been a brilliantly mischievous stimulus and friend. Nick Taylor has been a stalwart confidant and sounding board throughout. The encouragement of my beautiful peers in Bergen, Maud Ceuterick and Álvaro José Lopes de Seiça Neves, has meant worlds to me. And my reading group as I was finishing this book—Nate Stormer, Bridie McGreavy, Jennifer LeMesurier, John Ackerman, and Candice Rai—reminded me at just the right time why texts and talk still matter.

Last but most, Caroline, Mayer, and Naomi. If this book's creation has meant suspending some pleasure, thanks to you it has never meant doing without delight. I hope readers will find some in this too.

THE SHAPE WE'RE IN

A reporter once asked Muhammad Ali, the American boxer, how many sit-ups he did in a day. Ali answered that he didn't know—he only started counting once they started to hurt. The idea was that only those actions matter whose effects have a perceivable consequence. The rest are just the status quo, the kind of condition our condition is in. This book is about a whole class of ordinary actions that resemble Ali's sit-ups in that they seem not to "count" for much because we seldom experience them as having much effect. I call such efforts gestures of concern. Maybe they involve some volunteering, or attending a protest; maybe it's just posting a photo online, or forwarding an email. Examples could as well include bringing a reusable bag to the grocery store as sitting phone-faced on a couch, scrolling through a newsfeed. Whether more forward or recessive, gestures of concern are efforts people make to join in public affairs in ways that feel participatory and beneficial, though their measurable impact remains imperceptible.

In contrast to the physical gestures people make with their bodies or tools to execute a task or to express a feeling or idea, "gestures of concern" names a way to distinguish another kind of gestural action, one that isn't quite separated from a body's gesticular movements (as if that were possible), but is rather primarily *an expression into form of an affective relation*. Such gestures might involve language, gifts, artworks, and more, but what they share is an expressive concern that acts as both a means and as an end because their most instrumental effects are exhausted in their expressivity.

The best example may be the "Get Well" card. When you send a "Get Well" card to an ailing friend, it's not likely that the card will expedite their recovery. The card is a gesture. Its value lies less in being effective than in being expressive. Expressive acts of this kind do not seek causally to influence an outcome. They seek to express a sense of concern. These gestures enact a spirit of sociality that builds an affective commonwealth. When referring to gestures throughout this book, it's primarily these sorts of noninstrumental expressive acts that I have in mind. Concerned gestures may well be as timeless as the more principally physical gesticulations humans and animals have always made in social groups, but they are prominent enough now to merit their own attention.

When the digital affordances of our time enable more opportunities to communicate with public audiences, the resultant glut of information available for our attention tends to reduce our social participation to gestures of the sort performed knowing they will have little discernible consequence. Liking, sharing, posting, pinning: these and other concerned gestures are rhetorical in the way that rhetorical questions are. No one expects them to inspire a response. The impact of concerned gestures is rather to spread an affectability, begetting new capacities for what can be or be done, and what can be known or felt in the thereafter of proximity to their encounter. In this sense, all concerned gestures share the tendency for their power to reside in a layer of sociality that is not the layer of meaning. It's not that such gestures are *without* communicable meaning or significance, but that they require no readable response to exercise their importance. In the same way that a lawyer "practices" law or someone might refer to their yoga "practice," concerned gestures are practices that operate in service of some objective while already embodying its attainment.[1] "Get Well" cards and other concerned gestures find people beckoning toward some potential that they seldom see actualized except through the realization of reaching for it. It could be the potential for equality, or beauty, for social justice, or happiness—or many other things besides. But whatever the aim, because its deferral does not extinguish its potential, the gesture of reaching for it typically fails to achieve a new *state* of being, while affirming a new *manner* of being instead.

Recent modes of liberal governance have bequeathed us a particular manner of being in the world. Whether these go by the name of late liberalism, neoliberalism, surveillance capitalism, or something else, it's hard not to notice that we've been drawn into more than a political-economic system— into what Wendy Brown laments as "a peculiar form of reason that configures all aspects of existence in economic terms."[2] Inclusion and communicative participation in public life now reign as arch values of democracy, while near omnipresent connectivity and social technologies make it easier than ever for people to enact these ideals as regular parts of their everyday experience. It was not just Obama who wanted people to believe that "Change" and "Hope" are reasonable expectations of life in the present day, politically and otherwise. Those promises are built into the very policies of participatory culture.[3] But no matter how much we Tweet, post, occupy, or doth protest, it can be difficult to survey the historical present and not feel overwhelmed. We're facing a sixth extinction of our own doing. Oceans are rising. Health epidemics are rampant. If it's not COVID-19, Ebola, HIV, malaria, then it's cancer, ALS, Alzheimer's, Parkinson's. Yet still there's genocide, nuclear armament, terrorism, shooting sprees. The planet is overpopulated. Refugees and immigrants have fewer places to go. Extremism rules much of global politics and religion. And everywhere the same old carnival of brutal -isms. All this amid a growing disparity between the rich and everyone else. But not to worry, we're told, there's an app or pharmaceutical for everything. Markets are bubbling. Surveillance is ubiquitous. Drones are overhead, and algorithms are calling the shots.

Against the melancholia invited by this state of affairs, this book aspires to affirm and justify our concerned gestures as affectively generative within a present nevertheless deserving of critical resistance. Such a project shares affinities with feminist and queer ways of addressing the feelings of exclusion and precarity, optimism and ambivalence that pervade so much of everyday experience, not just for those othered by the threat that their body or skin type, sexuality or citizenship gets taken to pose to dominant and normative exceptionalisms, but also beyond identitarian politics to those who already have everything they need to configure the worlds they want, but don't seem to want the worlds they've configured. Rosi Braidotti, for instance, describes such projects as paradoxical: "how to engage in affirmative politics, which entails the production of social horizons of hope, while at the same time doing critical theory, which means resisting the present."[4] At its most ambitious, to affirm inconsequential gestures as affectively generative is to reorient our modes of thinking or searching such that we see the potential for things to be otherwise than they are. To do so is to cultivate a sense of interdependence and connectivity that makes us worthy of sustaining such an attitude without succumbing to the cynicism wrought by its recurrent disappointment. In short, the problem is how to resist the present while still being worthy of it.

One approach to this problem—the one ventured here—is to explore some ways in which people are concerned to engage with public life through creative and critical gestures that disclose the potential for a new kind of togetherness, even if that disclosure is all they accomplish. To the extent that any potential is always expressed as a manner of being, an orientation toward a possible future that is not yet attained as a state of being, its disclosure can only be understood as a process, not its result.[5] We are hence given to acknowledge registers of communication that matter experientially, in-the-act, as much as they might matter meaningfully, in the act's interpretation. That is, to understand the power intrinsic to those many vectors of ostensibly ineffectual public engagement today, we will need to identify a stratum of sociality whose significance cannot without loss be reduced to its propositional or symbolic content. Once we fix this engagement into an interpretable meaning, we toggle away from the *zest* that accounts for a more elusive register of any concerned gesture's influence.[6]

There is no reason to maintain that we never see results from our concerned gestures. If you serve food to the hungry, you also watch them eat. Nor is there cause to suppose such gestures and the relations they actualize are without meaning. Meaning is like adventure on a journey; it's easy enough to find for those who go out looking. Yet, as an epiphenomenon of communication, meaning alone does not account for the "presence-effects"[7] that concerned gestures also actuate, and it is these effects that are especially important in a time when we are so inundated with information that now nearly anything can be signal and anything noise, depending on whom you ask and which algorithms are doing the sorting. Considering that communicative participation in public affairs has never been easier, while not much seems to change by way of socio-political uplift, it is becoming clearer that the usual modes of communicative participation alone are insufficient to bring about the kind of world one would like to make a home in.

Though this book does not directly take on the political-economic apparatus of our historical present, I am much persuaded by arguments about its shortcomings. Jodi Dean's important 2009 study of "communicative capitalism" has proven to have legs as her thesis is as true in today's time of diplomacy-by-Twitter and the op-edification of journalism as it was in the American political climate that inspired it with its own this-can't-be-happening realities. As a byproduct of neoliberalism, communicative capitalism promotes a complacent fantasy: namely, the belief that our communicative engagement in public affairs is a guarantor of democratic legitimacy, even a means for achieving political justice, when really the materialization of such ideals through participatory technologies tends to reinforce the standing order and entrench corporate and global power structures.[8] The pages ahead also indicate a partiality to Lauren Berlant's thinking, which seems to capture something of what it feels like to be alive today when she worries that our optimistic attachments to desires about "the good life" are actually cruel obstacles to such a life's realization.[9] But if communication's potential to bring about a better world is only a fantasy, and if our personal optimism is a cruel impediment to attaining its object, then that presents a grim outlook on change and hope. Where is the place for replenishment? What good are gestures of concern?

THE AFFECTIVE COMMONWEALTH

Gestures of concern help to build our affective commonwealth. In classic Western treatises about governance, the idea of a commonwealth reflects an earnest political obligation to constitute society in ways that enable all of its members to share its benefits in common. While globalization today may have created a kind of common world, brought us all under one roof, so to speak, that roof covers a house of many mansions—and of far too many shanties. Evoking the common need not imply some bluebird-on-the-shoulder utopia, nor the possibility of (still less the desire for) the homogenization of cultures or persons. A commonwealth accommodates pluralism and difference by providing those resources from which we all might draw in order to thrive in our own characteristic way. In its primary register, a commonwealth refers to the shared wealth of the material world: oxygen, water, sunlight, soil, stone, all of nature's cornucopia. "Nature," Michael Hardt and Antonio Negri remind us, "is just another word for the common."[10] By identifying an *affective* commonwealth in particular, I mean to indicate more than just our natural and more-than-human shared inheritance. For Hardt and Negri, the common also includes "the constitutive elements of human society, such as common languages, habits, gestures, affects, codes, and so forth."[11] In this sense an affective commonwealth is a bounty of nature and culture alike, or better yet what Donna Haraway calls "natureculture."[12] It references a shared sense of what it feels like to be alive at the present time, but as if that feeling were a resource anyone could draw on to make sense of their worlds and to affirm more sustainable ways of being interconnected within them.

Readers who hear in "affective commonwealth" a variation on Raymond Williams's "structures of feeling" are right to do so.[13] Both concepts are ways of designating a "social experience *in solution*"—a lived and felt experience *while* it is lived and felt.[14] Williams knew that because the felt experience of any social totality is only accessible retrospectively, at which point the feeling is calcified and gone, structures of feeling can only ever be a "cultural hypothesis" about a "social experience which is still *in process*."[15] There is always a differential remainder between what lived experience feels like and our ability to articulate it. For Williams, art makes up some of that difference by showing, he writes, that "in the only examples we have of recorded communication that outlives its bearers, the actual living sense, the deep community that makes the communication possible, is naturally drawn upon."[16] Where "structure of feeling" emphasizes the actual living sense as a residue, then, "affective commonwealth" emphasizes the deep community as a resource. Both are preconditions for any type of collectivity, yet also formed in the process of coming together into new relations, the experience of which leaves behind a set of new conditions with new possibilities for commonality—or its rupture.

When we talk about a commonwealth, we talk about those public resources, both material and intangible, that support a collective flourishing. But a commonwealth is always as much under construction as it is ever an existing resource from which we can draw. As I show in chapters 5 and 6—where I discuss a British community that built its own library, and various tactical attempts to disrupt Google Street View surveillance—to build an affective commonwealth through gestures of concern is to participate in fashioning a world capable of replenishing what it takes from us as we build it. As we labor in our jobs (or in trying to find one), as we talk with each other (or at each other), what we produce is more than just a public work or outcome (a profit, a road, a resolution, a policy). We produce a set of dispositions that orient us to one another and to the prospect of a shared future. All dispositions are affective. They involve the condition of experiencing social moods or ambient tones that influence how we perceive and respond to the world around us. Dispositions, we might say, are the affective shape we're in during any encounter; and, like Ali's uncounted sit-ups, the shape we're already in often isn't taken to matter.

This book urges that our dispositions do matter. They matter not just within the supposed limits of an individual human body, but within the social field itself. Our moods are as ambient as they are autonomous, as social as they are solitary. Many of those who theorize affect have observed that we all absorb one another's affectivity, which both builds a "me" that is more than "I" and a "we" that is less than "us." Social moods or tones are always shared, even as they contribute in shaping individual dispositions at the level of an enfleshed body. All dispositions are also predispositions, before *and* after they become readable, just as all conditions have already been preconditions, and are always becoming new preconditions in-the-act.

The "affect" in an affective commonwealth accordingly names a *condition of experiencing* a disposition, a mood, a social tone, but not the disposition, mood, or tone itself. This is why, to talk about particular "affects"—say, fear or desire, contempt or love—is already to be talking about something outside of affect: something only readable from a vantage beyond the unfolding condition of experiencing it as such, a condition in which the best we can say of any inchoate feelings there is that they are becoming what they eventually will have been. Affect, in short, as I use the term here, is fundamentally not representable or reducible to the expression of any particular feeling in the form of a readable emotion or semanticized explanation. Affectivity is only capable of being experienced in-the-act. Gestures are our best hope for reading the in-the-act itself as a collective process, as a commons.

At stake, ultimately, is the receptivity we have, often without realizing it, to being among others. These others may include family and friends, or strangers, but also the other-than-human, our very planet and its many animacies—everything for which we may endeavor to fulfill an obligation of togetherness that is in some way commensurate with our sense of an obligation to us. Gestures of concern build affective commonwealths by producing a set of dispositions that orient us to one another with an imaginable future in mind. In this way, affective commonwealths enable our astonishing appetition for carrying on in a characteristic matter and manner, even while disclosing that we are constantly changing as we enter into new relations, each with the potential to refigure the known limits of what we can be and do.[17]

MEDIA EPISTEMOLOGY

This project's exigences can be tied to its academic and philosophical commitments, and one of my foundational commitments is to the belief that what we can be and do is largely determined by our media: not just "the media"—where representation is paramount, as everything from fake news to Hollywood's dismal diversity makes evident—but rather media technologies in the materialist sense that Friedrich Kittler acknowledged with his quotable maxim that "media determine our situation."[18] John Durham Peters illustrates this epistemological power of media as well as anyone in his work to rehabilitate the notion that media are elemental (air, water, fire, clouds, etc.). A philosophy of elemental media supposes that media are "modes of being," the "always in the middle" infrastructures that both contain us and support how we are.[19] Media are the means by which we live (though often oblivious to us, the way a fish is determined by water but unaware of it). How my commitment to elemental media shows up in this book is through my corresponding interest in thinking through some of the ways that communicative capitalism's wider algorithmic culture acts as a media environment in which gestures are beginning to reconfigure the social.

For example, in the summer of 2014, a small startup known as Yo became the #1 social networking app in America. Billing itself as "the simplest communication tool in the world," Yo allowed people to text someone the eponymous greeting and nothing else. "Yo," you could send to a friend. Full stop. Even within digital culture's radical economy of symbols—all the acronyms, emojis, shorthand, and .gifs that have become ordinary parts of everyday exchange—this was an extreme distillation. Twitter's 140 characters seemed outright logorrheic by comparison. Were social relations really now being built or maintained through a *syllable*? Yo's success was short-lived, and likely owed much of its appeal to frivolous novelty. But the app's popularity among millions of people exemplifies one of the ways we may now be confronting the widespread validation of communication's essential distillation into *gesture*.

The time is right for such a confrontation. Yo's precipitous spike is one among many examples of technologies vaunted for their novelty and festooned with utopian promises (not to mention bounteous start-up funds), as if communication media could improve the content of our communication by making its transmission faster, more efficient, more multimodal. Having found word counts too general, in technologies from text messaging to Twitter we have identified a smaller unit—the character—by which to limit our exchanges. Across social media, in our profiles and feeds and webpages and texts, pictures too are replacing words. Efficiency is all. Swipe left for toward, swipe right for away. More than phatic communion—Bronisław Malinowski's term for the types of human illocution that preserve an "atmosphere of sociability" rather than convey any meaning[20]—digital communion strives toward the maximal efficiency of countability. Meaning is no longer primary; the countability of space occupied is.

The irony behind our gestures of concern having no readable effect and going uncounted like Ali's sit-ups, then, is that counted effects is about all that they are in their digital form. Kittler proposed that communication strives toward digitality as its ultimate expression: the elimination of noise. Whereas critiques of ideology throughout the twentieth century showed that ideology conceals itself by introducing noise into a modulated and layered structure of mediation, today we see that digital media eliminate that noise altogether. The indifference of digital technologies to the information they are capable of processing into binary code, which now includes nearly all kinds of information (sound, pictures, video, text), blunts the edge of ideological criticism that is inattentive to this indifference by focusing only on what is said rather than the conditions that make it sayable at all.[21] Digital communication technologies, that is, by being indifferent to the *content* of the communication they facilitate, have succeeded in translating the world into data. Google's computations don't care about ideology. Whether churning out a search result or targeting an advertisement to its ideal viewer, what matters for computational logics are the *effects* of collecting, storing, and processing some types of data and not others—effects measured by the onset of monetary data flows, clicks, eyeballs on a screen.

When communication is thus reduced into fungible and capitalizable units, those individuals producing or receiving it also get sorted into demographics, focus groups, and target markets.[22] Sneaking ideological content into public discourse is no longer the same when algorithms, working with exabytes of data, have so succeeded in fine-tuning media processes that they have minutely isolated the value and measurable impact of all digitally mediated information for its target. Witness the scandal that disclosed how Donald Trump's 2016 campaign team had hired the political firm Cambridge Analytica to help its cause, which it did in part by taking private data from millions of Facebook members in order to target ads to the most vulnerable potential voters. Although the public conversation about the scandal focused mostly on the problems raised for the invasion of privacy, conversation could just as well have focused on the reduction of political identity and conviction to static psychometrics. When attitudes and dispositions are rendered empirically measurable, they are presumed alterable less by argument or eloquence than by mere formula, by a rearrangement of some numerical recipe. Regardless of the effectiveness of such methods, it becomes clearer that the critical projects of most urgency for the twenty-first century will need to do more than look into the ideological content of our public engagement; we will also need to investigate those media processes and cultural techniques that control human behavior by quantifying our contemporary modes of being.

Because these modes are always contingent, I operate with skepticism toward the hermeneutic premise that meaning is "always already" available in any text or event, and presume instead that nothing is intrinsically meaning-full.[23] It is more accurate to say that everything is intrinsically meaning-able, but that this ability is only operationalized when so sanctioned by different configurations of an epistemic context. In this sense, I am inspired by the non-hermeneutic affinities and methodologies of Kittler, Peters, Hans Ulrich Gumbrecht, and others who are less interested in interpretation than in processes of meaning constitution.[24] How do such processes determine what among the meaning-able to make meaning-full? Processes of meaning constitution occur materially, in the conditions of possibility determined by our technical objects, for instance, but also affectively, through adhesions and cohesions that are no less material but more impalpably dispersed across a social field of bodies in motion (I discuss such "stickiness" in chapter 2).

Now that the digital age is several decades old and even so-called new media are growing hoary, we are finally in a better position to recognize some of these cultural techniques within the new ordinary they have wrought. What we begin to see is a great proliferation of concerned gestures owing to the conditions of widespread digital communication technologies amenable to their flourishing. The media epistemic exigence for a study of such gestures accordingly emerges from a particular conjuncture of primarily American and western European liberal democracies post-millennium, which has come to valorize "sharing" as the new great virtue of the social and political alike.[25] I am drawn to the sharedness of these gestures, and compelled by the prospect that there's enough "something doing" around their sheer prevalence as to merit a corresponding need for a critical analysis suitable to the cultural politics of their ascendance and circulation.

Though *Gestures of Concern* does not set out a theory of gestures as such, its commitment to media epistemology involves thinking of gestures as mediated acts.[26] The mediality of gestures is self-evident when thinking of gestures as physical bodily movements, but less so when thinking of concerned gestures like a "Get Well" card or holding a door open for a stranger. Along these lines, I am influenced by Giorgio Agamben's theory of the gesture as an act that exhibits the ongoing mediality of being human, what he calls "the being-in-a-medium of human beings."[27] If a gesture signals the conditionality whereby we are always *in* a medium—in society, in language, in our animal bodies—a gesture is not a message *representing* that mediality so much as a performance of the mediality itself. Paradoxically, a gesture is both a means and an end (and hence both *not* a means and *not* an end). A gesture, Agamben says, is the "communication of a communicability."[28] If there is one easily italicized definition of "gestures" I follow across these pages (and across different types of gesture), this is it. As the *communication of a communicability*, a gesture's fundamental inbetweenness acts as an ethical opening to the possibility of being otherwise. Agamben shows us that no theory of gesture is not also a theory of media. To the degree that our networked media environment today gives us participatory access to those public issues whose stakes many share, attending to the mediality of gestures (and to the gesturality of media) is also to confront the daily practice of democracy.

CREATIVE DEMOCRACY

The second of this project's foundational commitments also leads to one of its exigences, and that commitment is to what could broadly be described as a pragmatist set of methods and tenets surrounding the idea of communication. The denial of hard dualisms; the supposition that all experience is open-ended and in process; the belief that any idea's meaning, any truth proposition, any would-be action's value depends upon the consequences of its adoption—all are tendencies of thought with which I am, for the most part, in sympathy.[29] What pragmatism offers the study of communication is far more than its being somehow practical, at least in the sense so often colloquially misconstrued as synonymous with prag-matist doctrine. To the extent that what's practical in any given case depends on whom you ask—that is, on a situated point of view—pragmatism is anything but practical. Rather, a pragmatic view of communication privileges the *communal* aspects of being-with, of coming together mutually to participate in creating a collective world. This shared project, at least for John Dewey, makes communica-tion among strangers central to public life and politics, hence to democracy itself.

In 1939, at age eighty, Dewey prepared a short speech for a celebration of his birthday. Observing that he had lived over half as long as American democracy itself, he addressed the task for democracy that he saw still ahead. For Dewey, democracy was not a passive inheritance, vouchsafed by laws and statutes, institutions and procedures. Nor was it maintained through the occa-sional trip to the polling booth or by dutifully paying one's taxes. It was, rather, something to be created anew, again and again, and cultivated through a daily faith in the common person's ability to contribute valuably to its creative sus-tenance. These two pillars—creativity and faith—made democracy, for Dewey, an ethical ideal. Creative democracy was a daily practice of communicative participation with others, grounded in a reflective faith in the validity and worth of all humans, regardless of their differences. Accordingly, Dewey said, democracy privileges "the process of experience as end and as means."[30]

Gestures of concern, similarly, as end and as means, are one embodiment of such a process. They instantiate the ideal of creative democracy by virtue of the concern with which they are invested, not by virtue of the outcome of their effort. But concern is not always joined by intention. By invoking the idea of "concern," I will particularly draw from the concept's importance for Alfred North Whitehead, a process philosopher with pragmatist leanings for whom concern was the essence of all experience. Concern is that impalpable compulsion that calls one to action, not just from within, as a kind of auton-omous volition, but from without, as a distributed energy within the social field, impossible to ignore. I discuss concern at some length in chapter 1, but presently it suffices to say that it is concerned gestures (and not just gestures of a more generic type) that contribute to affective commonwealths (and not just to commonwealths of a more generic type) because concern is what inflects all experience with the affective tone peculiar to it. What matters is that today we encounter creative democracy as an affective mode-of-being that is character-ized by unprecedented cultural production and participation.

Online or off, expert or amateur, sublime or inane, nearly anyone can now contribute "content" for the public measure. Free market values encourage, and technology facilitates, the expression of oneself through creative media and the subsequent sharing of that expression with others in a public way. Today's forays into public life often take broadly aestheticized forms (as when people share pictures, post videos, dance in flash mobs) or involve making public one's critical faculties and aesthetic tastes (as when people review books, create playlists, "like" their favorite fashions). A widespread democratization of creativity is validating and enabling everyone to be an artist or maker, while an equally widespread culture of curation is legitimating and encouraging everyone to be a critic or trendsetter.

As I show in chapters 3 and 4, these developments are deeply entangled. As more ordinary people make aestheticized contributions to the cultural landscape, we have more need to spoon through the gallimaufry and determine what's nourishing. Yet the increasing value placed on encouraging and facilitating everyone's contributions runs fundamentally counter to the values implied by the need to curate culture as a way to sort the signals from the noise. The former value extols the virtue of free individual expression, as if all resultant communication is equally important as long as it comes from one's true inner voice. The latter, meanwhile, suggests that some types of expression indeed are better than others (they're more culturally salient, more deftly executed, more aesthetically rich, etc.). As more creative expression circulates, there's more need to curate it; as curation becomes more important, curatorial acts themselves become a form of creative expression. In turn, the tension between the different suppositions behind the drive both to democratize creativity and to curate culture gives rise to new forms of sociality surrounding public involvement in that class of cultural goods loosely associated with the name of art.

Art may seem like too stately a title for most of what goes on from Flickr to Facebook, YouTube to Pinterest, Tinder to TikTok. In using it, I echo an insight that Dewey had in 1934, when he wrote that "the arts which today have most vitality for the average person are things he does not take to be arts: for instance, the movie, jazzed music, the comic strip, and, too frequently, newspaper accounts of love-nests, murders, and exploits of bandits."[31] Dewey's account sounds curiously redolent of parallel conditions today, when some of the most vital arts include ASMR videos, viral "challenges," deepfakes, and trending Tweets about the latest reality star. Jazzed music? *How pretentious*. When referring to art in these pages, then, as when to "cultural goods" or any of various other near-synonyms, the aim is not to define a singularly complex category of human creativity according to any of its supposed values or necessary and sufficient properties, aesthetic or otherwise.[32] Rather than endeavor any this-is-art-and-this-isn't disjunctions, my pragmatic approach seeks to think about and enhance the ways everyday encounters with the aesthetic (including both its "high" and "popular" variants) can increase individual satisfaction and intensify presence to the common, inasmuch as it ever is.

The strange predicament we're in, however, is that the capacitation of people as artists or critics is making the social modes of their publicness more and more indissociable from the modes of their artfulness. Ordinary people are simply engaging with art more often and more publicly. It is nothing new to observe that we are now all photographers, writers, filmmakers—or can be with the easy click of some buttons. As art-historical treatments of participatory art have shown, the effluvia of our information age and its neoliberal rationalities over the last few decades have implicated technology and the arts alike in the commodification of sociality itself. The very notion of political engagement, of citizenship as a public subject-formation, is taking an aestheticized form. Creative democracy, in short, has become more "creative" than ever. And like democracy, art is less valuably treated as a finished product than as something always in process. It is, as Auden said of poetry, "a way of happening, a mouth."[33] The failure of any fixed *objet d'art* to represent a constantly shifting affective commonwealth is of a feather with the failure of any fixed political ideal, democratic or otherwise, to fulfill its promise without the daily public work of sustaining its possibilities—in part through our concerned gestures.

Another exigence for this study is therefore the unprecedented convergence of art and public engagement today in ways that seem so neatly to match Dewey's wish for creative democracy, while nevertheless leaving it hard to imagine that *this* is really what he had in mind. If there is something to be gained in Dewey's plea for a democratic practice that privileges "the process of experience as end and as means," then studying the concerned gestures that operate as ends and as means of their own might offer one way to gauge what that could be. A contemporary climate of political extremity makes it easy to lose sight of the ways that expressive concern for our social interdependence can take less overt or effectual forms as it gets refracted through public participation with the aesthetic. As troubling times beget troubled resignations, the less vociferous and more "idiotic" gestures that serve as their own reward become a margin at the center of public life that needs to be acknowledged.

The important question is less what concerned gestures *are*, than what they do or don't contribute to our affective commonwealth.[34] And we still don't know what repercussions the socio-aesthetic processes of our information age might have, particularly when it comes to evolving principles of Western liberal democracy, its ideals of citizenship, and the virtues of different modes of publicness. As the creative industries and creative classes rise in the global economy, infiltrating the quotidian exchanges of everyday life, the realm of stranger relationality known as the public sphere converges with a broad range of aesthetic practices, both creative and critical, and reconfigures how ordinary people publicly express and communicate their desires for a better life amid prevailing conditions of precariousness. Regardless of where one stands on questions about the collapse or corporatization of public spheres, about their digital revival or their transformation via social media, about their actually existing capability to hold the state accountable for its actions, and so on, there can be no mistaking just how "participatory" public life has become.[35] But public participation in issues of shared attentiveness is changing its communicative form, foregrounding concerned gestures nowhere more visibly than in cultural public spheres.

RHETORIC AND CULTURAL PUBLIC SPHERES

The cultural public spheres that often form the backdrop for *Gestures of Concern*'s scenes of investment are the contemporary efflorescence of the historical literary public sphere that Jürgen Habermas traced to eighteenth-century Europe.[36] As an "apolitical" precursor to the political bourgeois public sphere, the literary public sphere found the arts figuring prominently both as a vehicle for addressing society's supposedly common concerns and as a catalyst for discussion about them. In Habermas's Western-centric account, for the first time in human history, in coffee shops, salons, and reading clubs of eighteenth-century England, France, and Germany, strangers gathered to discuss matters of concern to them as individuals (such as troubles with their children), as distinct from their concerns as citizens (such as problems with the exchequer).[37] People could avoid discussing the particulars of their specific circumstances and instead refract their concerns through the safe medium of a story or theatrical performance known by many. The political stakes of such conversation may not have been overt, but by diffracting them through works of aesthetic mediation, politics could be left tacit within a more explicit conversation about identifying and achieving the life of one's desires. According to Habermas's well-trodden argument, the historical literary public sphere served to inculcate rational-critical debate as the standard bearer for public discourse when it eventually turned political.

Today, however, the reverse has occurred. As a retreat from the bewilderment and frustration of political discourse, cultural public spheres are predominantly an alternative to the space where people engage directly with politics and the larger problems of society, about which they may well feel rather disaffected because such problems are so vast as to be perplex, and because people are not confident that their voices will be heard in a way that makes any measurable difference behind the closed doors where political choices are made. Instead, cultural public spheres are sites of avid engagement with popular culture, including smaller fan cultures in all their vernacular and online variants, to which many people, of course, do feel more emotionally accountable.[38] When such engagement happens, as Jim McGuigan suggests, it "more often than not takes a predominantly affective mode, related to the immediacy of lifeworld concerns, instead of the cognitive mode normally associated with the experience of a remote, apparently unfathomable and uncontrollable system."[39] Cultural public spheres inculcate gestures of concern as valid ways of engaging in the more everyday implications of our social interdependence.

This leads to the third and most architectonic commitment that distinguishes my project: namely, its supposition that the lessons drawn from the study of rhetoric over the last two and a half millennia may be our best resource for thinking about what concerned gestures do for our public associations today. It is in the study of rhetoric, after all, that we find the first known writing about gestures. *Cheironomia*, the custom of hand movement and gesticulation, was commonly taught by the Greek Sophists as essential for effective rhetorical delivery. Later, Cicero and Quintilian described gestures as a visual accompaniment to the verbal: the gesticulating wave, an emphatic fist, shrugging shoulders. For the Roman orators, these and other such gestures showed a speaker's emotions, drew an audience's eyes in a particular direction, and amplified or reinforced the cadence of spoken language. The trajectory cast by the first treatment of bodily gestures within the study of rhetoric is with us still, though these sorts of physical gestures differ from the concerned gestures that are my focus. (As I discuss in chapter 2, the distinction is convenient but unsatisfactory because it belies the ways all gestures are endowed with some modicum of physicality and concern.) The concerned gestures that permeate cultural public spheres today may be more than supplements to speech or corporeal forms of nonverbal symbolism directed at persuasion, but that makes them no less "rhetorical." Similarly, the concern with which they're inflected is more than just an expression of emotional investment, though it is no accident that the first extensive theory of the emotions is found in Aristotle's *Rhetoric* (where *pathos* conditions the very possibility of rational communication). If gestures of concern help to build the affective commonwealth, then the rhetorical tradition is an indispensable guide for understanding how.

Above all, emphasizing rhetoric brings the question of politics to the fore. Since its beginnings in ancient Athens, rhetoric has been entangled with the role of discourse in a democracy: how ordinary citizens influentially communicate their will to those in charge, and how people reach common ground about issues of mutual consequence despite their different prerogatives and opinions. Insofar as any public sphere is organized by and through its discourse, all public spheres are rhetorically constituted. Among the many ways of thinking about public spheres available, I follow Jerry Hauser's because of his insights about their rhetorical nature and the vernacular role that ordinary citizens play in their constitution. For Hauser, the public sphere is "*a discursive space in which individuals and groups associate to discuss matters of mutual interest and, where possible, to reach a common judgment about them. It is the locus of emergence for rhetorically salient meanings.*"[40] In forwarding a rhetorical model of contemporary publics, Hauser suggests that although the norms of the Athenian polis are long gone, rhetoric's role in democratic life today has not diminished; it has merely changed its face.

Of course, rhetoric has always been an art with many faces. One of these is the practice of producing public discourse. As such, the study of rhetoric has been attentive to those axioms that a communicator needs to bear in mind in order to speak and act persuasively. Taken in this way as a practice (*rhetorica utens*), rhetoric is a reproducible and purposive art of composition, a *techne*, whose flexible principles make reliable guides for influential communication across contexts and situations. But rhetoric has also worn the face of a critical study (*rhetorica docens*), a framework for recognizing the ways we are influenced and persuaded by others. As a critical lens, the rhetorical tradition offers a vocabulary for thinking about the leveraging of power and the manipulation of truth (perhaps its very "creation") through the influence stimulated by social relations and cultural practices. In both faces, *utens* and *docens*, practice and theory, rhetoric is central to the ways people try to fulfill their desires or respond to the desires of others being foisted upon them.

Heretofore, rhetoric's long tradition has taken its basis in the presumption of humanity's symbolic wiring. From this view, it is because of our intrinsic capacity to be enchanted by language, or what Kenneth Burke more generally calls symbolic actions,[41] that rhetoric can exist at all. Short of sheer force, that is, it is the artful tongue, the sidelong glance, not always the argument that's best, but the one that most *moves* its audience—in a word, it is rhetoric—that draws people to form their beliefs, reach decisions, cast judgments, dispense praise or blame, and, ultimately, act. A rhetorical model of public spheres supposes that these symbolic-discursive associations are the means by which citizens come together around issues of mutual import and reach a sense for what matters most in order to act amid the contingencies of their civic and social circumstances. Indeed, Hauser describes rhetoric as "*the symbolic inducement of social cooperation*," linking his thinking explicitly to the prevailing view that rhetoric is possible because its symbolicity suits the innate human disposition to respond to symbols.[42]

But this book tells a different story. Instead of privileging the public speaker whose persuasiveness is held to benefit others through the passage of critical judgments, I try to privilege the conceptual figure of "the idiot," whose more recessed and unassuming contributions to the social fabric are nevertheless of consequence for how we get on together—or apart. To do so, I've tried to think beyond what Carole Blair also bemoans as the "tendency to equate rhetoric with the occurrence of symbols"[43] and instead to consider the para-symbolic, affective force of our rhetorical sociality. To stress rhetoric's symbolicity is to regard the generation of *meaning*—"the referential resources of symbols"[44]—as its principal interest. A worthy task, to be sure. And certainly, when it comes to conceptualizing public spheres, Hauser's focus on "rhetorically salient meanings" reveals a strong predilection to privilege rhetoric's symbolic character. But all persuasion entails *pre*suasion. The shape we're in. It is a matter of recognizing, as Thomas Rickert has put it, "that what is public is as ambient as it is salient, indeed, that to get at salience, we already reach for and work within what is ambient."[45] If the para-symbolic rhetoricity of embodiment among an ecology of other bodies, more-than-human things, places, sounds, environs, and so on affects our public lives just as much as the meaning or importance we customarily hold human agents accountable to produce through the whole range of rhetorical symbolic action, then the challenge is to envision cultural public spheres beyond the symbolic-discursive aspects of their rhetorical constitution without losing the precept of their fundamentally rhetorical nature.

That challenge charges another of this study's animating exigences: the need to push affect theory and the study of rhetoric closer together by addressing the reciprocal ways that affect capacitates rhetoric and rhetoric activates affect. While scholars of rhetoric have been taking stock of affect theory and its implications for rhetoric (particularly in rhetoric's tangle with public affairs), affect theory in the main has shown no evident doings with the insights that rhetorical studies might contribute to the study of affect. "Rhetoric"—including its scholars, students, and practitioners, as well as whatever that energetic thing is that goes by the name—has had to defend itself since Plato first attacked it as mere cookery thousands of years ago. But the productive ways that affect theory has animated (and been animated by) work in feminist, queer, and disability studies, among other disciplinary sites that ask after the politics of exclusion, attests that affect theory and rhetoric are alike in sharing a degree of separation from the status that would obviate the need for attuning to those vulnerabilities and privileges that delimit the political by constraining and enabling the social terrain. Running quietly in the background of *Gestures of Concern* is accordingly an effort to make kin by making conversant two areas of scholarship that have much to give one another: a rhetoric of affect, an affective rhetoric.

PROVISIONAL AFFINITIES

When I first began reading affect theory, an outsized part of its gravitational draw was its more poetic drifts through ways of languaging the ordinary yet wondrous weave of what living can feel like. Work by the likes of Katie Stewart or Lauren Berlant, and more recently by the likes of Joshua Trey Barnett or Marnie Ritchie, has felt importantly different than the trained conventions of the staid academic set that can seem, by comparison, to "all cough in ink / all wear the carpet with their shoes."[46] Though the illusion that there is something "truer" about the habitable *poiesis* of writing in a more speculative key may only be a byproduct of language's intrinsic legerdemain, it is a sensual magic that I believe in conjuring and letting enchant us nonetheless. Part of this belief comes from a sense that so much of felt experience is impervious to capture, always more-than-human, and inviolably more complicated than it seems.

> World is suddener than we fancy it.
> World is crazier and more of it than we think.
> Incorrigibly plural.[47]

Affect theory has opened a way of feeling through the "more of it" of worlds in ways that exceed whatever citable takeaways or tidy deliverables its insights may yield to scholarship.[48]

Though I try to do justice to that capaciousness in what follows, I confess to feeling somewhat amiss when writing about affect in the context of digital cultures, where the screened flatness of things, logical and clean and efficient, seems so inhospitable to the messy texture and topography of affect's many energies and movements. At their comfortable distance, digital connections just don't feel, for me, the same as the affective proxemics of bodies in a room, sharing air, occupying nearness as sensation. Part of my aim, then, is to enlist such an assorted archive of examples and cases as to keep a movement happening across the scenes and sites of this book's investments. To keep that movement happening, much of the discussion in what follows has been offloaded to endnotes. Readers wanting more might start there. Though this project may read at times as theoretical, it should not be read as advancing "a theory"—not of whatever it is we call rhetoric, not of gestures, not of concern, not of affect, commonwealths, "the idiot," or any of the other concepts I've enlisted as shoes to shepherd its feet.

There are good reasons, urgent reasons, for the (re)turn to affect and more nonrepresentational thought over the past few decades, one of which has to do with the overemphasis on language as the end-all and be-all of our reality. As the grim facts of a heating climate make evident and our increasing reliance on technical processes and devices utterly indifferent to their content makes tangible, the experienced world is as obdurate and filled with asignifying matter as it is provisional and created through signs. As convinced by affect's hereness as I am sympathetic with critics of its theorization,[49] what I'm trying to take on is a way around the baby-for-the-bathwater dilemma of how to conceptualize our public associations with strangers as organized beyond their symbolic-discursive registers without at all abandoning the crucial importance of the symbolic-discursive in their constitution. In an attempt to do so, I assess and theorize cultural public spheres circa the second decade of the millennium as affective spaces where public dispositions are formed and the conditions of rhetoric's persuadability emerge.[50]

The convention in academic books to preview the chapters ahead does no favors for suspense. While this book has no designs on being a thriller, its commitments to unfolding experience and processes of becoming leave me disinclined to do a précis of its chapters. Suspense is less about anticipation than about presence: the ongoing creation of what is still ahead from out of what precedes it.[51] Nevertheless, some words about structure are in order. The book is organized into three sections of paired chapters. Each pair works together to advance a modular argument across the book's speculative paths. Chapters 1 and 2 try to establish that argument's theoretical footing by addressing the central ideas of concern and gestures, respectively. Chapters 3 and 4 address the dynamic of "citizen artists" and "citizen critics" posed by an algorithmic culture that has democratized creative and critical participation in public life. And chapters 5 and 6 turn to the production of affective commonwealths before leading into a short epilogue that searches for some takeaways by rereading an essay by the poet W. H. Auden.

While the cultural and political ambit of this book is limited to Western liberal democracies, and particularly to American and western European contexts, I have tried to write in a way that acknowledges the larger purview of a time when networked technologies and globalized commerce—let alone global warming—make the topics under consideration fundamentally transnational in reach and importance. The three broad commitments I've traced above are not seeded like rotating crops in particular chapters or sections, but have been set loose to fill the book's rooms like a gas. Drawing on examples that range from TED Talks to stickers (chapters 1–2), from relational aesthetics to Goodreads.com (chapters 3–4), and from British pop-up libraries to hacks of Google Street View (chapters 5–6), I have tried throughout to show that gestures of concern—if not always understood, and if not always consequential—affirm a kind of togetherness just about anywhere we'd care to look. By being more call than response, and sometimes more ear than tongue, concerned gestures operate in between the symbolic and the affective. They carry both signification *and* its preconditions, both persuasive content and persuadability itself. Ultimately, then, the problem they pose is methodological.

The method I undertake in what follows can be understood as a nonhermeneutic rhetorical criticism. This is a speculative project that is not interested in interpretive "quests for meaning"[52] of specific texts or how they achieve ways of being understood. Instead, I feel around for the emergent and evanescent intensities of things, seeking those very conditions of experience within which affective encounters with cultural artifacts transpire. Enlisting an odd archive of everyday examples and cases, many as one-off illustrations, others pursued in greater depth, I tamper with the unanswerable. How to characterize something that is as semantically evanescent as it is ineffably lingering, a relation that can only be known in-the-act, only experienced, not represented? Even in writing at length on the subject, I have often found my only recourse in speculation, metaphor, tonal emphases, and partial glimpses. While true to the nature of concerned gestures, these may be unsatisfactory for a reader wanting the concreteness of "a stone, a clod of earth, a piece of wood."[53]

Nevertheless, I have tried to make the concept tall enough to reach the ground by approaching the texts and ideas under discussion with an attitude of *provisional affinity*.[54] This has meant starting not from a point of inherent skepticism, but rather from a hypothetical alignment, taking propositions seriously as "What ifs . . ." by trying them on to see how they feel. This is what I have tried to do by way of method with my curious assortment of everyday examples, and it is all I can ask of my readers in return. What follows from belief? Where does it take us? Though concerned gestures sometimes take us nowhere, they disclose the freedom locked within where we are right now.

Becoming more attuned to gestures of concern is not important for enabling us to produce more effective gestures, or somehow for scaling them up in politically efficacious ways. Rather, I wish to speculate about what happens if we suppose that before political change can take hold, people need to be primed for it affectively. How does that priming happen when overt political participation doesn't suffice? If one answer is through gestures of concern, then the payoff is not that such gestures alone are the solution to social stagnation or a route to political emancipation. Instead, I argue that without the daily work of building our affective commonwealths we cannot expect any meaningful change to take hold at all. Often, indeed, the very process of undertaking such creative struggle can itself be democracy's great promise and reward.

IDIOT WINDS

Consider the idiot—not the imbecile, but the introvert. It's a figure that goes back at least to ancient Greece and the assemblies of early democracy. A mass as large as 6,000 men (and only men), rich and poor, elite and commoner, is elbowing outside on Pnyx Hill, getting sunbaked. As citizens, their entreaty is nothing less than to weigh the course of society. Without loudspeakers or screens, they do so by using some of the oldest media imaginable: their voices. In these assemblies, those who stepped up on the *bema* and spoke, raising a motion or delivering a speech, became *rhetores*, producers of rhetoric. These were politically active citizens invested in the power of speech to help find and mobilize a "common good." Meanwhile, those who showed up but didn't bother to speak were known by a different name. They were called *idiotes*, "private persons" presumed by their silence to be either disinclined or unfit for the task of political action. Meet here the idiot, born from the presumption that public speech is the most legitimate mode of political activity. Anything else is idiotic.

One contemporary inheritance of ancient democracy has been the implicit maintenance of the fundamental *rhetores/idiotes* distinction made long ago. This has contributed to the glorification of discursive participation in public affairs, an enduring belief that the best and most effective means of working through the conflicts posed by our interdependence is to talk publicly about mutually impinging issues. Given the need to act at times when the outcomes of our decisions cannot be known in advance, rhetorical communication is what helps us to determine what matters and to reach a critical judgment that enables moving forward through exigent contingencies. At the root of this inherited approach to political and cultural organization are some other aging distinctions: between the public (*polis*) and the private (*oikos*), and the corresponding differentiation between a shared orientation toward public life (*koinos*) and a solitary nonengagement with it (*idios*). It is because of such splits that the very idea of communication, when it first arose in classic liberalism *as* an idea, came to be understood as a way of overcoming the taken-for-granted rift between public and private life, between society and self, between shared and individual interests.[1] Today these rifts are harder to discern.[2]

Yet, in our own always-on age of digital exposure we remain entrenched by ongoing ideas about communication and political activity that suit a different time. There is good reason, in other words, to consider the idiot. Doing so will mean endeavoring a new social imaginary about legitimate modes of public subjectivity and their communicative features. In these pages, I operate from the supposition that communication, as John Durham Peters once characterized it, is "the project of reconciling self and other."[3] As several histories of communication have shown, this project can take innumerable material, sensory, and ambient forms, spoken or written language being only a fraction among them.[4] But what would happen to our inherited norms regarding the role of communication in public affairs if we collapsed the very distinctions that characterize communication as a reconciliatory project and considered the idiot more seriously instead? "Suppose," Peters has asked elsewhere, "that we could imagine a society or a style of thinking in which the great divisions of self and society, private and public would not be the condition of our inquiries. Would we still think of communication as we do?"[5] Would we, I wonder, still regard those "idiots" up on Pnyx Hill as disinvested from the political project of cultivating a common good?

To consider the idiot means operating from different assumptions about what's involved in engaging the political as a project of configuring the "common" or the "good" in the first place. What if these early idiots, the so-called private persons who must certainly have made up most of the *ecclesia*, were not *withdrawn* from their stakes in public life, but rather *drawnwith* them into a different mode of the political? The question is not merely historical. I am interested in how the figure of the idiot might be reevaluated today when the planetary crisis we all share has never made the common more palpable, while at the same time the growing economic inequality, fractiousness of party politics, and social segmentation happening globally have made the very notion of a truly common purpose seem illusory. If to be withdrawn is to have been pulled away from the social, to be drawnwith is to be produced by the social.[6]

And if we are so inescapably enmeshed in a field of relations and encounters that even to withdraw from it is to exert some influence on the field itself, then it's possible we are missing an essential mechanism whereby the political happens as a common but still heterogeneous process of world creation.[7]

Recuperating the idiot is not a charge to legitimate ignorance. To validate the idiot as a conceptual figure is a way to resist the didactic, dogmatic, and missionary thinking that would deign to make assertions that can accommodate everyone. There's a queerness to the idiot, and a queerness to considering such idiot as a political exemplar for troubling times.[8] Acting with what Mel Chen calls "the ambivalence of queerness,"[9] the idiot does not know the best way to proceed from contingency to contingency. To the question of what's best for a so-called common good, the idiot draws a blank. The idiot doesn't have *the* answer to much of anything. What the idiot offers instead is hesitation, an interstice. As Isabelle Stengers puts it, "the idiot demands that we slow down, that we don't consider ourselves authorized to believe we possess the meaning of what we know."[10] By refusing the conclusive and decisive, the idiot holds open a space to think the indeterminate as a way of acknowledging that *the* common is always and only ever *a* common. From this gesture of refusal, the idiot accepts difference as fundamental without rejecting the shared as that which we are complicit in creating.

One way to cultivate such a new social imaginary might be to treat the inherited distinction between passive *idiotai* and active *rhetores* as more fluid. And with good reason. The reality in ancient Greece was that *idiotai* sometimes did speak up at the assembly, while *rhetores* were those who did so regularly.[11] *Idiotai*, in other words, were not necessarily unconcerned about politics or public affairs; they rather expressed their concern in less vociferous ways. There is no need to reject the proven benefits of more overt communicative action in order to think about how communicating in less strident and more oblique ways can still be a forceful kind of political activity. What follows, that is, if we presume that it is the *idiotai*, not the *rhetores*, who offer the more compelling model for thinking about the ways many people enact their concern for the public interest today?

To begin with, we would need to revise long-held suppositions about the importance of discourse to the maintenance of liberal democratic societies. We would need, that is, to undertake a scalar change in focus from situated rhetorical acts to the incessant rhetoricity of all being. And rhetoricity, as Kendall Gerdes has observed, involves a radical passivity: no matter how detached or apathetic, we are always on, always taking calls, always responding.[12] Rhetoricity in this sense is a command with no power, as it refers to a fundamental inability to not be affected. Shifting from an emphasis on *rhetores* to *idiotes* would accordingly also involve legitimating modes of public subjectivity that would otherwise be regarded as passive, distant, or disengaged. Doing so entails identifying less visible and demonstrative ways the body politic holds together, about like supposing that human bodies are held together more by our fascia than by our bones. The "idiots" up on Pnyx Hill may have been silent, but could we not suppose that their bodily presence "spoke" while their voices did not? This quiet presence would not be less important or, perhaps, even less influential than those rhetors who endeavored to make their influence felt by actively soliciting attention through their speech. It would just be less demonstrable. It would be less operative as an instrumentally communicated message, and more as a disposition or gesture—indeed, as a gesture of concern.

In the introduction I described concerned gestures as those that feel participatory and beneficial, though their measurable impact remains imperceptible. Gestures of concern convey *a sense of something*, a kind of involvement, maybe, or an effort, but seldom something itself. "What does it mean," Lauren Berlant has asked, "to want a sense of something rather than something?"[13] Amid the bewilderment of today's globally corporatized, information-saturated age, having an impalpable sense of civic involvement is often more compelling than being involved through a more substantive investment, particularly when such investments are a heavy emotional burden and so seldom seem to pay off. As Berlant has argued, although we have become good at attaching optimistically to the idea of a better future, communicative efforts to achieve it often falter—or worse, make it more unattainable.

Gestures of concern are those "sense of something" actions whose efforts typically yield no perceptible effects, while nevertheless building the affective conditions in which more deliberate modes of engagement might gain some purchase. If we take the idiot seriously, that is, we are compelled to think about different registers of the political, including the "aspirational ambivalence" that would hold the common open as an unanswered question so not to be depleted when its completion leaves you out.[14] And here's why gestures of concern are so important: attending to the "idiot rhetoric" of such gestures enables us to acknowledge how our affective commonwealths are built through expressive acts that serve little instrumental end, while still going some way toward building a shared mood or affective disposition that may become the ambient backdrop through which more overtly consequential actions are perceived and interpreted.

In chapter 2, I'll explore the gestural aspect of such actions at greater length. For now, the focus is *concern*, which is one reason the so-called idiots of ancient Athens are so exemplary. While they may not have done much else at the *ecclesia*, they were at least concerned enough to show up and listen. As a near analog today, and as a way to circumscribe the empirical and political locus of this chapter, I will focus on TED Talks, the global institution that glorifies speech as the best way to change the world. But instead of attending to what the speakers say, or to how and why it's been represented, the challenge will be to think about those "idiots" whose concern at least compels them to watch and listen. And the first part of that challenge will be to make conceptual sense of the concern that does the compelling.

CONCERNING CONCERN

Colloquially, the different ways English speakers use the word "concern" reflect its conceptual complexity. We might speak, for instance, of "being" concerned, or of "having" some concerns, just as we might say, "Pay attention, this *concerns* you." Each of these usages carries different inflections, here positioning concern as a generalized *state*, there as a *property*, elsewhere as a *relationship*, making it a difficult word to parse. Without wishing to elide these differences in usage, as I use the term in this book, "concern" names a way to talk about the constant activity of being affected by scenes of investment beyond one's conscious control. These scenes might include other people, things, stories, facts, moods, memories, attitudes, ideas, "skirts that trail along the floor—/ and this, and so much more." My interest, in short, is to think of concern as a more existential condition, in line with several philosophers who have done so before. Alfred North Whitehead has been my primary guide in this regard, but echoes of others resound here as well. Kierkegaard, for instance, called concern "the relation to life" itself.[15] Heidegger called concern (Besorgen) "the Being of a possible way of Being-in-the-world."[16] More recently, Bruno Latour has made "matters of concern" the cornerstone of his politics of critique by emphasizing the "whole scenography" of our problems, not just their facticity.[17]

For all these thinkers, concern is not just a way to describe the kind of orientation one has to something specific—a particular fact or some looming misfortune, for instance. It's a way to describe a more ineffable *sense of something*. "Concern" is a word for the broader condition of always having a vector of one kind or another. When we say we're concerned about something, what we're really disclosing is that we have such a vector, and all vectors have a magnitude and direction. The magnitude of any particular concerns depends on how an array of historical precedents are intensified through the immediate experience of the present. The direction of any such concerns then comes from following the force of that intensification toward a future yet to come. This means that regardless of our concern's *content*—whatever we're identifiably concerned about—the *form* of all concern follows a predictable set of inclinations. Maybe it's looking for a new change, or not wanting one to come, or wanting things to go back to the way they once were.

Here's another way to put it: all concern has the quality of being active. To be concerned about something, yet to take no manifest action, should not be mistaken to indicate any passivity inherent in the concern itself. If you worry about the melting permafrost but don't take measures to abate it, that doesn't make your *concern* less active. Maybe you just figure the odds of actually making a difference are too high. Maybe you're still gathering information. Will ancient viruses really be unlocked as the ice thaws? Whether because we are unwilling, unsure, or unable, our failures to act manifestly in service of our concern does not mean that our concern isn't actively influencing our ways of being in the world. All concern is active insofar as it designates an inclination toward or away from a particular constellation of attitudes about certain ways and conditions of living. In other words, we are never dispossessed of concern, never in "neutral," though it would be as accurate to say concern never dispossesses us. Concern is that chorography both "out of which" and "in which" all creative activity takes place.[18]

As "concern" accordingly names the constant existential activity of being affected from multiple directions, to name any specific "concerns" is always to reduce our more spread-out condition of concernedness to an isolable locus. Though there often is some object or event, a state of affairs or situation that seems to make our concern coalesce around a particular locus, to identify it is a misleading convenience. Concernedness is just too manifold and ever manifesting to be fixed completely on any single object. Moreover, to name specific concerns, to talk about them, and of course to act deliberately in a way consonant with their amelioration, suggests that they are intellectually known to us. But this isn't always the case. The pervasiveness of concern means that any specific concerns can also be incipient, preconscious, inarticulable. They arise from the inescapability of phenomenal experience itself, a living organism's ongoing sensorial encounter with that which is outside it—or better, that which it finds itself among. Though a human body might register an impalpable concern through its autonomic processes—dilating pupils, goosebumps, constricting blood vessels—often we don't realize we're concerned about something until some superadded factor brings it to our attention. It might be a headline or hashtag; a bite of a madeleine; some litter on the roadside. Maybe it's a heart-gutting photo or a sticker on a laptop. Awareness of our concerns can arise from contemplation or from conversation. It is often inadvertent. Sometimes the awareness is as subtle as an intuition: *something's off.* Other times we aren't fully aware until the particular concern has gone away: "I had no idea how much that was weighing on me."

In the same way that you've been drawn to these pages by some concern of your own, this book (like all books) is a product of its author's concern. What's been weighing on me is a sense that to the extent people notice the concern of others at all, we tend to do so only within a limited fraction of the many modes through which concernedness can be expressed. To continue thinking and orienting in terms of the old *rhetores/idiotes* distinction will entail continuing to disregard the latter either as ineligible or illegible. If someone expresses their concerns overtly in speech or writing, or even more subtly in nonverbal signs like a furrowed brow or quivering lip, it is easier to suppose their concerns are identifiable and representable. And because they often are, outward manifestations of concern have become associated with legible signs or codes that, through habituated cultural norms and techniques, we take to have agreed-upon meanings. Yet, if we could cultivate a better sense-ability, a better attunement to the active character of concernedness, we would begin to notice it in more places, and in doing so build the groundwork of an affective commonwealth. This isn't just about being perceptive or "really good at reading people's cues," which plenty of people may well be. This is about how misconceptions regarding the nature of concern can lead to misconceptions about productive forms of any particular concern's manifestation.

For Whitehead, concern refers to the "affective tone" that colors all experience: nothing we perceive and experience, even raw sense data, "can be divested of its affective tone, that is to say, of its character as a 'concern' in the Quaker sense."[19] Notably, whenever Whitehead mentions concern, he makes the qualification that he means it "in the Quaker sense"—without ever elaborating what the Quaker sense entails. We know, though, that Quakers treat concern as a divinely inspired calling to personal responsibility. Concern is what weighs on someone with the revelation that a problem or situation exists about which something needs to be done. Concern is the un-ignorable energy, often beyond self-awareness, that draws people toward one constellation of relations and away from others; it is the basis for any personal sense of duty to do something, if only manifest as a compulsion to give it one's attention.[20]

In practice, this notion of concern becomes clearer in light of Quaker meetings, which aren't led by a sermonizing pastor or priest or any of their ordained equivalents. Based on the principle that religious faith should begin in private, within each individual, Quaker meetings rather involve sitting in collective silence. From amid this shared privacy, which is meant to foster contemplation and, ultimately, to elicit a disciplined religious experience, sometimes people are moved to speak. When that happens, anyone may stand and say what's on their mind. Maybe it's a concern about the latest wildfire, or about paying that month's bills. Maybe it's about the local family with two young children whose parents have end-stage cancer. Whatever the topic, *concern* is both what occasions these expressions and conditions their very possibility. It is concern that draws Quaker Friends together in the first place, concern that incites some of them to speak, and hence concern that could be said to shape both the collective experience of individuality and the individual experience of collectivity.[21]

Whitehead is proposing that the conditions for subjectivity do not preexist the occasion of experience that forms those conditions, even though we always enter into relations in some kind of precondition, carrying affective traces of prior encounters. Emotional neutrality—true impassivity—does not and cannot exist. We are always, in one way or another, invested intensively in that which we encounter, whether we consciously realize it or not, and even as our encounters contribute to determining our very emotional register. The process of "prehending" any occasion cannot be separated from the concernedness with which we do so. The register of feeling that's activated in that process *is* our concern. And its centrality to all relations suggests that reason, the cognitive mode of disposing intellect rationally, is not a primary orientation toward experience, but that all decisions (calculated or impulsive alike) pass first through some kind of affective filter—"a background of feeling" that is always there.[22] This is why affective commonwealths are of such consequence; they give us a way to acknowledge those traces of prior encounters that remain dispersed collectively, beyond signification, as affective preconditions attached like stickers to certain objects, modes of relation, works of art, and so on. When we are compelled toward or away from these attachments, it is concern that does the compelling.

LISTENING TO TED

Despite the active character of concern, it is often expressed in relatively passive ways, as the mundane act of listening to a TED Talk underscores. The transmedia juggernaut of "Technology, Entertainment, Design," TED operates under the slogan "Ideas Worth Spreading." To assess the formidable influence of TED around the world today, the temptation might be to look at the content of those ideas its speakers and various ventures seek to spread. This would turn us toward the motivations of a global brand attached unavoidably to certain ideological commitments and agendas. What sorts of ideas recur in TED Talks? Do they share a common thread? Are there subjects or values that TED seems to exclude? Though potentially fruitful, to pursue such questions—for instance, by undertaking a rhetorical criticism of specific TED Talks, or through a content analysis of talk themes over time—would ultimately be to privilege modern day *rhetores* as the active arbiters of the political fields in question. By default, such methods would neglect to consider the important effort of those *idiotai* concerned enough to watch a TED Talk in the first place. How can we understand acting in these more ostensibly withdrawn ways, ways that seem to have no functional consequence, to be an important mode of political action?

Instead of locating political action *in something* (e.g., in the interpretable symbolic content carried in words, logic, or images), an emphasis on modern day *idiotai* will involve looking for political action *through a sense of something* (e.g., those moods, sensations, or feelings that constantly establish new conditions for what's possible).[23] This method could be described as nonhermeneutic in that it does not tamper with interpretation of meaning-effects through reading the usual suspects of sign, signification, and context. Instead, it seeks to identify the affective capacities for different modes of encounter, and the ways perceiving subjects are often unwittingly channeled into legible parameters for an encounter's sensibility. Nonhermeneutic criticism strives to discover a *sense of something* (presence-effects) before a sense of something in particular (meaning-effects).

One way we miss this sense of something is when we neglect to identify listening as one of concern's active modes of expression. When it comes to civic participation, certainly, we have inherited the tendency to valorize speaking as a more active contribution to public life than listening. The focus on speech at the expense of listening is odd considering that listening is at least as integral as speaking when it comes to processes of rhetorically fashioning our realities.[24] After all, speaking would be ineffective without listeners at the other end to do the important work of making sense of speech to begin with. Within the constraints of our corporeal medium, the human body does not overtly announce when listening is happening, and it's for this reason that we've developed ways to perform listening, what in Japan is called *aizuchi*: the verbal and nonverbal interjections people make to demonstrate that they're paying attention. Despite these performances (which, of course, can be deceiving), merely *to listen*, even to matters of widely shared concern, does not tend to be recognized as an active contribution to the work of sustaining a democracy. Instead, it's closer to a baseline expectation, the premise of any free democracy that citizens will stay informed about the news of the day, and that they must do so in order ever to make an actual contribution to civic life by weighing in through language or other forms of symbolic action. It's the vociferous *rhetores*, not the quiet *idiotai*, that have always been acknowledged as those whose involvement in public affairs matters most and carries the most consequence.

This is unfortunate. It's unfortunate because the ostensible withdrawal associated with merely listening is misleading. Listening need not be taken as recessed or disengaged, but rather as a different mode of civic participation, one that is just as essential (if magnitudes subtler) than the more overt communicative acts that any listener might be listening to. Listening is a social practice; hearing is a physiological process. Hearing therefore operates more or less uniformly across all normatively able-bodied humans, whereas listening takes many forms and varies across social contexts and categories. More specifically, as Daniel Gross has argued, our *purposes* for listening can vary; the *scope* of our listening can change; we can listen for different *subjects*; and listening can involve different tacit *assumptions*.[25] For instance, within a biblical model we might listen in order to receive God's word or grace (the purpose), which is expressed in commandments or prophecies (the scope) that are about the faithful or faithless (the subject), all with the premise that the spiritual world has a voice (the assumption). By contrast, in a classical model inherited from Aristotle, listening makes us members of a persuadable audience (the purpose) in judicial, deliberative, or epideictic contexts (the scope), where citizenship is publicly performed (the subject) in the belief that society has no place for a private sphere of self-interest (the assumption).[26] What Gross has observed with these and other examples is more than the insight that it's possible to listen in biased and partial ways. He shows us, I think, that if listening is a social practice, then it's important not just for us to become better listeners for the sake of understanding. It's important for us *to listen to listening itself*: that is, to become more attuned to the different conditions of contemporary life whereby we are disposed to listen in particular ways.[27]

A SHORT HISTORY OF TED

To understand how TED Talks have entrained millions of people to listen in particular ways—in a mood of intensified concern—it's helpful to know something about TED's history. TED Talks are three- to eighteen-minute speeches, delivered by individual speakers before live embodied audiences at TED events all over the world—everywhere from a floating hotel on the Amazon to the bleak icescapes of Antarctica. They're also filmed and edited, potentially to be posted as web videos online, broadcast on television, streamed on airplanes and mobile devices, or downloaded as podcasts, among other forms of distribution. Speakers are typically selected by invitation or through a competitive application process based on the supposed merit of the unique "idea" they hope to share. These ideas have subject matters as disparate as can be (the general parameters of Technology, Entertainment, Design leave a wide berth). The most popular TED Talk of all time, by Sir Ken Robinson, is about the educational system's threat to children's creativity. Other popular talks include a neuroscientist's analysis of her own brain after having a stroke; a "Mathemagician" performing astonishing mental calculus; someone teaching us the proper way to tie a shoe; and the singer Bobby McFerrin "playing" the audience as a kind of musical instrument, to name just some of the more than two thousand eclectic talks available on TED.com.

The history of TED follows two iterations: the first under its founder Richard Saul Wurman's eye, from 1984 to 2001, and the second under Chris Anderson's, from 2001 to the present. In its origins, TED is the brainchild of Wurman's dream to create a kind of super conference that would bring the best minds in Technology, Entertainment, and Design together to expound on the promises and problems of the coming millennium. Wurman had worked as a graphical designer and architect committed to the pragmatic principle that complexity should be made clear and communicable (he's perhaps most known for his Access City Guides, and for coining the term "information architecture" in the mid-seventies).[28] Under Wurman's guidance, TED conferences have from the start been associated not merely with innovation and novelty, but also with bringing the innovative and new to those entrepreneurs and corporate mavens positioned to give them wider cultural traction.

Though Wurman lost money at the first conference, struggling in 1984 to find three hundred guests to attend, by the next, in 1990, it did much better, and by the third, in 1992, his TED conference had become so popular that subsequent annual conferences often sold out a year in advance. Wurman's TED conferences were a yard sale of curiosities on public display, many of which have gone on to become cultural and commercial mainstays. Some of the first public demonstrations of the original Macintosh computer, of compact discs, Adobe Photoshop software, the Segway, the groundbreaking animation behind the movie *Shrek*, all debuted as TED Talks. *Wired* magazine began as lobby talk among conference attendants. Even Larry Page and Sergey Brin's first effort to publicize Google took place in an early TED Talk.[29] Such celebrities as Frank Gehry, Herbie Hancock, Bill Gates, the Dalai Lama, Steve Jobs, and others were known to come as speakers and then stay after their talks as members of the audience.

While Wurman's TED conferences drew an elite (if overly male) crowd, and had its fingerprints on many incipient commercial successes, it nevertheless promoted a conference-for-conference'-sake attitude, as if aspiring to bracket any ulterior motivations other than getting smart people together to see what happens. While many of the speakers under Wurman's watch did come from universities, others were entrepreneurs, independent scholars, inventors, artists, or just generally curious people who brought their intelligence and creativity to bear on interesting problems and ideas. In selecting this motley bunch, Wurman was more or less a one-man curator. His career and intelligence gave him the intellectual cachet and connections, and his propensity for the iconoclastic and provocative played well in keeping his conferences entertaining. (He once had a duo called the Raspyni Brothers emcee proceedings while juggling knives onstage as he stood between them, and for another early talk he asked a Microsoft executive, Nathan Myrhvold, to deliver a speech on "how dinosaurs fuck."[30]) While Wurman had no qualms about the high bar for innovation and ingenuity of TED speakers—a bar whose height he appears to have kept the discretion to set all on his own—the conferences also operated with the ostensive principle of inclusivity. Invitations weren't required to attend. *Anyone* could go, provided they paid the price. And here's where things get tricky.

At thousands of dollars per seat, Wurman's TED conferences consisted of a coterie of fairly elite and committed participants. Although these events provided some of the first public exposure to what are now among the most commonplace names and innovations, they certainly did so with a top-down vision of how ideas ought most effectively to be disseminated. Despite their nod toward inclusivity, then, Wurman's TED conferences can be read from the outset to have operated within the neoliberal paradigm that promulgated free market ideals as justification for what amounted to major exclusivity. Anyone's idea was free to compete for Wurman's consideration, but it needed already to be "in" enough to get his attention. Likewise, anyone was free to attend, in theory; all you needed was a ticket to get through the door. But the tickets weren't easy to come by.[31] Its conference-for-conference-sake ethos aside, then, the vision of TED that Wurman began in 1984 was never *not* implicated with tacit neoliberal assumptions and, accordingly, with the power brokers of a cultural and economic elite who might make it possible for the conference's "ideas" to be actualized on a wide scale. Apple, the Segway, *Shrek*, Google, *Wired* . . . it's no coincidence that TED had its fingerprints on their incipient public life. That's not to say there is necessarily a traceable, direct correlation between the presentation of such ideas at TED and their eventual success or growth into the mainstream. But we can say that TED under Wurman sold the *ideal* of a free exchange of ideas at a price that ensured those already included in the economic and intellectual elite very much remained there.

What amounts to the entrepreneurial bent of TED's first iteration would merely be an interesting observation if TED didn't also imagine itself as a fundamentally *communicative* enterprise. From the start, its whole structure as a conference involved individuals giving speeches to a captive audience, to whom the speakers attempted to make exciting but complicated ideas comprehensible. In other words, TED began not only as a tacitly neoliberal project; it was a quintessentially rhetorical one as well—rhetorical in the oldest sense of the word, in that oratory was its currency. This has remained the case ever since, as became still clearer in 2001, after the bursting of the early dot com bubble created an opportunity for a Pakistani-raised British entrepreneur named Chris Anderson to take over, and for TED's second iteration to begin.

It's under Anderson's guidance that TED became a global brand name. Though its flagship events are still highly exclusive conferences—a cultural equivalent of the World Economic Forum in Davos, with ticket prices anywhere from $5,000 to $250,000—TED has, in a way, gone public. Its major conferences are now only part of what the TED brand offers to an ever-widening audience, including online classes, a book series, a philanthropic wing, salons, forums, a social network, blogs, fellowships, podcasts, residencies, and, of course, its most popular offering, the filmed version of TED Talks that serve for most as their exposure to the brand. In a story all too common after the turn of the millennium, TED's website accounted for the biggest expansion of its audience. The site wasn't launched until June 2006, when Anderson and a partner, June Cohen, decided to make the talks at the conferences available as free web videos for anyone who might be interested. And interested they were. In November 2012, discrete views of talks on the TED website eclipsed the one billion mark worldwide, meaning TED Talks were watched by a global audience 1.5 million times per day, at a clip of seventeen videos watched per second.[32] These numbers have only increased, as TED Talks aren't just available on TED's website. They're now streamed on Netflix, broadcast on BBC television, made into podcasts, played on NPR, downloadable online, and can be watched on the seatbacks of airplanes. In addition, they have been translated with subtitles into more than one hundred languages.

The in-person TED events are growing rapidly, too. Under Anderson, TED began offering its brand name and operations procedures to community organizers around the world who were interested in bringing independently organized TED Talks to their local communities. These talks have taken place everywhere from Lagos to Leeds, Baghdad to Bangalore. On any given day, between five and seven "TEDx" events now happen somewhere on the planet.[33] Each of these events includes several speakers and hundreds of audience members. In total, over 65,000 talks have been given at TEDx events in over 3,000 cities and more than 170 countries. Most of the speeches end up on the TEDxTalks YouTube channel, if not featured on TED.com or elsewhere. Their staggering popularity attests to the sense of great promise and import that almost magically attends them. In a time of far more spectacular entertainments, TED has managed to spawn a veritable renaissance of oratory.

THE IDEA IDEA

How is it that this happened? The peculiarity is not just the anachronism of public speaking having become so popular again, hearkening back to the heyday of nineteenth-century orators and their soapboxes, and back further to the oral cultures of antiquity and their *bemas*. The bigger mystery is how—among thousands and thousands of these talks, many of them seen by millions of people, and many multiple times—almost invariably any given TED Talk manages to exude a sense of great occasion. There's a keen sense of eventfulness and promise that comes with a TED Talk, irrespective of its subject matter or quality. This vague sense may well be too preconscious to quite be articulable, too dispersed to quite be individuated, but it seems to invite a disposition to be moved and inspired by TED *in advance of* whatever specific aspects of the event end up inspiring or moving members of the audience. The power of TED, that is, lies in exciting in its audience *a sense of something* as much as in promoting something particular through novel and innovative thinking. For all its stress on "ideas worth spreading," it may be that TED's popularity has no more to do with the signifying content of any particular ideas than it does with the affective power of the "idea idea" itself. Yet, this notion that good ideas are capable of making a difference for civilization, however beautiful, depends on a still more fundamental belief that their clear and cogent communication is the way to make it happen.

Jodi Dean uses the term "communicative capitalism" for what she describes as "the materialization of ideals of inclusion and participation in information, entertainment, and communication technologies in ways that capture resistance and intensify global capitalism."[34] The concept is Dean's way of critiquing the reductionist thinking of the American left, specifically "the reduction of politics to communicative acts" with the result that, when it comes to socio-political protest, "doing is reduced to talking."[35] "Communicative capitalism" is thus a term for the state of affairs that finds the old ideals of talk, deliberation, and discursive inclusion to be ineffectual forms of critique and political engagement under conditions of neoliberalism—despite these conditions nevertheless vaunting communication as the great solution. These days, Dean suggests, when more people talk and fewer respond, the ongoing fetishization of communication fails as a politics of resistance before it ever gets off the ground.[36] Though she doesn't historicize the problem as a lingering consequence of the *rhetores/idiotes* distinction from which we've inherited the tendency to privilege talk as the quintessence of political activity, her indirect critique of that paradigm's shortcomings are self-evident.

Nevertheless, there is reason to be cautious about accepting Dean's thesis wholesale. Hers is decidedly not a project of recuperating the idiot. Although Dean may well be right to say that communication is often ineffective or, let's say, a necessary but not sufficient condition for a successful politics of resistance, it is also worthwhile to acknowledge a corollary truth: namely, that although they often go ignored, our subtler gestures of concern do have a consequence for rebuilding our commonwealth on less appropriative terms. Just because these gestures may tend to be more recessed and subtle forms of political action than the "communication" Dean worries we overvalue, that does not make them ineffective or unimportant. The force of our concerned gestures may not always be felt directly, or always intensely, but they have a force nonetheless. We will accordingly miss an important register of the political in everyday life if we neglect the affective power of such gestures and the concern that inspires their creation.

The concern with which millions of people are drawn to TED Talks is not just the naïve idealism of investing hope in the possibility that an idea can change the world. It's a concern that is conditioned in us through an apparatus that has become perniciously good at hiding its ideological basis. The question is partly how the concern with which people soak up TED Talks can be regarded as an important contribution to creative democracy, and also how TED Talks elicit such concern in ways that constrain its tenor and vector. Dean's critique of communicative capitalism suggests that the very principles once thought to vouchsafe a healthy democratic practice have, by being incorporated into a neoliberal agenda, become the very things that render public discourse ineffectual as a means of critique and contestation. Across her work, she has been consistent in her attempt to reveal the extreme limitations of publicly formed political critique when such critique emerges already sanctioned by that which it seeks to resist. For Dean, the virtues of "free" inclusiveness and participation resemble democracy but in practice fortify a system designed by nature to squash resistance and retain corporate dominion.[37]

In many ways, then, TED is a quintessential example of communicative capitalism's materialization. The pernicious trouble with communicative capitalism is its all-consuming reach, its ability to incorporate even critiques of its manifestations into support for its own program. For example, in 2013, the interdisciplinary scholar Benjamin Bratton gave an excoriating TED Talk *about* TED Talks. Describing TED as no better than "middlebrow mega-church infotainment," he unleashed a critique strikingly similar to Dean's worries about communicative capitalism, attempting to lay bare what he called TED's false premise that "if we talk about world-changing ideas enough, then the world will change."[38] Predictably, nothing changed. What instruments we have agree: the talk didn't go viral; it didn't succeed in hampering TED; it didn't even close the program at its own TEDx event (though pity the speaker who followed him). What it did do was prove Bratton's and Dean's very point. Talk just isn't enough. Feed even the hard talk to the beast; the beast burps and goes on its way.

What this all suggests is that TED does a lot more than just spread ideas through its talks. Its more powerful impact is to spread an affective disposition to believe that talk is important and consequential—to privilege the rhetor over the idiot. Here's how Chris Anderson put it in a 2008 interview with Charlie Rose: "When you think of how you could make a difference in the world, with limited resources, one approach is to nurture ideas, to find a way of communicating them and shaping them so that they can take on a life of their own."[39] In other words, TED is self-avowedly invested in improving the world through ideas so packaged as to thrive and develop beyond the immediate rhetorical situation of their expression. Ideally, this thinking goes, the best of these ideas will take on "a life of their own" by surviving in something like a Holmesean marketplace of ideas. And in that sense, TED's whole enterprise can be read as a tacit acceptance of the neoliberal paradigm that would value the expression of ideas on the principle that the marketplace will sort out the best ones, even in cases when an idea would endeavor to resist the policies that sanction their free expression in the first place.

In short, TED champions talk but only by tacitly conceding its dependence on a background set of not-yet-conscious expectations that go on to delimit the validity and worth of its content. A speech isn't only filled by its speaker with its idea; it's filled in advance by an audience made predisposed to believe that its idea might matter. By commodifying the public circulation of the very ideas that its enterprises are so devotedly committed to spreading, TED instead privileges the notion that *affectivity* is the most vital and galvanizing mode of rhetorical circulation in the cultural field. In TED's neoliberal logic, under the auspices of a free market ideal, it doesn't matter *what* the ideas are, but rather *that* people are attuned to them in optimistic ways—this is what gets eyeballs, impressions, bodies in seats.

The issue is that TED's commitment to "ideas worth spreading," no matter how laudable, carries with it an unseen contradiction. On one hand, it suggests that such ideas have an autotelic value by themselves, merely by virtue of being expressed; on the other hand, and simultaneously, TED suggests that ideas only really have value if they survive in the marketplace of their reception. There is, in other words, a tension in TED Talks between the beauty of inflection and the beauty of innuendoes: the beauty of an idea's mere expression, and the potential for that idea to "catch on" and lead to a new and better world. TED's steadfast insistence on privileging a particular kind of speech reveals that TED is hardly inclined to let all ideas and forms or media of expression run unregulated. Rather, in its strict oversight of its various enterprises—manifest through its curatorial, editorial, and ultimately rhetorical policies—TED's own big idea becomes glaringly apparent: the commitment to "ideas worth spreading" seems instead to be a commitment to spreading a certain affectability.

AFFECTIVE AND SYMBOLIC ORDERS

Many affect theorists warn against the temptation to conflate affect with emotion or feeling.[40] One way to differentiate these terms can be illustrated with a simple example. Suppose you're in the kitchen cooking dinner. Without warning, you clench in fright. You've just noticed that you've burnt your hand on the stove. But the pain comes with a strange realization: your hand must have been there for some brief time before you felt the pain. Cursing and wincing, you run your hand under cold water and look to assess the damage. In this scenario, the pain you experience is a feeling. It's private, personal, biographical. Because the same stimulus might cause one person more pain than another, the feeling is only your own. But your visible reaction—the fright, the cursing and wincing—is an emotion. It's social, perceivable, representational. Because your face and noises and bodily comportment convey to anyone watching a sense of what you must be feeling, emotions are semanticized forms of communication.

So where does that leave affect? If feelings have a private character and emotions a social character, what is affect's character? In this example, affect is the manifesting of a new potential world during that precognitive gap between when the flame began touching your skin and the registration of pain as a fright.[41] Because the body needs time to process all sensation, our consciousness is not a perfect reflection of an empirical situation, but a virtual simulation approximated by the cable-strong thread between the past and the unspooling present.[42] Inevitably, this simulation—what Brian Massumi calls the "virtual"[43]—misses phenomena beyond our conscious perception. What's missed is affect, the softest bullet ever shot.[44]

In the calculus of any experience, its division by the sum of its feelings and emotions, affect is the remainder. It is what will have been registered, often in the form of a feeling, and expressed, often in the form of an emotion, though it is neither of those things so much as their incubation. It is in this sense that affect is pre-personal, not-yet-conscious, asignifying, and nonrepresentational. Affect is independent of meaning. Because of this, it is misleading to talk about "affects" as if they were discrete, knowable, and nameable things, already full of meaning. Similarly, to label affects as "positive" or "negative" not only ignores the key question—positive or negative for whom?—it also reifies affect as a thing to be possessed or a tool to be wielded, limiting it presumably to a human agent and therefore according to a predetermined notion of a subject who delivers and receives it. If affect is subjectless, or at least intersubjective, then autonomous agency is less at issue than social capacity. Affect accordingly operates as a kind of shared reservoir wherein the potential for incipient meaning pools up, until, overflowing, it becomes personal in the form of feelings, social in the form of emotions. Affect, then, can never be accessed; it can never be named or expressed; it is only ever a processual pooling up of intensity that potentiates the innumerable ways, wincing and flailing, we might feel and emote our way through the world.

This, anyway, is one position of affect theorists in a tradition often traced to Baruch Spinoza's *Ethics*, in which he distinguished between affect as a manifest bodily state (*affectio*) and affect as an intensive force (*affectus*). For Spinoza, *affectio* referred to a body's patent emotions, specifically the great triad of desire, pleasure, and pain. *Affectus*, meanwhile, referred to the generative and mutually affecting force of one body's encounter with others, be it a human body or a flame on a stove. Theories of affect as force—the tradition I firmly track with here—invite us to recognize that a proto-phenomenological process establishes the whole basis on which our sociality might attain its various potentialities. In other words, when used as distinct from feeling or emotion, the concept of affect acknowledges that all volition has a basis in autonomic bodily processes and social energies that are blocked from consciousness yet responsible for organizing the whole realm of potential actions that guide how we find ourselves situated in the world. As Nigel Thrift describes this precognitive gap where affective forces accrue, it is "that small but significant period of time in which the body makes the world intelligible by setting up a background expectation."[45] I want to suggest that inasmuch as this notion of a background expectation gets formed not just within individual bodies but also between them, it comes to pass within an enveloping affective order that operates in a different phenomenal register than the symbolic order where our actions and language offer themselves to interpretation. The notion is not of a causal chain (of one order initiating the other) or of separate "events" (of a two-way relationship between orders). Rather, in a formulation Spinoza would approve, affective and symbolic orders involve coexisting attributes of the same activity, the way an exploding firecracker emits both sound and light in the same burst.

Imagine, then, an affective order of all experience that traffics in intensities, sparks, shimmers, glisks.[46] The affective order operates through folds and creases in experience, the surprises and habits that orient people to the energetic relations at play beyond conscious cognition between all bodies, human and otherwise. Now imagine its coextensive symbolic order operating through signification, representation, indexicality. It moves in discernible channels between sender and receiver, and always offers itself to translation or interpretation. For the affective order, moods. For the symbolic, meanings. For the affective, virtuality. For the symbolic, actuality. Affectivity is manifesting, symbolicity is manifested. Affectivity: expression. Symbolicity: representation. Relations for affectivity, objects for symbolicity. The affective order involves *pre*suasion; the symbolic order involves persuasion. At issue in the difference are all those ambient factors that dispose people to the possibility of being influenced, even though that disposition may precede an attachment to any particular object, signifying encounter, or legible text. We are dealing, in short, with different phenomena of sociality, of our fundamental *togetherness* with people and nonhuman things alike as an always-in-process dynamic that makes communication necessary for navigating the strange concatenation of forces we invariably find ourselves enmeshed among.

Walter Ong once observed that "ideas, even the most abstract, are formed not simply by interaction between ideas but also by the whole climate of an age and by an emotional atmosphere."[47] In other words, symbolic action never happens in a vacuum, but always comes stained in advance by an affective element that colors the horizon of its interpretability and influence. TED offers the aestheticized form, in microcosm, of the ways that everyday citizenship in Western liberal democracies now operates through a mash-up of the symbolic and affective orders that organize our entire realm of social life. These coextensive orders of influence account for how people creatively and critically respond with concern to the many adventures of social experience. Though it may not seem so, both orders of influence are equally as rhetorical, though the affective is fundamentally asignifying, not yet conscious, and only reductively attributable to an individual human agent because it always operates in between percipients in a distributed social field. Affect is always more than me and less than we.

The role of symbolic action in organizing and influencing the course of human civilization has been exhaustively argued throughout the twentieth century. The symbolic order accounts for this vast purview of language in everyday life and social organization.[48] My project is not to develop a theory of semiotics or to engage with those who have. Instead, I wish to feel and think about how the symbolic affordances of our public associations are always entangled within the affective orders that surround us. There is little to be gained from privileging one order over the other, but much to be lost in neglecting the affective on account of its apparent illegibility and the perplexity of discovering methods to access it. An affective order is terribly difficult to describe without calcifying it through the representational modes that its very value as a concept lies in evading. We have no recourse to explicate the nondiscursive except through discourse. Even just to identify the asignifying requires some level of signification, shearing the wool from the very sweater. And yet we might, I think, make some progress by reading for affect in those preconditions that endeavor to constrain symbolic action in a given context. As it turns out, TED makes that easy.

THE TED COMMANDMENTS

If you've seen just a few TED Talks, you might recognize their standard formula. Talks typically begin with a catchy, direct address to the audience and then segue into a narrative of the speaker's personal investment in the topic before offering a distilled research summary, an outline of potential applications, and a concluding entreaty to Go Forth! and save the world.[49] Almost without exception, TED Talks involve a single individual speaking onstage before a live audience; they're all strictly kept between three and eighteen minutes long (parameters TED considers the minimum and maximum limits for a succinct but thorough presentation); there's also almost always a snazzy visual component or demonstration, a slice of autobiography, a dash of humor, and a garnish of anecdote, all of it steeped in such genuine high purpose and idealism that white doves practically circle overhead. Unmistakably, inspiration is the unstated aim, and it's not uncommon to find audience members delivered to tears or drawn to their feet for a thunderous ovation—an impact that TED's editors make sure to include in the videos they post online. It's said that over half the talks at TED's major conferences earn a standing ovation, for which TED insiders have even developed a name: "TED moments."[50]

If it has become the rule rather than the exception that nearly any given TED Talk is affectively impactful, that is not because TED recruits only eloquent public speakers. Instead, TED mitigates the wide variability of its

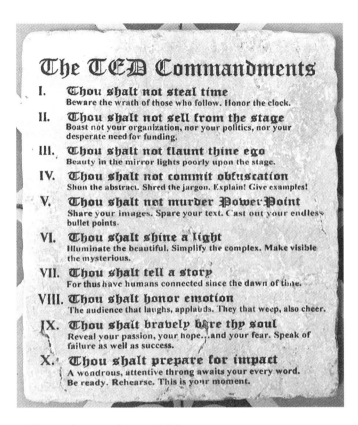

The TED Commandments

I. **Thou shalt not steal time**
Beware the wrath of those who follow. Honor the clock.

II. **Thou shalt not sell from the stage**
Boast not your organization, nor your politics, nor your desperate need for funding.

III. **Thou shalt not flaunt thine ego**
Beauty in the mirror lights poorly upon the stage.

IV. **Thou shalt not commit obfuscation**
Shun the abstract. Shred the jargon. Explain! Give examples!

V. **Thou shalt not murder PowerPoint**
Share your images. Spare your text. Cast out your endless bullet points.

VI. **Thou shalt shine a light**
Illuminate the beautiful. Simplify the complex. Make visible the mysterious.

VII. **Thou shalt tell a story**
For thus have humans connected since the dawn of time.

VIII. **Thou shalt honor emotion**
The audience that laughs, applauds. They that weep, also cheer.

IX. **Thou shalt bravely bare thy soul**
Reveal your passion, your hope, and your fear. Speak of failure as well as success.

X. **Thou shalt prepare for impact**
A wondrous, attentive throng awaits your every word. Be ready. Rehearse. This is your moment.

Figure 1.1. The TED Commandments, 2012.

speakers' oratorical talent by providing every speaker with specific guidelines—commandments, in fact—for how to deliver the most effective talk. They call these quasi-rhetorical handbooks the "TED Commandments." And for full evangelical effect, they even come delivered carved on a stone tablet (fig. 1.1). Similar to the way John Durham Peters has read the biblical Ten Commandments as media theory, I'd like to read the TED Commandments as affect theory.[51] These tablets, after all, exert an affective, nondiscursive impact that works alongside but differently from the message they communicate through the symbolic language etched upon them. The tablets, that is, operate at a layer of perception that has as much to do with mood and disposition as with what their commandments signify. There is an eventfulness to a stone tablet that supersedes whatever might be engraved upon it. With all its physical and connotative weight, the stone tablet itself disposes its receiver to perceive its content in a particular way, in a particular frame of mind—or better yet, within an affective atmosphere that invariably, if unconsciously, permeates the interpretive reception of everything encountered from within it.

What are we to make of these TED Commandments? Ironical fun? Arch gravitas, delivered as from on high? Each begins with the faux-imperious "Thou shalt . . ." and goes on to prescribe both TED's general rules (no product promotion, restricted time limits, etc.) and a set of ideals and axioms about what makes an effective public speech. Taken, that is, as a list of those rhetorical fundamentals most equipped to sell an impactful idea, the commandments disclose TED's version of what constitutes a successful impact in the first place. And a successful impact within TED's ecology of values, it appears, derives more from an emotional influence than a rational, cognitive one. Not only does the stone tablet convey an affective tone that colors it in a particular light; the TED Commandments reveal that TED wants each of its talks to create a particular atmosphere in which its "ideas" will be received:

1. Thou shalt not steal time
   Beware the wrath of those who follow. Honor the clock.
2. Thou shalt not sell from the stage
   Boast not your organization, nor your politics, nor your desperate need for funding.
3. Thou shalt not flaunt thine ego
   Beauty in the mirror lights poorly upon the stage.
4. Thou shalt not commit obfuscation
   Shun the abstract. Shred the jargon. Explain! Give examples!
5. Thou shalt not murder PowerPoint
   Spare your images. Spare your text. Cast out your endless bullet points.
6. Thou shalt shine a light.
   Illuminate the beautiful. Simplify the mysterious. Make visible the mysterious.
7. Thou shalt tell a story.
   For thus have humans connected since the dawn of time.
8. Thou shalt honor emotion.
   The audience that laughs, applauds. They that weep, also cheer.
9. Thou shalt bravely bare the soul.
   Reveal your passion, your hope . . . and your fear. Speak of failure as well as success.
10. Thou shalt prepare for impact.
    A wondrous, attentive throng awaits your every word. Be ready. Rehearse. This is your moment.

The TED Commandments have been through at least three iterations since their outset (apparently, nothing is etched in stone, even what's etched in stone). But closer inspection of even just the first version reveals something different and more essential than what we could learn from a rhetorical criticism or content analysis of any TED Talks themselves. Take Version One, Commandment VIII: "Thou shalt honor emotion. The audience that laughs, applauds. They that weep, also cheer." This prescription seems to hold audience applause and vocal approval as a talk's objective (as opposed, say, to the audience's ratiocinated comprehension of an argument's validity). To "honor emotion" seems less to mean encouraging the *speaker* to emote than to elicit the audience's emotion, in this case its laughter or tears. But to do so is, at the same time, an entreaty to avoid the robotic and calculated, the cold and imperious, the preachy and high-handed. In a way, we are right back in the Scottish Enlightenment, when George Campbell sought to upend the age-old Western tradition of taking reason as the principal doctrine of evidence for the validity of ideas and, by emphasizing the passions, to relocate it instead in the percipient's commonsense intuition, a common sense grounded in "truths so plain, that no man can doubt them."[52] Certainly this plainness is codified in Commandment IV: "Thou shalt not commit obfuscation." But it's also evident in Commandment V: "Thou shalt not murder PowerPoint," which entreats speakers to "Share your images. Spare your text." As with all these guidelines, the goal is an efficient enthrallment, in this last case better achieved through a picture than the thousand words it's worth.

At first blush, each of these rules seems to instantiate what Richard Lanham calls the C-B-S ideal of communication, so named for its emphasis on clarity, brevity, sincerity. There's something pure and noble, certainly simple, about a C-B-S or "informationist" conception of communication, which holds as its ultimate value the conveyance of meaning. Lanham identifies the C-B-S model as "the standard model we use for human communication" and notes its "economic basis."[53] As an economically based model, it treats language essentially as a commodity, making its expressive ideal a matter of maximally efficient transmission. All ornamentation and stylization, all flourish and fluff—in a word, the wrappings that most people call "rhetoric"—are therefore to be avoided. "'Rhetoric,'" Lanham says, is "the general term of abuse we now use for everything not conforming to C-B-S code."[54] Defenders of the age-old study of rhetoric, Lanham among them, have accordingly indicted the C-B-S model as overly simplistic and ignorant of the context-dependent nature of all communication in a lived world where case-by-case variability demands changing necessities.

But for TED and its mission of spreading worthwhile ideas, the C-B-S view does seem like a perfect fit given the striking similarities between its economic basis and the informationist or mathematical model that underwrites digital culture today.[55] Where an economic approach imagines words as things, as fungible deliverables for efficient, unadorned transmission, a mathematical model imagines communication as a process of sorting the signal from the noise, hence of reducing all excess and distraction.[56] Both would deny the relevance of any superadded element—emotion, volume, rhythm, and so on—to communicative transmissions, seeing them instead as distortions or distractions from the goal of being efficient, fast, and lossless, which ones and zeroes are really good at doing. (By contrast, it is precisely these intangible superadded elements that theories of rhetoric have widely understood to give communication its influential force.[57]) In short, if the TED Commandments abide an economic-cum-mathematical approach to communication, manifest in its general adherence to a C-B-S model, that would make some sense in light of TED's inclinations toward free market principles and the Silicon Valley utopianism that sees in digital technologies their materialization.

But in practice TED does something different. The Commandments' explicit emphasis on clarity (Commandment IV), brevity (Commandment I), and sincerity (Commandment IX) is not alone for the purpose of delivering an idea as if it were a thing packaged in words and stripped of all fluff to achieve maximally lossless meaning transmission. Behind each of these rules, it is hard not to see another unstated mantra: *Make them feel as much as you make them think.* Why else the emphasis on pictures over bullet points, stories over politics, emotion over jargon, beauty over complexity? Taken as a whole bigger than its parts, the TED Commandments are interested in prescribing a general template for TED Talks that would restrict them to a relatively narrow band of oratorical diversity. It is as if a range of singers were told to sing whichever song they like, provided they sing it in the style of a courtly ballad. This doesn't remove "the rhetoric" from TED's speeches (how could it?), but it endeavors to conceal it behind a C-B-S approach whose very parameters for interpretability exclude up-front the validity of an "idiot rhetoric" that would sooner stammer than speak in well-turned phrases.[58]

TOWARD AN IDIOT RHETORIC

This chapter began with a tentative entreaty: to consider the idiot. The fifteenth-century theologian Nicholas of Cusa was probably the first to consider the figure of the idiot with any concerted focus,[59] but the better cue to follow may come from Gilles Deleuze and Félix Guattari, who wrote in their last collaborative work about two kinds of historical idiot, the old and the new. The old idiot, they explain, "is the private thinker, in contrast to the public teacher."[60] While the public teacher "refers constantly to taught concepts," the private thinker forms concepts on his own, using "the innate forces that everyone possesses on their own account by right ('I think')."[61] This old idiot—modeled on the *idiotes* from the Athenian *ecclesia*—wanted indubitable truths, but wanted to arrive at them by himself, without being told. By contrast, Deleuze and Guattari's "new idiot"—modeled on the eponymous hero of Dostoevsky's 1874 novel—has no wish for indubitable truths, but "wants the lost, the incomprehensible, and the absurd to be restored to him."[62] To consider the idiot is to challenge the illusion that's baked into TED Talks and so much of the cultural field today: specifically, the fantasy that the social traction of communicative acts comes from the fixed "content," "information," or "ideas" they convey, and not at least as much from the affective scenography in which they're received.

When it comes to TED Talks, that scenography is subtle but powerful. Whether it's the TED Commandments, the high production values of their videos, the 136-page manual that TED gives TEDx organizers to micromanage their events, or many other ways besides, TED events conspire to inspire a feeling that now seems nearly atavistic: the possibility that an individual can stand before an audience and, with the power of words, communicate an idea that can change the world. But if these communicable ideas themselves circulate in the symbolic order, the ineffable feeling around them circulates more affectively, as an idiot rhetoric impervious to capture. Where the rhetorical judgments made symbolically serve to achieve the communicative transmission of a message, rhetorical orientations formed affectively may never reach the layer of meaning at all. If the former works its influence to achieve understanding, the latter works its influence to create cohesion.

The difference can be mapped onto what James Carey has described as the transmission and ritual views of communication. In the first case, the transmission view supposes that the idea of "communication" involves the transmission or transportation of signals, messages, or goods—i.e., *information* of one kind or another—across space to control people and distance.[63] A ritual view of communication, conversely, does not bother with the extension of messages in space so much as maintaining society over time, "not the act of imparting information but the representation of shared beliefs."[64] We might think of one's morning coffee or tea along these lines. Brewing and drinking your daily cuppa can be viewed as a transmission, the functional transference of caffeine from the beverage into your bloodstream in order to wake up. Or it can be viewed as a ritual, the ceremonial routine that paces your participatory entrance into a new day. If the former is measured in milligrams (a quantity), the latter is measured in wafting steam and clouding milk (a quality).

What we're beginning to see today, and TED Talks are only one example, is the confluence of transmission and ritual views of communication, particularly vis-à-vis emergent ideals of "democratic" and "participatory" engagement in public life. Though Carey himself acknowledged that the transmission and ritual views were not incompatible, that each could coexist with the other in the same communicative act, he did not address the extent to which their convergence has come to indicate a third view altogether. We might call this view the "ritual transmission" model. Insofar as the transmission view is linked with control over space and people through organized efficiencies, and the ritual view with the maintenance of society through shared symbolic practices, the former can be associated loosely with the political and the latter loosely with the cultural. By extension, this makes the "ritual transmission" view the realm of cultural politics.

In ritual transmissions, the ritual *is* the information. That is, the ritual itself has become that which is transmitted as an abstract exchange. Here, the spiritual, experiential, and community-building qualities of ritual communication do not disappear, but they get flattened into a deliverable, into data. When ritual becomes transmitted as a sum of its parts, there is no room for an affective remainder beyond what can be appropriated by the logic of transmission. The ritual, reduced to its reducibility, becomes fungible: still ritual—social, temporal, shared, felt—but always a transmission insofar as the ritual is set up to transpire on information's bald horizon. An "idiot rhetoric" is one that refuses this reduction, restoring the incomprehensible, the unfinalizable, and the unpredeterminable as a source of rhetorical influence even if it operates adjacent to or outside symbolic means.

Rhetoric has long depended on the valorization of a unified subject, whether on the speaker's side (what Quintilian called the "good man speaking well") or on the audience's side (by preconstituted notions of those for speech to be *subjected to*).[65] Such versions of rhetoric are representational insofar as they always re-present a subject formation already there.[66] But no change can happen when the speaker is already regarded as one subject, the audience as another, and each taken as givens of the conditions necessary for rhetoric to exist. Considering the idiot as a conceptual figure for troubling times enables a new way of "thinking the subject" *without* thinking the subject—that is, a way of thinking about political subjectivity without presuming it to take a predetermined communicative form or to come from a source already known in advance. As Mikhail Bakhtin once wrote of Dostoevsky's writing, the aim is to resist the "degrading reification of a person's soul, a discounting of its freedom and its unfinalizability."[67] If we do, we see that the *idiotes* from antiquity were just as "rhetorical" as the *rhetors* who bore that designation, though their influence operated in a different key.

The concern of the listening idiot is always commanded by an affective scenography of material and technical factors that capacitate its extensions. The TED Commandments do this materially, irrespective of what they literally command, just by virtue of arriving packed in dissolvable starch peanuts and being carved on stone tablets. Of course, the signifying content of the commandments also promotes what appears to be a C-B-S model of communication premised on the maximally lossless transmission of meaning, while meanwhile advancing a more affective project that has little to do with meaning as such. The commandments, in other words, have far more to do with creating those conditional moods imbued with the right concernedness, the right affectability, to gain an influence. By seeking to minimize the influence that any particular speaker's unique rhetorical flair might have on a talk's success, TED seeks to leave the purported substance of each talk's "content" to stand out as its most distinctive characteristic. If all talks do more or less the same thing at the level of their arrangement, delivery, style, and so on, then no talk's formal characteristics can uniquely account for its impact or lack thereof.

In effect, the TED formula tries to subtract all demonstrable "rhetoric" from the talks themselves (though of course doing so follows a rhetorical calculus of its own). One function of making all talks formally the same, in other words, is to allow each talk's content to stand out as autonomous from the form of its expression. This doesn't mean that TED somehow ruptures the eternal relationship between form and content that characterizes all oratory and language, providing the study of rhetoric one of its most fundamental tenets, that *how* something is expressed shapes *what* is expressed and vice versa. But it does mean that the form of each speech appears rendered away, that is, neutralized and naturalized, by its standardization, with the ostensible result that a talk's "idea" is all that remains to distinguish it. As TED accordingly presents its talks as ceremonial packets for their ideas, we are invited to listen out for their meaning as inherently stable, context independent, and losslessly communicable through symbolic language. We are, in short, encouraged to invest great hope and promise in the symbolic order, when something beyond signification is really more primary. As Whitehead wrote in a different context, "The ceremonies with their output of emotion become the mode of expression for the ideas; and the ideas become an interpretation of the ceremonies."[68] Such is the nature of ritual transmissions.

Communicative capitalism thrives on the simultaneous reverence for experience as singular with the reduction of experience as reproducible. To promote talk as the solution to our social ills, and then to foster only the kind of talk that fits within a narrow bandwidth of oratorical diversity, is to imbue the *experience* of that talk with special salience. Naturally, this experience will be informed partly by whatever symbolic content and message is being delivered, but not primarily. To suppose that the received communication of an "idea" (a signifying thesis, proposition, claim) is what accounts for communication's impact is to neglect the preponderance of asignifying, affective aspects that condition the influence that a symbolic order is or isn't able to achieve. As with TED, so elsewhere in everyday experience: the constraints imposed on our ways of communicating create an ambient mood or atmosphere that dispose people to encounter communication in particular ways.

To draw toward an "idiot rhetoric" is to become more attuned to those ways we are drawn in certain directions over others. The idiot's rhetoric is the idiot's presence, sometimes merely listening in the background, but expressed one way or another in concerned gestures that don't authorize any predetermined claim over what matters and for whom. An idiot rhetoric is one that presumes no unified subject, has no interest in the "putting into equality" of people, or things, or ideas.[69] Instead, an idiot rhetoric is one that pauses over the question of who can speak and for whom, and in doing so "precludes any shortcut or simplification, any differentiation a priori between that which counts and that which does not."[70] The idiot in this sense is not a skeptic, least of all in the Cartesian way where the presupposition of a thinking subject is the baseline presumption of existence. Thinking is not the source of his being. His own opinion, the innate "here's what I think," is of no consequence next to the timidity of the idiot's hesitancy to claim to know what it means to say what's "good" for anyone else. An idiot rhetoric slows us down before moving always on to the next big idea.

Otherwise, when we listen to a TED Talk, the old democratic desire for symbolic-discursive communication to resolve the challenges of our interdependence kicks in. A modern-day orator stands before us, smartly appointed, holding a clicker to punch through the slides. A rhetor speaks. We are right back in the *ecclesia* on Pnyx Hill, seated now and charmed. Idiots merely, listening. A cut to a tight angle close-up of the speaker, a pan to the rapt audience. We see the arresting slide with its irrefutable data, the lights are bright and beaming just-so on stage. And as it all ends, count on it, crashing applause. TED's sonic branding starts to play. The next talk begins in 10, 9, 8 . . .

2

STICKINESS

Has anyone written about the pleasure of peeling the back off a sticker? The removal of that attachment, the parting of its togetherness? With one side sticky, the other not, there's a care that stickers require so not to stick one to itself or to misplace its quasi-permanence: a modest handicraft. And they're everywhere. Bumpers, billboards, skateboards, street signs, laptops, water bottles. There are now entire museums devoted to stickers (and to think, you used to only get one to show you'd paid the admission). Libraries catalog and preserve them. Kids play with them. Even the freshness stickers affixed to take-out sushi trays have a place in the Smithsonian's permanent collection. We use stickers to label things, to communicate messages, to convey identities, to post our mail. From their outset, stickers have been communication media. Both metaphorically, and as operative cultural techniques, they exemplify our gestural engagements with public life.

This chapter takes the motif of stickers as a running example to help unpeel some of the complexity still sticking to the concepts raised in the last. In that chapter, I sought to reorient the privileging of public symbolic action as an intrinsically validated means of engaging the political in favor of less symbolic and more affective actions: "idiot rhetorics" expressed through ostensibly inconsequential gestures of concern. Through the example of TED Talks, I considered how, although symbolic action in the form of speech continues to be heralded as the best way to inculcate ideas that can "change the world," more subtle gestures like listening to a TED Talk become politically laden insofar as TED entrains people to listen in rhythm with a neoliberal logic that is not, of course, the only way to listen. If the TED Commandments helped us accordingly to consider the "concern" in gestures of concern, presently stickers will help us to consider the "gestures."

Let me reiterate from the start that what "gesture" refers to in this book has only an indirect relationship to those bodily movements and gesticulations most often associated with the term's primary meaning.[1] Though such gestures as hand waves or shrugging shoulders are close kin to the sorts of gestures discussed herein, they are not the focus. Instead, by "gesture" I mean to designate those acts performed—sometimes for show, sometimes to express a feeling or intention, sometimes devoid of forethought—with at least the tacit knowledge that they will have no major effect. Sending a "Get Well" card; saying "Gesundheit" after someone sneezes; kissing a child's boo-boo; "liking" a social media post; showing up at an assembly. All are small gestures of the sort that this book is about. No one expects such gestures to accomplish that much, even to start a conversation or be reciprocated, and seldom to bring about meaningful change, though they sometimes do all these things and more. The affective force of such gestures affirms a sense of something more intangible. Call it kinship, empathy, solidarity, kindness. In this book, I call it concern. If we wish to consider the idiot as a figure with an essential political capacity despite an apparent ambivalence or distance from the fray of public affairs, then it is necessary to understand how their endowment of concern can be expressed through such gestures.

The phrase "gestures of concern," as with "concerned gestures" (a term I use as its interchangeable counterpart), offers a way to distinguish this kind of gesture from the more classical kind that refers to visible bodily motions.[2] But the distinction can also be misleading, as the two are often entangled. For instance, when you let a car merge in front of yours in busy traffic, that's a concerned gesture: doing so brings into form an affective relation of concern for another. But it also involves a physical gesture, indeed a whole operational chain of them: holding your hand on the steering wheel just so, pushing the brakes with appropriate force (too hard and you're being aggressive, too soft and you're reluctant), nodding your head to the other driver in your own characteristic way, and so on. "Gestures" and "gestures of concern," in other words, are neither synonymous nor coterminous, even as they are often entangled. Not everything is a gesture; nor are all gestures "concerned" in the active sense of concern as an existential condition. My aim is not to measure out gestures in coffee spoons, putting each in its proper cup, or to forward a theory of gestures as such. I am not trying to join academic conversations in the old and manifold field of gesture studies (and accordingly endeavor no typology of gestures, no physiology of gestures, no history of gestures, no account of gesture's relation to speech or to the origins of language). But if, as Bruno Latour suggests, mutual concerns are what hold people in common more than any other set of values or principles,[3] then attending to the gestures that express such concern becomes a viable way of worlding a commons—an affective commonwealth.

The simple act of unpeeling a sticker offers as good a starting point as any. And a video posted to YouTube in 2013 can begin to show how. A Turkish collective of street artists going by the name of Vandalina posted the three-minute video, which they had produced to depict their presence in the Turkish capital of Ankara. With high production values and an electro-ambient soundtrack, the video consisted primarily of a montage of anonymous hands unpeeling stickers and putting them up in public places: on walls, signs, windows, poles, turnstiles, in and outside subway trains. The hands without a face could belong to anyone, be anywhere. In swift and supple gestures, these hands peel away one palm-sized sticker after another and slap them up on surfaces, all with such ease and speed that the motion seems nearly automatic. Sometimes there are already stickers there where the hands put up a new one. The camera cuts to whole sheets of peel-and-stick stickers spooling out of printers, then large posters doing the same. Outside by night, we see a hooded group of people kicking the crumbled backs of stickers along the urban sidewalk, as if there are so many you can't help but step on them; then they're wheat-pasting posters on walls; more peeling and sticking, peeling and sticking. The overall impression is as if to say, *We're already among you. We're everywhere. And we're not going to stop.*

By all appearances, they have stopped. The activity on Vandalina's YouTube page has long since gone dormant, as it has on their accounts with Twitter and Facebook. The video nevertheless illustrates something of what I'm trying to take on by invoking the notion that gestures are important for building our affective commonwealth. The short video confronts us with several gestures at once. There's the *physical* gesture of unpeeling sticker after sticker, seen in close-up shots of kinesthetic bodily movements so seemingly fluid for the anonymous subjects executing them as to appear as habitual as waving to a friend or dashing off a signature. There's also the apparent *expressive concern* of these peel-and-stick gestures: in this case, it's a gesture to raise more awareness about the growing rates of femicide in Turkey, where (the stickers announce) five women are being murdered per day. Both of these gestures—the body's active movement and that movement's expressive function—are represented in another gesture, that of producing and posting the video itself. By creating and posting the video, Vandalina gestured reflexively to itself as a collective concerned enough to intervene in public affairs by attempting to redirect social attention to issues that they believe merit collective action.

Gestures of concern can involve all three of these layers: physical, expressive, reflexive. They're unavoidably embodied; they express some concern; and they make visible that very expression *as* expression. I don't see these as a checklist of properties needed for something to "qualify" as a gesture of concern or not. Classifying different types of activity is useful to the degree it helps us to understand them, and what is most important to understand about gestures of concern is not what they are, but what they do. One thing that concerned gestures do is perform an expressive function to greater affect than an instrumental one. In other words, the force of their affectivity tends to eclipse the force of their symbolicity.

During its active period, the Vandalina street art group exemplified the idea.[4] As their video depicted, the group operated by designing and disseminating protest stickers around the urban center of Ankara. Each month they chose a different social issue for the stickers to address (the issue of femicide featured in the video was their debut campaign, and it received considerable attention). One way that Vandalina distinguished itself was by its democratic methods. They crowdsourced public input through social media, giving anyone a say in choosing the issues covered and in designing stickers to address them. Once the collective settled on its monthly concern, they created their stickers—some all text, others images—and shared the designs on Facebook for anyone to download, print on sticker paper, and slap up wherever they chose (fig. 2.1). Moving from issue to issue, month to month, it would be hard to say Vandalina held a strong ideological commitment to any particular set of problems. As one of their members acknowledged somewhat indifferently, they chose only "obvious social problems that anyone would list without a breath."[5] In that case, it's easier to see Vandalina as less invested in any pointed political agenda than in the effort to convey what Katie Stewart might characterize as "a vague but compelling sense that something is happening."[6] Or, to put it differently, they may have mobilized around some specific concerns, but the collective existed as a vehicle for expressing a more general, active state of concernedness.

Equipping each of their team members with around two hundred stickers per night, the collective tried to generate maximum coverage across Ankara until the stickers were so ubiquitous that people couldn't help but notice: *there's something happening here.* If what it is ain't exactly clear, that could be because, while gestures of concern certainly express *something*, it's often their more impalpable contribution to a *sense of something* that makes them so affective. As we saw with TED Talks in the last chapter, an interpretive reading of a particu-

Figure 2.1. Vandalina sticker. The wording translates as "Everyone Should Know."

lar sticker will only get us so far in this one. Instead, a nonhermeneutic tracing of the "stickiness" in gestures of concern will require shifting the focus from what a given representation means to the conditions of its representability.

STICKERS AS CULTURAL TECHNIQUES

German media theory has a concept that is useful for this approach. *Kulturtechniken*, or "cultural techniques," are what Bernhard Siegert describes as "inconspicuous technologies of knowledge" that organize everyday life.[7] Doors, chalkboards, ampersands, clocks, stamps, grids . . . Stickers, too. *Kulturtechniken* is an ambiguous concept, with translation difficulties in both its halves (in the first, as to whether *Kultur* denotes "civilization" or "culture," and in the second, as to whether *techniken* denotes "techniques" or "technologies").[8] As Geoffrey Winthrop-Young points out, the term's use and meaning have also changed over time, with at least three different inflections that are all still in use, the one operationalized in any given case dependent on the agenda of whoever deploys it.[9] My interest here is not in theorizing cultural techniques as such, but in leveraging the concept's nonhermeneutic emphasis on the materiality of communication to think more about stickers—to the end of revealing more about gestures of concern.

Not all concerned gestures involve cultural techniques, but all cultural techniques have a gestural component. "Techniques," André Leroi-Gourhan has observed, "involve both gestures and tools."[10] Though Friedrich Kittler is typically the one most associated with media theory's turn to *Kulturtechniken*, in many ways Leroi-Gourhan is the fire that lights the cave.[11] As an archaeologist and anthropologist, Leroi-Gourhan has an interest in media or technology that is secondary to his interest in the fundamental technicity of bodies and their operational entanglement with the tools they use. He shows us, though, that unlike many animals, humans do not operate through instinct alone but according to patterns of behavior learned from social experience. At some point in our evolution, that is, human animals began combining objects as tools with manual gestures they'd picked up from social memory. Whether a stone blade for digging or a remote control for turning on the television, the tools humans use as part of our social and cultural lives involve chains of operations mediated by technologies of one kind or another. Over time, as the needs fulfilled by operating these technologies have become more integrated into daily life, we've developed cultural techniques to harness them. Cultural techniques, in this sense, are what Winthrop-Young describes as "the skills and aptitudes involved in mastering a given technology."[12] The operational processes involved in such mastery sometimes involve the creation of new technologies, which in turn leads to new cultural techniques. The history of stickers offers a good example.

Stickers don't have a tidy origin story. As I use the term, the invention of stickers coincides with the initial discovery of the means by which to affix through adhesion (as opposed to another supervening tool like a staple or string) one markable surface onto another—almost always in defiance of gravity and for the purpose of communication. On these criteria, proto-stickers date to the wheatpasted signs of ancient Egypt, which took the form of papyrus affixed to walls using an adhesive made from mixing wheat and water (a technique still popular among street artists today). There were also the stamped wax seals that had been serving as adhesives in mailed communications since the Middle Ages (which, of course, conceptually can't be disarticulated from the signet rings bearing the stamps themselves, which have been found in the earliest civilizations of the Indus Valley and Mesopotamia). Not until 1839 did Sir Rowland Hill invent the first "pre-apply" adhesive paper, the kind you lick. Only a year later was it to be used for the first postage stamp, the Penny Black.

And by the 1880s, labels began showing up on tin cans and packing crates in the form of colorful paper, printed using lithographs and affixed to surfaces using gum paste. These all, certainly, are proto-stickers, too. But if the simple, peel-and-stick variety is what sets the bar, then the key date is 1935, when R. Stanton Avery invented the self-adhesive label that soon became a commonplace office supply. After that, stickers went just about everywhere.

Take the bumper sticker. The bumper sticker as we know it is likely the invention of an American screen printer in Kansas named Forest Gill, who, in the years after World War II, designed stickers specifically for automobile bumpers by experimenting with wartime materials such as fluorescent Day-Glo ink and pressure-sensitive paper stock.[13] But Gill's innovation was not entirely technological; he relied essentially on the same technology that Avery had used to make self-adhesive labels for the office. Gill's innovation was to realize that because automobile bumpers (first introduced on the Ford Model A in 1927) were safety mechanisms designed to be dinged and scuffed, manufacturers tended to leave them unadorned, leaving veritable blank canvasses visible on every car to anyone trailing from behind.[14] Stickers didn't belong in the office. They belonged in public. Gill took his invention to promotional product marketers and, soon enough, in the first years of America's national highway system, bumper stickers began promoting tourist attractions, products, civic events, and public-safety campaigns.[15] Not until the Eisenhower-Stevenson presidential election of 1952 did people begin using bumper stickers to express their own politics. Today stickers do a lot more than that.

It wasn't long after bumper stickers became popular that smaller stickers moved into the home, eventually being marketed toward children and sold in packs of trading cards or in peel-and-stick books. Instead of the text-based stickers on a bumper, designed for viewing from middle distance, these newer stickers tended to be image-based and colorful, designed for viewing up close, and often portraying or parodying characters from television, video games, sports, comics, and other realms of pop culture. Their smaller size made it easy to peel and stick them anywhere, and being marketed for children to a certain degree domesticated and depoliticized them. Such stickers served as aesthetic tags to express tastes, creativity, and personality via cultural referents, be it Roberto Clemente or Pac-Man. Undoubtedly, part of this story is another chapter in the general merchandising of culture that had been happening well before peel-off stickers were around. But if the ostensible depoliticization of stickers for children amounted to their culturalization by contributing to creating a visible presence of fan cultures that could display these stickers in public, peel-off stickers as swiftly became *re*politicized when such subcultures as skaters and punks, those not so keen on the merchandising of their identities, began creating homemade stickers of their own.

The story here is part technology, part technique. The spread of xerographic photocopy machines, lower printing costs, and the widespread availability of blank labels enabled the homemade production of sticker art in ways not so easy before. These widely available blank labels ranged from the standard Avery office-supply labels to "Hello My Name Is . . ." labels to the USPS Priority Mail Bluetop 228 Labels (which American post offices made available for free in 500-label bricks), not to mention commercially available sheets of crack-and-peel self-adhesive paper. Different techniques for the handmade production of these stickers produced objects that could either be one of a kind or widely reproduced, that could have lesser or greater durability, and that could look more home-cooked or professional depending on the chain of operational techniques used to produce them. The use of toxic vinyl inks and adhesives, for instance, gave such stickers more gloss and durability, but required a different handicraft than the slap-and-go ease of a 228 label you could draw on with a marker. By the 1980s, such sticker art had become another form of graffiti, an adhesive analog to the "aerosol arts" that were becoming popular around cities on the American coasts.

The spread of stickers into public life as a cultural technique for communicating matters of shared concern marks an important shift in public communication. It made more empirically legible a broader social attitude shared by ordinary people, which until then was mostly intuited and guessed at. If the aim is to ascertain a regnant public attitude or structure of feeling, that is, stickers make good barometers. Every so often a new thematic cluster of stickers seems to appear in public space as if all over, all at once. This weird synchronicity can give the impression that something's happening, as if some felt activity were becoming an emergent attitude and passing through public space like a weather pattern. The activity might be plainly political; often it's a fan culture coming out to play; sometimes it's a kind of lifestyle or value. With Vandalina in Turkey, initially, it was attention to femicide. Lately, *reading* makes a good example.

Though there may well be street art collectives promoting the importance of reading, it's the dispersion of reading-related stickers from different sources that conveys the sense of something doing. "I ♥ Books." "Reading is Sexy." "Eat. Poop. Read." "Keep Calm and Love Reading." "Read Motherfucking Books!" (fig. 2.2). These and many stickers like them—and not just on bumpers—are concerned with something hard to pinpoint: a socially dispersed disposition toward reading that enables and legitimates different modes of public engagement with books. Though they're all different, the messages on such stick-

Figure 2.2. As seen in New Orleans, 2011, a DIY sticker attributed to "The Reader."

ers are clear enough, even dogmatic and put forward without disguise. These aren't arguments about any particular *way* of reading, or even especially about which books have most value. They're not quite conversation starters. Bumper stickers are too pithy and condensed to be much more than gestures. Peeled and placed on a bumper or a street sign, such stickers are cultural techniques that facilitate gestures of concern. They need no response or measurable impact to serve their purpose. But that just makes them harder to figure out: if some concerned gestures aren't *without* a representational message, yet don't achieve their primary force therefrom, then why convey a message at all?

READING GESTURES, READING AFFECT

The readability of affect does not require its representability. As Eugenie Brinkema has shown, there is no inconsistency in arguing that affect is "non-intentional, indifferent" while also arguing "for affect as having a form and reading for affect as it inheres in form."[16] To read for affect in its formal elements, however, as Brinkema does through light, color, sound, and so on in films, and as Vilém Flusser has done through the body's movements in everyday gestures like shaving, writing, or smoking a pipe,[17] is to risk missing that affect always inheres *between* bodies and forms as much as it ever inheres *in* them. As expressive social actions, gestures make such terrific vectors of affectability because, measured more by the impressions they garner than by whatever intentions might motivate them, they exhibit the very mediality of being human, of being both *between* other bodies and *in* one. It's not, then, that the gestures of interest to me *can't* represent states of mind, feelings, and ideas, or even do so intentionally. It's just more accurate to say they represent a representability; they communicate a communicability that exceeds what intention can capture.

For example, if someone puts up a sticker that says "putyourfaceinabook," "Freadom," "Fight Evil. Read Books," or any of their other variations, it may be clear enough what any of these slogans signify. It's also likely these slogans will be perceived as an intentional message from whoever put them up, and plausibly so. But assertion should not be mistaken for argument, and a floated "here's what I think" not confused with a polemic. The rhetorical function of such stickers, in other words, is not contingent on persuading an audience to drop what they're doing and start reading. To fulfill their purpose, these stickers need not be very good at inspiring more readers or cultivating the sustained engagement with ideas that's more than just a headline to see and move beyond. Though such stickers aren't without representational salience, that is, their primary consequence has less to do with their persuasive outcomes than with the more impalpable affective tone they achieve by displaying a mode of concerned expression that contributes gesturally to the social fabric.

What we are dealing with is something close to what Kenneth Burke described as "pure persuasion." For Burke, pure persuasion was principally something affected through symbolic actions performed for their own sake and not in order to achieve a perceivable response or outcome. As Burke writes, "Pure persuasion involves the saying of something, not for an extraverbal advantage to be got by the saying, but because of a satisfaction intrinsic to the saying. It summons because it likes the feel of a summons. It would be nonplussed if the summons were answered."[18] Burke notes that pure persuasion in any absolute sense is nonexistent. All communication, all rhetoric, seeks *some* influence, some advantage. Gestures of concern, similarly, are never "pure" in this absolute way. By virtue of the concern that compels them, it's hard to imagine concerned gestures being performed without at least a nonconscious motive of having some signifying effect, particularly when they're so often delivered via symbolic actions available for interpretation, as in the case of stickers about reading.[19]

We've seen this before in the ambiguous intentionality of the concerned but introverted *idiotai* from ancient Greece; and we've seen it in the act of listening to a TED Talk. There's a tentativeness to these concerned gestures—what Burke calls the "standoffishness" of pure persuasion—that stops short of a full-out appeal or entreaty.[20] As a result, where such gestures "land" is seldom universal. The inaccessibility of their directedness means a concerned gesture remains always unfinished, "incomplete" inasmuch as its para-symbolic action resists the interpretive capture of being reduced to its meaning-effects. Instead, the presence-effects of a gesture that could land anywhere, and differently for different audiences, privileges the sensibility of an encounter above its interpretability. If we concede that concerned gestures like these play a role in public affairs whether or not we can read their intention, then it should at least be clear that their more affective and recessed nature gives them a different role than the more vociferous and deliberative ones that have been the birthright of democracy since its outset.[21]

As Jenny Rice has argued, "Today's key mode of publicness produces subjects that inhabit a kind of public-private limbo," some eager to participate publicly, others eager not to do so.[22] Those who participate actively in public life, shaping and defending the shared stakes of our social interdependence through discussion and debate of shared issues, are no more legitimate public subjects than those who remain altogether distant and absent from public engagement, gesturing their concern through stickers and watching TED Talks. This is not just a matter of legitimating one's right to remain inactive in public affairs, or of emphasizing everyone's shared stake in public issues, whether or not they actively engage it. Rice suggests, paradoxically, that remaining distant from public life is itself a form of public engagement—though, I would add, it's a gestural one. "It is not helpful," she maintains, "to think about the nonparticipant as separate from the polis. Instead, we are better off thinking about multiple forms of public subjectivity, one of which includes the 'apathetic' public subject."[23]

Rice collapses the distinctions that have long been taken for granted as essential to understanding all public forms of communal action. In doing so, she argues that understanding public life through a participant and nonparticipant divide fails to account for ways that public affairs activate affective registers that sometimes leave quite invested and caring people more inclined to remain distant. This affective orientation to political activity, Rice argues, makes it easier to "understand how today's key public subjectivity allows us to remain actively and productively distanced from intervention, while never being outside of its discourse."[24] Her argument unfolds in the context of her book on crises of urban development. But more than development crises, and more even than harder-hitting issues like global warming, immigration, abortion, and the like, it is the cultural field—the aesthetic—that brings forth the "public-private limbo" where our affective orientations toward participation in public life become viable as public *actions*.

No one has more artfully made this point than Lauren Berlant. It is the aesthetic, Berlant ventures, that "provides metrics for understanding how we pace and space our encounters with things, how we manage the too closeness of the world and also the desire to have an impact on it that has some relation to its impact on us."[25] In recognizing the importance of the aesthetic for shaping our affective disposition in the world, but wary of the state's likelihood to respond to our minor gestures, Berlant identifies an "intimate public sphere" where our public subjectivity might be expressed more recessively.[26] In Berlant's intimate public sphere, affective relations precede and outweigh any rational or discursive standards, and hence legitimize the individual's affect-ability alone. For Berlant, then, "public spheres are always affect worlds, worlds to which people are bound, when they are, by affective projections of a constantly negotiated common interestedness."[27] Intimate publics, by contrast, are more specifically those in which "matters of survival are at stake."[28] Berlant's intimate public is an "affectsphere," a public of affectively shared privacy, one mediated aesthetically less through discursive associations than through cultural forms and gestural modes of interaction that attend to the ongoing and always shared struggle of persevering through life's desires and pains. Both Rice's and Berlant's separate efforts to collapse traditional categories of public and private into a more liminal state of "limbo" (for Rice) or "impasse" (for Berlant) indicate a change in what it means in catastrophic times to be a public subject, someone invested in identifying the concerns we do share in common, even if their gestures and their readability cannot always be reconciled.

CONTRIBUTIONS AS GESTURES

One of Jodi Dean's most trenchant critiques about communicative capitalism targets its tendency to impoverish public discourse by reducing the exchange of "messages" into fungible "contributions." Now, she says, "messages are contributions to circulating content—not actions to elicit responses. The exchange value of messages overtakes their use value."[29] The sort of condensation and simplification of ideas evident in TED's C-B-S model or, for that matter, in just about all bumper-sticker wisdom illustrates part of her concern. When the message is a news report or political speech, the condensation often takes the form of a headline or sound bite, and increasingly a Tweet. Though this often leads to a dangerous reduction in the depth and nuance of the messages themselves, it does not always diminish their strength. To the contrary. As Megan Foley has argued in the context of public address, "Sound bites emphasize oratory through the very gesture of leaving it behind."[30] The ironic result is that this supposed loss—both the loss of a message's complexity, reflected in its condensation, and our loss of any sense that our own political messages can make more than a sound-bite blip on public affairs—is precisely what sustains the ongoing circulation and recirculation of messages-as-contributions.

Like Dean's critique, Foley's insight that "sound bites have turned public speech into a fetish" is as applicable to what TED does for ideas as to what trending headlines and presidential Tweets do to news stories, or to what bumper stickers do to "wisdom" itself.[31] There's a pernicious circularity here. If the reduction of deep and dialogic messages into flat and interchangeable contributions is a fetish, then it serves as a substitute for a communicative ideal of exchange and depth perceived as having been lost—even though that substitute, Freud would say, is "precisely designed to preserve it from extinction."[32] Despite communicative capitalism's astonishing efficiency and all-consuming go at facilitating the circulation of more communication, in other words, it might be that our complicity in the constant circulating and recirculating of messages-as-contributions is as much borne from our sense of loss as from any sheepish compliance with the circuits of communicative capitalism itself. At the same time that this makes communicative capitalism seem more sinister, it may also point to the cruel optimism we maintain as a kind of quicksand hope for its escape.

One of this book's main postulates is that many of our public communicative engagements today are gestural in a mood-inducing way. The fetishized reduction of messages into contributions illustrates how that might be so, and it's perhaps nowhere better exemplified than in the digital spaces of social media. In networked media platforms where people now post, share, forward, follow, like, and pin "contributions" whose mere circulation constitutes their public value, discursive contributions to public life tend no longer to be valued for their substantive content, rationale, or "message," but for the depth and duration of the attention they receive. This attention operates in a dispositional, orienting mode. For instance, when a video goes viral through its circulation among a public attentive, say, to a cat taking a bath, its doing so attests to some trending interest emerging around that video's salience. The salience may well be inane. Indeed, popularity can often be ascribed to the plain attraction of humor or sentimentality—modes deadened by any recourse to discourse about them. But the video's popularity attests to its salience nonetheless, and hence to an experienced orientation thereto, even if that orientation remains vague because unattached to any known and substantive public opinion other than mere attention. To put this differently, if a tendency of public sentiment can be identified around viral videos and other web memes, it is not always (indeed, not even usually) because "deliberation" occurred.

So often now, distribution displaces deliberation. Videos typically go viral because individuals share or like them in ways that are publicly visible, and less often because we discuss them and their implications. To encounter a viral video is always to encounter its having already gone viral. It always gestures toward the virtuality of the public that has *elsewhere* ascribed to the video its salience, though at no single point can anyone say when, where, or how a trending recognition of that salience was achieved. Zizi Papacharissi gives the name "electronic elsewheres" to describe "an environment accessible to many publics that do not share the same geographic location."[33] It is on account of such electronic elsewheres that just by watching viral videos we enact the very tendency of public sentiment that, while watching, we experience already to exist around them. When we watch a video known to have gone viral, in other words, its having circulated through a distributed network of agents represents the trending of its salience that our attention to it actuates. The medium is not the message; the circulation is the message.

Under these conditions, participation in intimate cultural publics becomes an intervening end in itself. Jenny Rice puts it this way: "If affect is something produced through interactions between bodies, then public deliberation probably also produces something that does not coincide with the *telos* of civic judgment."[34] And what *something* is that? The mere production of talk. As Rice explains, "The talk itself—attention and investments in the act of communication—is also a *telos*. This is the 'affective circulation' of publics; talk itself becomes a *telos* even beyond the official content of that talk."[35] If we even provisionally grant the proposition that a move from messages to contributions now characterizes a significant bulk of public communication, then an important exigence for thinking gesturally becomes apparent. It's not just that gestures of concern have always been integral but neglected aspects of sociality; it's that their great proliferation in these contributory times makes it more important than ever to become attuned to their force.

GESTURES AS ART

Where Dean emphasizes and laments the "talk without response" configuration of public exchange,[36] gestures of concern offer creative and critical workarounds to an instrumental logic of contributions. On account of their ability to actuate aesthetic encounters that, for a moment at least, become an inter-vening end in themselves, concerned gestures create a new field of possibility for subsequent encounters. Experience of the aesthetic, within the duration of a vital encounter with it, is marked by a momentary freedom from needing to be otherwise: explained, counterargued, interpreted, shared, reduced. That freedom, which is nothing more than the pure potential of the virtual, the free-dom of a fleeting break from habit when true attention becomes possible, too soon passes back over into habit, routine, ritual. We want to share it. Digital inter-faces invite us to share it, and communicative capitalism all but commands it. But to read all this sharing and circulating as an unfortunate move from a message's use value to its exchange value, I think, misses that what we are often sharing is not the message but a ritual transmission of the experienced freedom it has momentarily created.

Homemade stickers in public places disrupt that freedom enough to call attention to the importance of its sustenance. Compared to the digital stick-ers that companies like Apple and Google enable people to share in text mes-sages or atop digital photographs, for instance, the peel-and-stick kind have a wider reach and a less fungible materiality. Whereas digital stickers in the form of animojis or masks superimposed over photos are typically shared on mobile devices directly with specific individuals, the stickers affixed to walls or poles in public spaces address an audience of strangers and passersby. These stickers accordingly attain their force-effects as much by contributing to an ambient mood as they do by communicating a particular message to an audience that can be expected to ascertain its meaning. Their quasi-permanence is part of the reason why. Although, as Malcolm McCullough has pointed out, "stickers don't last the way carved marble does,"[37] it's harder to unpeel a sticker on a street sign and share it with someone else than it is to share a selfie that an app has con-verted into a stylized sticker that can go anywhere with a few taps of a screen.

The circulation of a digital sticker may not serve any purpose other than as a gesture of sharing what may or may not inspire a glisk of poignant experi-ence before being passed over for the next. In such cases, increasingly common in a cyberspace of so much sharing, the ritual transmission of these passing moments is the sufficient purpose they serve. That is, conveying a message is secondary to conveying a kind of feeling: the feeling of freedom that comes from an affective order's pure persuasion, the self-sufficiency of needing no demonstrable effect for the gesture's communicative substance to have signifi-cance. Sharing then becomes a ritual of transmitting the contributions that we only share because they defy the logic of transmission in the first place. Our ritual transmissions are transmitting rituals.

The reason cultural public spheres make an especially good access point into the ecological dynamism of affective and symbolic orders is that the aesthetic tends to elicit affective experience more intensely than other communicative forms. To elicit affective experience is not the same as to represent affect through signifying processes. Affects, Simon O'Sullivan reminds us, do not have "to do with knowledge or meaning; indeed, they occur on a different, *asignifying* register."[38] Affects, he adds, are "the stuff that goes on beneath, beyond, even parallel to signification. . . . You cannot read affects, *you can only experience them*."[39] If art is not uniquely capable of eliciting such experiences, it is at least intensely capable of doing so. And in that case, art becomes a medium for accessing affectivity *in process*.

In turn, the role of art in public affairs gains a critical—or, less sharply, a functional—capacity for actuating experiences of the affective orientations that in turn prefigure the symbolic order of rhetorical action and the whole discursive realm through which cultural public spheres carry out their more empirical business. On this count, it can be helpful to think about the similarities between art and affect itself. O'Sullivan writes, "Art is less involved in making sense of the world and more involved in exploring the possibilities of being, of becoming, in the world. Less involved in knowledge and more involved in experience, in pushing forward the boundaries of what can be experienced."[40] Through an affective lens, in other words, what artworks represent or mean is of less consequence than what sensations or experiences they produce.[41]

The story of Shepard Fairey, the street artist probably most known for creating the Obama Hope poster, makes a telling illustration.[42] Fairey started out by making DIY stickers at a skateboard shop where he worked behind the counter. One of them was a black-on-white square sticker not much bigger than a postage stamp: "Andre the Giant Has Posse" (fig. 2.3). It began as a gag, a turf-tagging device he and his friends slap-tagged around Providence in 1989, when Fairey was attending the Rhode Island School of Design. Before long, the local indie paper printed a picture of the sticker and offered a reward for anyone able to identify its source or meaning. Fairey began making trips to Boston and New York to put the stickers there. He improved his production, from crack-and-peel stickers run through a photocopier to more rugged vinyl stickers and vinyl ink. Then he ran classified ads in punk zines and skateboarding magazines, offering the stickers for free. He sent them to friends all over. Soon he heard the stickers were showing up across the country and then in other countries.[43] Eventually, the homegrown "Andre the Giant Has a Posse" sticker grew into the OBEY GIANT campaign, first in the form of more stylized and pared-down stickers, then large wheatpasted signs and stencils, then shirts

Figure 2.3. Shepard Fairey's "Andre the Giant Has a Posse" sticker.

and hats, soon fine art prints, stationery, and the fully merchandised brand it's become today.

In a manifesto that he wrote about his initial OBEY campaign in 1990, Fairey cites Heidegger's phenomenology as an influence, specifically its aim, as Fairey put it, "to reawaken a sense of wonder about one's environment."[44] Stickers, for Fairey, are ways to create surprising public experiences, to stoke curiosity, revitalize perception, and reorient people with a newfound attentiveness to what's around them. "The sticker has no meaning but exists only to cause people to react," the manifesto explained.[45] Deliberately, then, he left the symbolic content of the sticker ambiguous to divest it of any clear ideological intention to deliver a particular message. Fairey seemed less fascinated by *what* message a sticker placed in public space might communicate than by its ability to reorient one's sense of being in some space at all. Another way to put this is to say that the force-effects of his stickers were designed to register more in an affective order than in a symbolic one. While this prospect may be viable enough, it does little to account for what is left when art has been appropriated, sometimes willingly, by the machines of capital or reduced to ritual transmission by being enclosed within a regime of interpretable signification and meaning. What happens to aesthetic experience when brick walls are cut down so that Banksy's stencils can be taken from the streets and sold in a gallery? What "sense of wonder" is left when the oddity of an "Andre the Giant Has a Posse" sticker becomes the cleaner and friendlier OBEY GIANT logo sold as stationery?

The best answer I have been able to reach is that we are left with a *gesture*. For Jean-Luc Nancy, "every work of art implies something other than signification, it implies an act, a gesture."[46] For Nancy, a gesture is "the accompaniment of an intention but one that, in itself, remains foreign to the intention. . . . Gesture is a sensible dynamism that precedes, accompanies or succeeds meaning or signification, but it is sensible sense."[47] If art is above all a gesture, it need not be directed toward a meaning or a message; indeed, its dynamism will only be closed off if so taken. In this sense, art is *directly and immediately* political and not, as is often understood to be the case, a gesture of signification understood to be a political gesture. Nancy's concern is that we not "transform art into some kind of production of signification."[48] Mine has been to speculate about what follows if, *pace* Dean's critiques of messages becoming contributions, we also regard gestural contributions to public life as aesthetically dynamic and powerful on a similar basis—that is, without needing to be transformed into a symbolic "meaning" to affirm the affective force of their social influence.

AFFECTIVE ECOLOGIES

One way we transform something into its meaning is when we count it. "Hey!" a child complains. "You gave *her* three apples. *I* only got two!" Meaning: *That's not fair*. And maybe so. But were all the apples the same? Were some rotten, smaller, bruised? The reduction of any state of affairs to what's countable about it will invariably miss what's not. Gestural contributions to public life are often those that don't add up in attempts to ascertain what they signify or produce. In theory, for instance, there is little reason for rational and self-interested individuals to vote. The cost-benefit analysis of doing so just doesn't pan out. Why bother to vote when a single cast ballot will never be powerful enough to sway an election? Yet, millions of people do turn out to vote, even in the knowledge that their individual ballot will have no practical consequence on the election's outcome. To explain this paradox, political scientists have developed a theory of "expressive voting," which suggests that people often vote with no expectation of having an actual influence, but rather merely to express their "feelings, desires, or attitudes."[49] Expressive voting accordingly falls into a category of behaviors "in which the only purpose is expressive—

Figure 2.4. The author's "I Voted" sticker from the 2016 U.S. presidential election.

where the intrinsic element is the sole one in the relevant decision-theoretic calculus."[50] Gestures of concern are another way to think of such a category.

But if the ability to count an individual vote isn't adequate to account for the concerned gesture of expressive voting, then how do we make sense of such a gesture? In America, it's done with stickers. All voters get a sticker. Different states and districts have their own renditions, but their spirit remains the same. "I Voted." They're badges of public pride, certificates showing off the fulfilment of a civic obligation, and encouragement for others to do the same—democracy's bathetic door prize. The precise origins of the patriotic decals are enigmatic, but the practice seems to have started in the 1980s, about a century after American elections went from being highly visible public events to being private and personal affairs with the introduction of the secret ballot currently in use.[51] As an affective antidote to the siloed experience of voting today, the "I Voted" stickers are meant to restore *a sense of* togetherness and co-participation in building a shareable society (fig. 2.4). By calling nonpartisan attention to the being-in-common that the right to vote creates for all citizens, the stickers affirm the building-of-commons that voting is felt to exemplify.

There are precedents for the practice, more or less, in antiquity, when Scythian slaves used a red-dyed rope to corral and mark Athenian citizens who were malingering in the agora instead of attending the meeting of the *ecclesia* (later, Athenian leaders began paying citizens to attend).[52] But unlike the motivational influence of being publicly shamed with a red mark, or of being bribed with a few obols, the "I Voted" stickers are more effective at creating an impalpable sense of in-this-together commonality than at motivating more people to hit the polls. Alas, as people all over America (at least) post photos of these stickers to social media, stick them on the gravestones of suffragists, or wear them over their heart, the dispersed and productive sense of commonness that the stickers evoke is already too late. The fecund affective conditions they create for the civil and public discussion of issues that could lead to rhetorical judgments about how best to move society forward is actualized only after the would-be fruits of those missed discussions have been harvested in the form of a cast ballot. Communicative capitalism's fruits don't ripen on the vine. They're picked early, taken to market, and left to ripen or rot once you've brought them home.

The beautiful yet elusive promise of any public sphere is that the right affective background for sympathetic conversations does exist, that civil deliberations and debates, arguments and agreements will happen, have a duration, be lived with in the mash and mess of everyday experience until eventually, maybe, they lead to something generative and good. Jerry Hauser's writing about public spheres, for instance, emphasizes the idea that ordinary communication, including the conditions in which it is realized, makes public engagement with issues of common significance possible. "Our communicative environment," he writes, "conditions our *publicness*, defines how we experience ourselves in a milieu of strangers, and shapes the character of those publics that actually do form. The communicative ecology shapes our *public spheres*."[53] Hauser's formidable contributions to public-sphere theory are often associated with what he takes as their constitution through rhetorical discourse: the varieties of symbolic transactions between strangers that "affect people's shared sense of the world."[54] But it may be in his reference to a "communicative *environment*," a "*milieu* of strangers," a "communicative *ecology*" that we can find a more profound insight. It is not just discourse, in other words, that matters for Hauser, but the relational conditions of such discourse, its "associative network." While discursive symbolicity still remains a public sphere's vital currency, the rhetorical salience of symbolic exchange—that which gives a public sphere its capacity to achieve consensus and reach its functional telos of critical judgment—still requires a context of shared assumptions and commonplaces. Hauser calls this context and the discourse circulating within it a "communicative ecology." I have suggested that we imagine our communicative ecologies operating through both symbolic and affective orders.[55]

To superimpose a public sphere's symbolic order and its less legible affective order does not just identify another "dimension" of public life and its complexity. Identifying in affective orders those conditions of possibility for meaningful symbolic exchange also means reconfiguring how we understand the distribution of those exchanges and their articulation with/in commercial or civil society. If a public sphere's symbolic order relies on or coexists with an affective order, however, neither of them alone will adequately account for the ongoing and dynamic process of articulations between rhetoric and culture that characterize everyday life in the first decades of the twenty-first century.

The superimposition of affective and symbolic orders therefore requires a more porous and dispersed understanding of the "situation" in which rhetoric (in its various manifestations of communicative action) occurs.

Jenny Rice has proposed such an alternative in her argument that rhetorical situations occur within a wider experiential network, an "affective ecology," such that "public interactions bleed into wider social processes."[56] The stakes are how we understand the ways rhetoric circulates through the social field to form public associations that might lead toward a common purpose and movement. The idea is that no single agent, no isolatable exigence, no discrete audience, no specific constraints can alone account for the whole processual complexity of rhetoric's emergence and distribution through public life. Other more affective factors are in play, and these distributed intensities are part of the wider communicative ecology that gives rise to the public creation of rhetoric around matters of common concern.

Rice supports her argument with an example from Austin, Texas, where concerned gestures by citizens and local businesses to "Keep Austin Weird," in the face of encroaching corporate development, utilized cultural techniques such as bumper stickers, T-shirts, and graffiti to create a dispersed public feeling and attitude. We could just as viably furnish the example of Vandalina's stickers about the rates of murdered women in Ankara, or stickers about the importance of reading, or stickers announcing that someone had voted today. The public feeling behind the aggregative and various pleas to "Keep Austin Weird" was not just occasioned by or about the exigent issue of urban sprawl, or of big-box companies overpowering local ones, but rather by a mood dispersed throughout the social field, predisposing the public's orientation to the constellation of issues surrounding Austin's commercial and residential development.

Rice's point is that neither the material reality of the encroaching development itself nor the discourse surrounding it can alone sufficiently account for the circulation of affective dispositions that influence how rhetoric's symbolic actions take shape and spread. I would add, crucially, that the "influence" of affective dispositions is what potentiates rhetoric's persuadability, which makes the affective *itself* rhetorical, leading to a conceptual circularity that is hard to breach. To distinguish affective and symbolic orders, then, is not to make an ontological distinction, but to draw a distinction between coexisting attributes. To separate one from the other would be like asking whether the sea or the land makes a beach.[57] The problem is how to understand them *in* their coexistence. Doing so may require deepening our understanding both of the nonsymbolic and of rhetoric.

Consider two inroads to the problem. In one, the more traditional approach, we could extend the range of the rhetorical to include, for instance, the body, and more generally the material "things" of this world, among those communications that have rhetorical salience achieved through symbolic means. In the other, we could recognize the corporeal and material as something else entirely: as things that lack the representational functions implied by the human tendency to perceive them symbolically, yet have salience nonetheless. If the former approach supposes that fundamentally nonsymbolic things have the capacity, in certain contexts of agreed-upon codes, to *mean* symbolically, the latter approach supposes that nonsymbolic things *have consequence* because they cannot viably be separated from the symbolic orders they support.

An illustrative example is the treatment of the body as an argument. Classical rhetoric, grounded in an oral culture, shows a precedent of acknowledging the body's capacity to influence through representation—for instance, through the display of hand movements, postures, and bodily comportment. It's in this lineage that the first approach I've described can be seen as traditional. Although proponents of such a position might acknowledge that the body itself has no inherent symbolism or discursivity, they equally maintain its capacity to mean and influence *by being used* in symbolic and discursive ways. Hauser, for instance, has observed that although the human body's "biological status is not symbolic," if we focus only on "its status as a biological organism" we risk missing "the body's symbolic significance and the numerous ways in which it is used as a form of signification."[58] Recognizing that the body can be "*used as a form of signification*" extends discourse into nonlinguistic forms of communication, so that the purview of the discursive now includes not just the body, but spaces and places, sounds, and materiality more generally, the implication often being that these things are wielded symbolically by an agent—a hunger striker, architect, musician, and so on—whose intentions activate the instrumentality of whatever extralinguistic media they use to achieve a certain influence. Inasmuch as rhetoric includes the realm of the discursive, which is to say that which has a capacity to mean through symbolic representation, an extension of the discursive also constitutes an extension of the rhetorical.

But against what I see as these incisive yet ultimately traditional approaches to extend the discursive and hence the rhetorical, another camp can be identified among those who would concede no distinction between the discursive and the material at all, supposing instead that matter is not used discursively: it is discursive. This approach is sometimes associated with what's called a flat ontology, and while it denies that the material and discursive exist on separate planes, it does so by recognizing an extra-symbolic aspect of material things held to have a salience wholly their own—that is, independent of any signifying capacities humans might ascribe to them.[59] As Félix Guattari has argued, matter's extrasymbolic nature vests the material with what, in a different approach, would be seen as nondiscursivity, if not a "discourse" somehow beyond representation, beyond symbolism, beyond signification.[60] This mode of thought also attends to bodies, spaces and places, sounds and images, and so on, but without attempting to separate their symbolic discursivity from their materiality through a correlationist principle that a mind is a necessary supervisor for all meaning.[61] Instead, such thinking flattens matter and discourse into a kind of asymbolic (hence, by its traditional model, arhetorical) material semiotics that operates in an affective key: things affecting others through assemblages of relations that are felt or perceived without meaning attached because to attach meaning is to fix and semanticize a set of relations better understood rather as emergent, as always still "becoming."

Through this thinking, affectability is the always-here backdrop of our rhetorical togetherness in the world. Rhetorical salience may remain the legible operator of public affairs, their most robust and vital currency. Yet the affective, or what Diane Davis calls "a fundamental structure of exposure," is rhetoric's most elemental sine qua non.[62] Both Diane Davis and Thomas Rickert equate affect and persuadability. In a quotable passage from her introduction to *Inessential Solidarity*, for instance, Davis writes that her "goal is to expose an originary (or preoriginary) rhetoricity—an affectability or persuadability—that is the condition for symbolic action."[63] Rickert writes similarly, in his *Ambient Rhetoric*, that "affect, or persuadability, already inheres, both materially and meaningfully, and is therefore prior to rhetoric. It is the condition of possibility for rhetoric's emergence."[64] Both their books do some heavy lifting, Davis's principally through Levinas, Rickert's through Heidegger. While their projects are quite different, then, if a commonality unites them, it is the desire to acknowledge that language is not the only show in town when it comes to the rhetorical. The nonsymbolic, "metaphysical" identificatory capacities of affect create the very conditions whereby rhetoric is possible. The affective order, in other words, is the necessary primer for those orientations toward otherness and togetherness that make rhetorical sociality possible in the symbolic.

One way to illustrate how symbolic and affective orders coexist in concerned gestures is through the Black Lives Matter movement's signature rhetorical act, "Hands Up, Don't Shoot." In a context of disproportionate and unnecessary American police violence toward people of dark skin, the gesture of raising one's hands is a sign of vulnerability, of nonviolent intention. It acts as a bodily means of giving pause by seeking to slow relations down before they get out of control. It would be hard to imagine a concerned gesture more emblematic of the figure of the idiot than two raised hands and a look that says, "Now let's be careful about what we're about to do." And it's easy to see how this is a gesture of concern: it literally mobilizes a gesture (raised hands) of concern (not to be shot). But the gesture operates differently depending on the body of the one enacting it. A white body raising its hands and asking not to be shot can merely *represent* through symbolic performance the gesture that a black body doing the same thing expresses through bringing into form an affective relation that speaks for itself. While we could say that one *means* more than the other, the gesture's intensive force comes from the affectability it creates by bringing into form an extrasymbolic, material structure of exposure to an encounter with another.[65] Different bodies of encounter matter differently, and differently across historical conjunctures.[66] Affectively speaking, that is, all encounters are sticky situations, though some stickier than others.

STICKINESS

If this chapter began with unpeeling a sticker, I bring us toward its close by saying more about what to do with its stickiness. At an elemental level, stickiness is a property of an adhesive's molecular bonds. The more stress needed to pull those bonds apart, the stronger the adhesive will be. To separate a sticker from its backing, then, is to exert enough stress on those bonds to break their adherence. Because you can't *talk* the bonds apart, doing so requires the movement of a body or tools in a kinesthetic action that involves the sense of touch. As Karen Barad has pointed out, though, touch does not actually involve making contact with something else, so much as it involves the illusion of contact. Not something, then, but a sense of something. Because atoms are mostly empty space, and the electrons inside them can't bear direct contact, what we feel as "touch" is actually just the force of electromagnetic repulsion: negatively charged particles pushing each other away.[67] When we separate a sticker from its back, that means what we feel as contact (between our fingers, the sticker, and its backing) is in fact a repulsion, and what we see as a separation (of the sticker from its backing) is in fact each part's cohesion.

As the very physics of touch reveals, connections are not always connections. Despite ecological thought's basic mantra that "everything in the environment is connected to everything else,"[68] it's plain enough to see that enormous disconnections characterize our social and political lives. Whether physical or abstract, the prevalence of these disconnections does not mean that *influence* isn't pervasive. As William James once put it, "Everything that exists is influenced in some way by something else . . . all things cohere and adhere to each other somehow."[69] Certainly, one way to think about influence is through the study of rhetoric. That study has often emphasized influence as the product of a situated, contextual relationship between form and content, between *how* something is represented and *what* that representation means. But if what matters about gestures of concern has less to do with their meaning-effects than their sense-effects, as I've suggested in the cases of Vandalina, Shepard Fairey, and unknown others, then tracing the stickiness in such gestures will require an understanding of rhetorical influence as operating in affective registers as much as the representational.

Yi-Fu Tuan once observed that "human adults dislike having sticky matter on their skin, perhaps because it destroys the skin's power for discernment."[70] Gestures of concern—exemplified (but by no means limited to) putting stickers up in public—can contribute to our power for discernment. As gestures, they communicate communicability itself, conveying a sense of a "happening doing"[71] across the social field, an emergent affectability that doesn't dull our faculty of exploration, but rather discloses the possibility of a public sensibility or mood from which we might gain new capacities to act in solidarity.[72] How that happens, how a generalized affectability rises to become something "sticky" or not, remains to be seen.

In *Promise of Happiness*, Sara Ahmed draws on Teresa Brennan's work to complicate how affectivity circulates. One way that Brennan illustrates her thesis that affect is transmitted socially is by using the example of someone who, on entering a room, picks up on the tension inside immediately.[73] Ahmed extends this theory by observing that affect isn't just transmitted "outside-in" (i.e., the existing affectivity in the room transmitting *into* those who perceive it) but is also transmitted "inside-out" (because our moods influence how we are able to receive the affectivity coming from elsewhere). "If bodies do not arrive in neutral," Ahmed writes, "if we are always in some way or another moody, then what we will receive as an impression will depend on our affective situation."[74] For Ahmed, then, affectability is akin to moods, ways of being oriented vis-à-vis others, both objects and people. The mutual influence of these moods or orientations, outside-in and inside-out—"toward" or "away," as Ahmed has also described them—gives the affective order a kind of stickiness.[75]

However, unlike a sticker with self-adhesive properties that the surface you might stick it to does not possess, the stickiness of affects is not intrinsic to subjects or objects. Rather, Ahmed insists, affects follow "a set of processes that might bypass conscious recognition (and are all the more affective *given* this bypassing)," and through this process they become something that "*almost comes* to reside as a quality of this or that object."[76] Ahmed's insight is that once we adapt an orientation toward objects and people that presumes certain "affects" reside in them, we lose sight of the history by which that orientation came to the fore.[77] We lose the perspective, for instance, to remember that a hooded stranger on the street, or an abandoned handbag at the bus station, is not intrinsically suspicious. They may have come to seem suspicious because of the orientations that have circulated in our wider affective order and become sticky. "Affect," Ahmed writes elsewhere, "is what sticks, or what sustains or preserves the connection between ideas, values, and objects."[78] Not only is the study of affect an ethically laden enterprise, then, in that it calls us toward mindfulness of the ways we have come to be stuck in certain dispositions toward others; thinking about affect as processual rather than situated means there is always hope, even in the face of apparent finality or obduracy, for a reorientation of affective dispositions that could make worlds otherwise.

The stickiness of affective orders accordingly has important consequences for understanding rhetoric's role in any public sphere's more legible symbolic order, where people empirically do discuss issues that have shelflives and serious social urgency for audiences of other people who are equally implicated in the various issues' consequences. Jenny Rice has noted that an affective study of public life means acceding that "'deliberative spaces' do not neatly originate with a *kairotic* exigence that sparks multiple voices responding to each other."[79] Public rhetorics surrounding particular issues—say, repatriating the Elgin marbles—are "not necessarily born from a single exigence, or even from subsequent conversations," but from already existing dispositions toward that topic, which may be unknown to us. The result, Rice supposes, is that public rhetoric is sometimes "less conversational and deliberative than it is additive and associational."[80] We bring to our discussion of the British Museum and the Parthenon a whole history of sensibilities toward colonialism and cultural heritage, some more entrenched, others still inchoate, and they spiral out toward related topics to which we invariably bring still more sensibilities and predispositions, on and on.

This point brings out one of the reasons it is so important to distinguish between affective and symbolic orders while retaining their coexisting inseparability. In our shared attention to public issues, the knowable basis for our disposition to these issues is often how people have discussed them: how the arguments appear to have developed, why some and not others seem to have prevailed, which points are given the most salience and which are sidelined or ignored. These factors all fall within a public sphere's symbolic order. Yet, beyond what is knowable, all the participants discussing, for instance, the ownership of cultural treasures looted or gained in conquest have affective histories that preconfigure and influence the discussions that constitute a public sphere's more empirically traceable instantiations.

Without acknowledging that our public communication always already occurs within both the symbolic and affective orders of a communicative ecology, we miss that the stickiness of affects offers what Nigel Thrift calls a "whole new means of manipulation by the powerful."[81] The unknowability of affects, coupled with their tenacity or their stickiness, lends a tacit but pervading uncertainty to social relations. We never wholly know the ambient motivations and preconscious orientations that affect how or why symbolic orders take the shape that they do. While a suspicion of "mere" rhetoric has become a relatively commonplace disposition in the popular press, and while many have developed a shrewd ability to detect linguistic manipulation, certainly to be skeptical toward power, the faculty of detecting affectability is not so easily developed. Meanwhile, the "idiot" continues to go unrecognized and unvalidated. In the same way that an "I Voted" sticker affirms a civic being-in-common while concealing the ideological differences that an "I Voted for So-and-So" sticker would proclaim, the uncertainty of affects can orient us toward others without the assurance of knowing whether our shared feelings and opinions, and the communicative expression thereof, are founded in a material reality that is more than imaginary. Increasingly, the very performance of citizenship has become an art of negotiating this uncertainty. And, as we'll see in the next two chapters, that's nowhere more evident than in processes of integrating creative and critical engagement with the arts into everyday life.

3

DEMOCRATIZING CREATIVITY, CURATING CULTURE

There's a good story, possibly apocryphal, about James Joyce composing some of *Finnegans Wake* through dictation. As the story goes, Joyce was sitting in a room dictating to his friend Samuel Beckett when someone knocked on the door. Joyce said, "Come in," and Beckett, who hadn't heard the knock, wrote it down. Later, as Beckett was reading back where they'd left off, Joyce didn't recognize the phrase. "What's that, 'Come in'?" he asked. Beckett reported that that's what Joyce had said. To which Joyce, after thinking for a moment, replied, "Let it stand."[1]

Whatever this anecdote may or may not tell us about Joyce's creative methods or playful tendencies, its allure hinges on a deeply ingrained attitude about art's relationship with lived experience. The story implies that Joyce had not initially intended for the command, "Come in," to be included in his book. He'd rather uttered the phrase in response to his immediately lived reality, an embodied social reality outside the fictional reality portrayed in his novel. By deciding to include the phrase in his manuscript, however, Joyce pierced the supposed boundary between art and "real life." This didn't make experience and its representation indistinguishable, but it hinted at the porousness of their borders. If the surface of the novel could be punctured, as it were, to allow the outside world also now inside it, then the reverse might also be true: the surface of quotidian life could be infiltrated by art in ways that don't just extrinsically modify experience, but rather constitute the intrinsic artfulness of sociality itself.

Panning out from a closed room almost a century ago to consider the broader conditions of public life today, I want to suggest in this chapter that we have begun to undergo changes in the social fabric that have made art and sociality increasingly interconnected. This is an important step in the argument advanced so far. Together, the first two chapters made a case for taking the figure of "the idiot" more seriously, first by thinking about the concern that draws people toward tentative investments in something beyond their private interests, second by identifying the gestural nature of those investments as more affective than effective. In this chapter and the next, it remains to be shown how the importance of concerned gestures has been intensified as a result of historical processes that have made engagement with the arts, creative and critical alike, an ordinary part of everyday social life. It is no longer as tenable, if it ever was, to suppose a realm of "art" on the one hand and "real life" on the other.

From a certain standpoint, this argument is nothing new. In the early 1930s, around the same time that Joyce was composing *Finnegans Wake* in Europe, John Dewey was lecturing at Harvard about the error of separating art from daily activity. Instead of what he called the "museum conception of art," which he thought falsely segregated and compartmentalized the aesthetic as if it were separate from ordinary experience, Dewey maintained that the aesthetic was as natural as any biological commonplace and that "art is thus prefigured in the very processes of living."[2] Back in 1932, when Dewey was giving these lectures, he could not possibly have foreseen all the changes in the cultural field and its communication technologies that, by the millennium, would come to effectuate such a widespread reconfiguration of social life as to make his thesis nearly self-evident. Though I will draw on Dewey's philosophy later, my aim in this chapter is less to advance a pragmatist aesthetics than to suggest that aesthetic expression today has become integrated into ordinary experience to such an extent that the very idea of separating art from our daily ways of being together is almost inconceivable.

And importantly: this has had consequences. By reconfiguring the social around the aesthetic, and the aesthetic around the social, the public communicative practices of everyday life are lately taking the form of creative and critical expressions that we can understand as gestural. As networked communication technologies blur the old boundaries between virtual and actual, public and private, expert and amateur, artist and audience, and so forth, a new mode of concerned publicness is emerging. On one hand, the democratization of creativity has made ordinary people into citizen artists; on the other, the curation of culture has made ordinary people into citizen critics. By offering two short variations on how we came to such a predicament, we can better see why attending to concerned gestures, along with the interplay of affective and symbolic orders, suits the dynamics of a contemporary culturescape that finds citizen artists and critics working in tandem, but also in tension.

In the first variation, "democratizing creativity," we encounter a historical present in which nearly everyone has been capacitated and encouraged to produce aesthetically mediated experiences. One of the more obvious manifestations of this phenomenon is the way digital technologies now enable people to undertake aesthetic practices that, for a long time, were the province of professionals alone (editing photographs or video, for instance, or recording one's own music). Yet the democratization of creativity is not just about the well-known technological capacitation of people to undertake creative practices, but also about a change in cultural attitude whereby the aesthetic has come to be adopted as a principal form of public communication for ordinary people. This change is not alone attributable to the advent and spreading of digital technologies and the creative economy to which they've given rise. The rise of citizen artists can also be traced to the so-called art world's evolving notions of participatory and relational art. The result is an everyday life wherein participatory democracy and participatory art are becoming ever more indissociable.[3]

In the second variation, "curating culture," ordinary people have been given the means and motive to become curators of the abundant cultural production that results from the democratization of artistic practices. Although "to curate" had become a mainstream buzzword less than a decade into the millennium, cropping up everywhere from clothing boutiques to food trucks, curating has meant different things and entailed different practices throughout history. Alongside the democratization of creativity, then, what registers today as a parallel democratization of cultural curation was not born yesterday. Curating has always been a means of organizing knowledge for the purposes of shared social benefit. It's only recently that ordinary people have been enlisted to perform everyday, vernacular acts of curation. These mediated acts may ostensibly appear devoid of the more substantive discursive qualities that constitute so much of public affairs, but they operate rhetorically in ways that have great social consequence. Still, their greatest consequence derives less from the construction of social meaning through symbolic action than from a more primary presymbolic contribution to the affective order that preconfigures any public's disposition to be rhetorically affected in the first place.

VARIATION I: DEMOCRATIZING CREATIVITY

Fundamentally, to democratize creativity is to tap into everyone's innate creative potential by eliminating the barriers to its expression. To eliminate barriers to creative expression is not just to give people crayons and paper, but to change the parameters of addressivity for creative acts, and to legitimate these acts in themselves as opposed to doing so on the basis of some aesthetic or alternative measure of merit. In turn, creativity's democratization promulgates a set of values that extol the individual and open the realm of the cultural to varieties and agents of expression not typically afforded a place in art's "world." Vera Zolberg notes that "conventionally, [democratization] has signified making available what has come to be viewed as traditional elite culture to broader publics, and inducing these publics to use or appreciate it. More recently, however, it has also come to encompass the enlargement of the content of aesthetic culture itself, by including cultural forms and genres hitherto unrecognized or previously excluded from this hierarchically defined construct."[4] By associating "democratization" with aesthetic culture—an association not implied by one of the word's cognates, "democracy"—we are invited to see the old democratic project of inclusivity, accessibility, and equality as one that's now being sustained through aesthetic production.

The reconfiguration of public life such that citizenship becomes artistic, and a citizen's art the self-sufficient sharing of experience for the public measure, would not have been possible without changes in those material conditions necessary to bring such a reconfiguration about. Over the last thirty-plus years, one major way our material conditions have changed has been through the enormous epistemological shift to networked and digital communication technologies. In new media scholarship interested in democracy during this period, these changes are reflected in the convergence of two robust areas of research. In the first case, a profuse literature has emerged around questions of the internet's potential to facilitate and revive the public sphere.[5] By now, so much has been written on this topic that many scholars have made much ado about just how much ado has been made.[6] Greg Goldberg describes the attention most bluntly when he writes, "More than an interest of scholars of new media, the public sphere is a preoccupation."[7] Certainly one reason for the preoccupation is that the accessibility and discursive freedoms of digitally networked communication platforms make them seem so neatly to fulfill the promise of Habermas's normative theory of a democratic public sphere.[8]

Meanwhile, though, scholars have been giving similarly widespread attention to a second set of issues: namely, the democratic potentiality of Web 2.0

(3.0, etc.) and the paradigm shift toward a mobile participatory culture now enabling ordinary people to generate and mediate the cultural content that circulates across networks accessible from nearly anywhere.[9] This strain of literature is not just about the Web-as-public-sphere, that is, about how the digitally networked technologies make it possible for more people to have access to cultural capital and to deliberate among strangers about mutually impinging affairs. Rather, it is invested in the consequences and implications of new media hardware and software platforms that enable more people to participate in cultural production by contributing, curating, and critiquing cultural content for the public measure.

Examples of this paradigm are plentiful to anyone paying attention. Whenever someone makes a YouTube video, designs a website, shares a photograph, livestreams an event, and so on, they are active producers of cultural content and not just its passive consumers. The age of the "prosumer" (a portmanteau of "producer" and "consumer" coined by futurist Alvin Toffler as far back as 1980) is fully upon us.[10] In turn, common parlance has changed cultural "audiences" (a passive formulation) into "users" (an active one), and what David Beer maligns as *a rhetoric of democratization* tacitly affirms the old questions about the internet's potential to revive the public sphere, despite how its power dynamics strongly delimit the means and ends of our online activities.[11] One of the ways this general trend of democratization has played out is in a particularly "creative" way, such that aesthetic practices once undertaken by a much smaller subset of the populace have become the purview of ordinary people and been presented as a viable means of enacting ordinary democracy.

AESTHETICIZING THE SOCIAL

Examples of the aesthetic converging with everyday communication and its media are manifold, from stickers to emojis, deepfakes to VR, and from the gamification of just about everything to the great global renaissance of "design." Communicating interpersonally via photographs, for instance, is in itself an inherently aestheticized mode of communication, certainly in a different way than speech or writing. As Robert Hariman and John Lucaites have put it, photographs "'aestheticize reality.'"[12] Considering that we also have the ability to edit those photos we post, text, or otherwise share with others, the artfulness of such everyday interactions is plain to see. When, before sharing, we crop a photo, add animations, digital stickers, filters, augmented reality features, or any post-processing techniques that deliberately change that photo's potential sense impressions without wholly changing its meaning, we have evidence of just how aestheticized ordinary communication has become. When the aesthetic features of our interactions supplant or suppress their signifying message in favor of a more affective tonality, we begin to see how such communication takes a gestural form.

One of the most straightforward yet rich examples of how aestheticized communication can become gestural is the photo filters that Facebook created after the bombings and shootings in Paris that killed more than 130 people in November 2015. These filters enabled those on Facebook to add a translucent French flag over their profile picture as a way to show their solidarity with those who suffered from the attacks. Within the first three days of the attacks, according to Facebook, more than 120 million people had added these filters over their profiles.[13] Since that time, concerned global citizens have created filters of their own—a Union Jack in the shape of a heart, various rainbow flags, and so on—and made them available for anyone to use for an issue of their choice. The idea of a "solidarity filter" wasn't just an affordance that Facebook's Camera Effects feature made possible; it is also something that private citizens have taken on themselves creatively to expand and utilize in different contexts as gestures of concern.

What's interesting about the French flag filters is not the measurable effects they had. On that count, they had no overt demonstrable effect, at least beyond inspiring more flag filters. By all appearances, the filters didn't begin any meaningful public deliberations about terrorism or the different geopolitical exigencies that may have spawned the Paris attacks. They weren't a form of critical-rational debate. Whatever "argument" the filters may have offered didn't follow the formula of a reasonably warranted claim supported by data. The solidarity filters could hardly be shown to have had a profound effect, at least not a direct effect, on making Paris safer or on stopping the larger problems that the tragedy underscored. Yet if we understand them as gestures of concern, we can see how they contributed to a dispositional background or mood that sets the tone for all other communicative interactions and engagements. Gestures of concern matter not primarily because of any message they may or may not forward. They matter because they contribute to forming a background of expectation and desire around how worlds are configured. What's important about this background tone is not the elicitation of strong emotions or feelings, but something more subdued: a shared and hence socially dynamic affective register that sets the conditions within which other communications transpire, be they wildly passionate, coldly rational, or any admixture thereof.

In this sense, the filters on Facebook are less important for transmitting a signifying force—whatever "message" they might offer—than for spreading an affective force that cannot without remainder be attributed to a single origin/

agent or made specific enough to be delivered for ready-made interpretation. The niggling trouble with affective forces is their impalpability. When subjected to interpretive analysis, there seems to be no there there. But, as Brian Massumi has noticed, that's a problem with forces in general: "No scientists have ever observed a force. Not even Newton saw gravity. Only force-effects are observable. 'Force' is a word used to designate the repeatability or iterability of effects."[14] So what force-effects do photo filters have if not at the observable level of signification? Massumi's answer would be that their effect is perceived through the senses: "a perception is a force-effect."[15] In other words, merely by registering in one's perception, the filters exert some influence, even if that influence moves beneath consciousness and cannot be explained without changing its nature by virtue of translation "into" explainability. Aestheticized modes of sociality often operate gesturally in this way, by supplanting their demonstrable consequence with mere expressiveness that, nevertheless, can register in perception and form a background set of shared dispositions and moods.

Moods are never fixed and irreversible, but they do have a way of lingering and being shared, like the weather. In this sense, the expressiveness of concerned gestures can coalesce into moods that act as a temporary affective "stasis." Among scholars of rhetoric, stasis theory traditionally concerns the place where different disputants stand relative to a particular issue. There's a great misconception that arguments begin from difference and work toward sameness, when just the reverse is the case. Until we can be sure we're disagreeing about the same thing, we don't really disagree at all. For this reason, if a bit technically, arguments begin from the same point and move toward difference. Though this seldom happens in everyday disagreements, stasis theory is a method of ensuring all parties are on the same page by establishing a figurative place where people agree to disagree, thereby identifying the central issue in need of disputing, at which point progress can begin.

The bald expressivity in gestures of concern doesn't lend itself to isolating a ratiocinated point of stasis that could be expressed in language and used as a springboard for logically coherent argument. While such expressivity also doesn't foreclose the possibility that such stasis could be achieved through more instrumental rhetorical means, the affective stasis imputed through expressive gestures that coalesce into a shared mood is too generalized to be attached to any object or proposition. Moods just don't have objects.[16] Like a hotel room that's been smoked in, or like the active, existential character of concern itself, moods affect whatever is within their reach. One reason gestures of concern are so important is that they do help to achieve a nonrepresentational, affective variation of the more propositional "stasis" that is sometimes regarded as important to communicative progress. Affective stasis discloses a temporary consensus, the sympathetic commons of a provisional affinity.

The expressiveness of photo filters like those on Facebook after the Paris attacks seems to have done this in a particularly prominent way, but memes do it all the time. Memes, as Eric Jenkins has shown, are expressions, not representations. "An expression," he writes, "actualizes the potential energy—the affects, feelings, intensities—already circulating in the social field."[17] Memes have a representational aspect, but as they circulate they don't just re-present themselves as the propositions of particular subjects addressing particular objects. People don't generally "read" memes as fixed arguments. We encounter memes as presenting themselves for ongoing remaking, provisional nodes in a collective process that arrives both already underway and capacitated for new remakings still ahead. Their affective force eclipses their signifying content.

A meme is decidedly different than the liberal blogs that emerged in America, for instance, as a form of critique and protest during the Bush-Cheney administration, though both can operate as vernacular ways of airing political concern.[18] The difference is not the concernedness with which they're inflected; the difference is that the expressive nature of memes makes them gestural. As the ongoing means *and* ends of a collective process, rather than the means *to* an end of an individual, memes work diachronically and affectively more than synchronically and representationally. In this sense, the trending shift from blogging's popularity in the 2000s to the popularity of memes in the 2010s may attest to a mood of perceived diminishment in the capacities of representational rhetoric to produce worlds not susceptible to capture by communicative capitalism. ("No one drinks rye anymore, someone said. / No one feels that way anymore."[19]) By contrast, the meme escapes capture because the speed and scale of its circulation, along with its constitutive shape-shifting, express its power in *a relation being called into question*, not in an object being advanced as a cause. The meme's mode is an idiot rhetoric.

It's important to note that these aestheticized forms of rhetorical sociality are often undertaken in the relatively unexamined way wrought by their being a quotidian "new normal" within the wider backdrop of networked digital culture. Concerned gestures are not often grand gestures or necessarily the product of much premeditation. The social moods they propel are ordinary adaptations of those social moods in which they emerge: both a response to and a building of an affective commonwealth. It was Deleuze who showed that the signifying, propositional content of language is insufficient to understand its asignifying, affective sense.[20] I'm suggesting that to the extent their expressive "sense" is what matters, and not strictly their "meaning," concerned gestures thus lend themselves more to expressing an affective force than to communicating a propositional message, a phenomenon made all the more commonplace within a networked culture that has made ordinary social interaction itself a mode of aesthetic practice.

SOCIALIZING THE AESTHETIC

Although one consequence of the spread of networked communication technologies has been to make social interactions more artistic for even those who don't regard themselves as artists, many of those who do see themselves as artists have for years now been trying reciprocally to make art more social. In an influential 1998 book of essays, the art critic and curator Nicolas Bourriaud dubbed this more collective and social approach to art "relational aesthetics." For Bourriaud, the common trait of artists who practice relational art is that they "all construct models of sociability suitable for producing human relations, the same way an architecture literally 'produces' the itineraries of those residing in it."[21] An artist operating in this vein might, for instance, sublet her studio apartment and then move its entire contents into a gallery space for the Whitney Biennial, as Dawn Kasper did in 2012. Visitors walked through and around the space while she inhabited it as if it were "actually" her apartment, which, during the course of the Biennial, it was. She'd play music, talk on the phone, do work, relax, and anything else she might normally do at home, except now in full view of visitors for whom the experience was both interactive and voyeuristic: it actualized a new kind of social relation.

As Bourriaud tells the story, relational aesthetics was a contemporary response of artists, beginning in the 1990s, to the perceived reification of the social bond and the reduction of all social relations into something marketable.[22] Its practitioners were therefore interested in achieving through art a form of social interactivity that could not so easily be reified or reduced—making art, in Bourriaud's account, "a political project when it endeavors to move into the relational realm by turning it into an issue."[23] Cultural commodification and social spectacle, of course, were not new in the 1990s when these relational art practices first emerged. What was new at the time was the onslaught of networked technologies creating unprecedented forms of communicative interactivity between humans, between humans and computers, and between computers and computers. In other words, relational aesthetics arose as a form of art from within the larger context of a spreading digital culture, precisely as the ascent of that digital culture was meanwhile starting to give social relations themselves a more aesthetic form.[24] The democratization of creativity, in short, has drawn citizen artists in two directions: at once making the social more artful and making art more social.

Although not all have accepted relational aesthetics as a novel aesthetic form or efficacious political project, there's no disputing that it created a huge stir in the art world.[25] Relational aesthetics raised questions about the nature of art, its social function and public character, the aesthetic properties of communication, and how art's history might need to be revised, among others. As anyone familiar with twentieth-century art history will note, though, art had taken participatory forms in various ways well before the surge of the 1990s. On or about April 1921 marks as good a starting point as any, when the "Dada Season" tried to involve the Parisian public in art. One such "artwork" entailed enticing over a hundred people to walk through torrential rain to the abandoned courtyard of the church of Saint Julien le Pauvre, where Dada artists gave them a tour of an area important precisely because it wasn't picturesque, historically relevant, or sentimental. Another project involved staging a mock trial of the writer Maurice Barrès and inviting the public to serve as the jury.[26] The public provocations of the Italian Futurists, the revolutionary agenda of the Russian Constructivists ("the streets our brushes, the squares our palettes"), Antonin Artaud's Theater of Cruelty: all attempted to reduce barriers between artists and spectators by involving audiences actively in the work of art. By the 1960s, conceptual art had arrived, and with it the "happenings," "events," "situations," and anything-goes assortment of participatory, collaborative, and interactive impulses that were largely an artistic response to the emergence of a commodified spectacle society.

In light of this longer history, the art historian Claire Bishop (one of Bourriaud's sharpest critics) has suggested that there is a key difference between, on one hand, the "activation of the individual viewer in so-called 'interactive' art and installation" and, on the other, "the social dimension of participation."[27] In other words, art might move beyond its medium-specific confines and physically engage with its audience, bringing the viewers closer to it, but that isn't the same as when artists "appropriate *social* forms as a way to bring art closer to everyday life."[28] Examples of art trying to bring the audience toward it with greater interactivity have included exhibits in which visitors get colorful dot stickers to decorate an all-white room (Yayoi Kusama); sidewalk chalk murals that fool pedestrians with three-dimensional illusions (Julian Beever; Edgar Mueller); clouds of six thousand light bulbs that audiences can individually turn on or off (Caitlind r.c. Brown); walkable roller coasters (Heike Mutter and Ulrich Genth); a 175-pound pile of free candy (Félix Gonzáles-Torres); cinematic flip-book sculptures (Robert Cohen); and a virtual tunnel under the Atlantic allowing viewers to see those on the other side (Maurice Benayoun). By contrast, examples of art taking more social forms tend to engage the audience in more ordinary, if impalpable experiences: dancing to funk music (Adrian Piper); eating Thai food (Rirkrit Tiravanija); hanging out in an artist's apartment (Dawn Kasper); talking politics (Joseph Beuys); talking progress (Tino Sehgal); organizing a garage sale (Martha Rosler); drinking beer (Tom Marioni).

Art-historical narratives notwithstanding, if this latter tradition is the lineage and model of relational aesthetics, perhaps its best precedent is a different kind of art altogether. After all, when it comes to public life and social change in particular, what more originary relational art do we have than rhetoric itself, that old art of oratory that was not complete without an audience to shape the form it took? As the long rhetorical tradition has shown, more than just needing an audience there to hear a speech, audiences creatively determine a speech inasmuch as the artfulness of the speaker consists in shaping words to suit the audience's disposition toward the occasion. Cicero, for instance, observed that orators must modify their speech and thought to "the understanding of the crowd"[29] and speak in a way that conforms with "the good sense of the audience, since all who desire to win approval have regard to the goodwill of their auditors, and shape and adapt themselves completely according to this and their opinion and approval."[30] As an art of shaping and adapting, of enlisting others as co-participants in creative invention, rhetoric is *the* relational art par excellence. There is no sociality that is not also rhetorical sociality.

In this light, relational aesthetics confirms that the static distinction between active artists and passive audiences is just as problematic as the ancient distinction between political *rhetores* and apolitical *idiotes*. Instead of separating art from daily life, or "engaged" civic participation from its apparently "disengaged" alternative, we are better off asking what happens to the felt experience of citizenship today when the aestheticization of the social and the socialization of the aesthetic coincide. The question, in short, is a matter of what accountability we have to strangers, and how forging new commitments therewith can facilitate actual or virtual social contracts that enrich our affective commonwealth. By way of example, let's look at a few cases of art and sociality converging in citizen artists who form social contracts from within the shared affectivity of being made accountable to one another.

CASE 1: BLAST THEORY

Blast Theory is a British artist group that originated in rave culture of the 1990s and has been capturing some of the felt zest and playfulness of that culture ever since. Initially, the group tried to do so by bringing audiences to account through scenes of play enacted in found venues that had the sense of coming to a party rather than a performance or art event. One of their early works, *Gun Men Kill Three* (1991), did this by giving people a chance to shoot paintballs at others who had agreed to be shot. By bringing an audience in as participants that were constitutive of the work itself, a Blast Theory project felt like a game or playful experience that immersed people in the real world in ways that challenged the players to put something at stake. In *Kidnap* (1998), for instance, the group held a public lottery of consenting participants who had agreed to be kidnapped for forty-eight hours if they won. The kidnappings were then broadcast live online (impressively, at a time well before livestreaming technologies had become commonplace). In *Uncle Roy All Around You*, a hybrid online/offline game from 2003, human players in front of computer screens guided human players who were somewhere out on the streets holding mobile devices. In another impressive technological feat for the time, the devices marked the real-time location of the street players on a map and enabled them to communicate with those playing from the computer lab somewhere else. Together, both types of player shared the goal of looking for a fictional character named Uncle Roy. Near the end of the game, the street players were asked if they were prepared to "commit to help a stranger for the next year." If so, they were asked if they'd release their personal contact details to that stranger. Those players who agreed were then paired up, face to face, and made mutually accountable to one another, despite being total strangers.

Four pillars seem to support the Blast Theory project.[31] First, they see the audience as a protagonist, that is, as a key member in the project, not just a spectator. Second, they like mixing different layers of reality, virtual and actual, often by integrating technology into their projects. Third, they seek to create a more permeable boundary between when games begin and end, removing the borders around "play" and creating a sense of pervasive gaming and play in ordinary life. Finally, they are interested time and again in presence and liveness, in creating real and felt stakes that involve an impact beyond the concocted experience itself. Overall, their work shows an interest in placing people in new situations that allow them to find new ways to be together and talk.

CASE 2: ADRIAN PIPER

Adrian Piper is an American artist and philosopher based in Berlin. Though her work is often discussed in the same wheelhouse as relational aesthetics, its conceptual emphasis has both preceded that moment and survived the hangover of its aftermath. Since the 1960s, she has produced works across

Figure 3.1. Adrian Piper, *The Humming Room*. Museum of Modern Art, New York, NY, 2018. Photo courtesy of Katherine Guinness.

media—drawing, video, dance, performance, participation—that confront audiences with difficult questions about gender, race, identity, and accountability both to oneself and to others. In a project named *Calling Card* (1986), for instance, she produced a set of cards, more or less resembling business cards with provocations printed on them, that people could give to those they saw acting publicly in racist or sexist ways. In *The Humming Room* (2012), she put a security guard at the entrance to her exhibit with the instruction that, in order to enter, visitors needed to hum a tune. Any tune would do, but to be admitted visitors had to approach the guard while humming and be heard humming as they went by (fig. 3.1). Piper's work often confronts its audience in a way that asks them to make a personal commitment. Though it might be frivolous or quite serious, this commitment constitutes a social relation that would otherwise not be activated but for the aesthetic context of its production.

Probably the best example of Piper's commitment-seeking art is an installation called *The Probable Trust Registry: The Rules of the Game #1–3*, for which she won the Golden Lion for Best Artist at the 2015 Venice Biennale. The work involved converting a gallery space into one that looked like three distinct corporate reception areas. Gray walls from floor to ceiling divided the areas, each of which had a lectern for visitors to read information, and a golden circular desk staffed by a receptionist dressed in black and working on a stool at a computer. Embossed in gold, all-caps letters on the wall behind each receptionist was a different statement:

I WILL ALWAYS BE TOO EXPENSIVE TO BUY.
I WILL ALWAYS MEAN WHAT I SAY.
I WILL ALWAYS DO WHAT I SAY I AM GOING TO DO.

Visitors to the installation were free to interact with the receptionist and ask questions. Indeed, such interaction was the only way for the uninitiated to know what was going on. The idea was for visitors to pick the declaration(s) about which they felt strongest and to enter into a signed and legally binding contractual agreement to follow through on its promise. Those who signed contracts were given a copy of it for their own records, while a second copy was kept in a registry among other signed contracts. Every contractual participant would have access to this registry of "probable trust" and in that way be made socially and morally accountable to strangers.

The installation not only required the participation of its audience, something Piper's work had been doing for some time. The artwork also invited its participants to enter into a contract both with themselves and with others, which would theoretically remain in effect for the rest of their lives. Of course, though it was free of legalese, the contract's legal enforceability was murkier than its moral claims on both personal and social integrity. By signing the agreement, participants became from that time on beholden both to themselves (to keep a promise that most often only they would know if they were breaking) and to strangers (to keep a promise to others who would be as capable of holding you accountable as you would be of them).

CASE 3: ADAM MILNER

Adam Milner is a refreshingly hard-to-classify American artist whose work, like Blast Theory's and Adrian Piper's, takes many forms and media: photographs, dances, installations, collages, drawings, collections of found and stolen objects, body parts and fluids, texts, tables, performances, videos, interactions. His projects often work by extending the personal and intimate into the social and shared—or rather, by refusing the separation between them. In one of his videos, for instance, he uses the light reflecting off the screen of his phone to "touch" artworks in galleries otherwise designated as untouchable and off limits. For a work of similarly tender beauty, *Body Fossils*, he took flowers that had fallen from plants, along with eyelashes that had fallen from his own eyes, and inset them on embossed paper to produce panels that gesture toward the fragile connection between a human body and the world. In *Body Fossils*, Milner isn't just using these things as a medium to represent something else; he's exhibiting the flowers and eyelashes themselves. By conceiving the artwork as merely a container for displaying the petals and lashes, he blurs the human and object world in ways that cultivate empathy and kinship across such divides.

In 2017, Milner began exhibiting his ongoing *Letting* series, which consists of bed sheets stained pink with his own blood and that of his partner, Fred. Without being graphic, the works gesture toward the intimacy of homosexuality and the difficulty of knowing where one body ends and another begins. Recently, Milner extended his work with blood, that most intimate of mediums, in a project called *Not a Pact, But Not Not a Pact*. The ongoing project involves both drawing his own blood and bringing friends into his apartment to draw theirs. Through these DIY blood drives, a community forms (both metaphorically and literally) by bringing people into proximity made more intimate by way of its vulnerability and hands-on tenderness. The exhibitable portion of *Not a Pact, But Not Not a Pact* involves the display of cotton gloves on metal stands, each saturated with the blood of a different contributor. But the exhibition, in many ways, is secondary to the embodied experience of the blood drive itself: the experience of coming into a new mode of relation with others.

Along these lines, much of his work pivots on enacting a more partici-patory social contract and commitment. For instance, in a 2017 performance called *I found the tallest man I could and buried him so we were the same height,* he did just that. The work required entering into a kind of unofficial contractual agreement with a stranger to share an experience that would open up a rela-tion not possible without the experience itself: standing together in the heat, talking, digging out soil with a shovel, stepping inside the pit to see if the depth was right, and so on. The performance explored what one kind of equality or being-in-common looked like—the literal if superficial equality of identical height—by enacting the trustful social relationship necessary to build it.

In another relational work, called *Still Life,* he asked visitors to his exhi-bition to answer a simple question as the condition of their being admitted: "How much of your body can I have?" Going beyond the embodied playfulness of Adrian Piper's *Humming Room*, the question at the heart of Milner's *Still Life* sparked conversations, rituals, and negotiations that often ended in the clip-ping of hair or fingernails, the gift of a contact lens or gum, the scraping-off of nail polish, and so forth. Those admitted then sat in pews beneath stained-glass windows, while Milner laid these objects out on long, narrow tables that he had built to fit down the length of the aisle. There was nothing else to see except what visitors had given. Like so much of his work, the performance required a tacit social contract and mutual trust between Milner and the participants—lovers, friends, or strangers. It not only gestured toward the sacredness of those embodied sacrifices we are willing to make for others in service of such con-tracts; it measured the results of that sacrifice by putting them on display.

If projects such as these have in some ways literally created a new body social, they have done so because Milner has asked something of others and built with them a confraternity that brought a new set of capacities into being. This work succeeds in part because of his own involvement in the exposures he creates. For Milner, art seems to engender and explore those circumstances necessary to foster the vulnerability it takes to subvert social distancing and incite the possibility of a social intimacy that is presumably always there between us, though it becomes more attainable through aes-thetic experience.

NEW SOCIAL CONTRACTS

Though Blast Theory, Adrian Piper, and Adam Milner are doing work of decidedly different purposes and execution, they do share a tendency to bring about experiences that would not be possible without the aesthetic gesture that activates them. While these experiences will naturally vary from person to person, if we see them as actuating new social contracts, we can begin to recognize how aesthetic experience and social experience become entangled in ways that influence how people might imagine their accountability to others in a larger social totality. Social contract theories from Grotius to Rousseau (and many others besides) concern the individual human's relationship with the state, and the extent to which individuals can, should, or must surrender some of their freedoms in exchange for receiving the benefits of a legal and political order. If these legal and political orders are not intrinsic to a "state of nature" but rather created by human invention, then it becomes important to think about the role individuals play in asserting their natural or given rights relative to the formation and sustenance of those legal and political institutions that could be their guarantor. Theories of the social contract are significant for democratic governance in particular when they concern how to position the individual as a participant in establishing that contract's terms.

Some of the richest examples of creativity's democratization, I'm suggesting, have been socially oriented works of art like *Uncle Roy All Around You*, *The Probable Trust Registry*, and *Still Life*, each of which enlist participants to create new kinds of social contracts through sharing an experience that may not feel like a work of art so much as a gesture toward art that has a social character. In these examples, however, new social contracts aren't made between the individual and the state, but between one individual and another in ways that help to build the shared trust amenable to a more civil society. They may do so through engineered experiences that are too extra-ordinary to feel like just another part of everyday life, but that's also one reason for their affective force. By converging the aesthetic and the social, if only in set pieces, these and other works show the folly of drawing hard distinctions between the relational and the aesthetic. Our rhetorical sociality is never separate from everyday life. To the contrary, our accountability to strangers is constant and therefore important to cultivate.

At the start of this chapter, by way of an anecdote about James Joyce, I suggested that thinking about the convergence of art and everyday experience will help us to account for new modes of concerned publicness today. I promised to offer two variations of these modes. Thus far, we have been considering one of these variations: namely, how the democratization of creativity has spawned the growth of citizen artists, evident both in "nonartists" who are engaging the social by way of the aesthetic and in "professional artists" who are engaging the aesthetic by way of the social. Each enacts a new mode of citizenship through the creative adventure of entering into a new relationship with strangers founded on some common ground. That commonality can show up as a kind of solidarity or affinity, as with a photo filter on Facebook, or it can be experienced as a kind of social contract or accountability, as in some more conceptual works of art. But whatever the case, citizen artists blur the line between works of art and the rhetorical sociality of everyday life—not unlike the knock Joyce heard on his door while dictating *Finnegans Wake*. Certainly, not all artists undertake participatory approaches to their work, anymore than everyone partakes of our time's expanded techno-cultural capacities to express oneself aesthetically. Nevertheless, rather than treating art as an individual or private experience (the model of aesthetic encounter following from the visual/sensory paradigm that has dominated thinking about art for centuries), we have never had more cause to think of art as an affective process of social cooperation.[32] The democratization of creativity, in short, is facilitating what John Dewey called "creative democracy." And that brings us to our next variation.

VARIATION II: CURATING CULTURE

Dewey's ideal of creative democracy hinges on a faith in the common person's ability to address public problems adequately, and to do so again and again in a process that constantly creates democracy anew.[33] If the democratization of creativity has put cultural production in the hands of nearly anyone, then it has helped to facilitate the dream of creative democracy that Dewey championed so long ago. But it has also created a corresponding need to classify, critique, and curate all public discourse in better ways. To put it differently, in an age of information overload, attention is the scarce commodity.[34] Under such conditions it has become essential that experts and trustworthy systems of organization can guide us to whatever "content" might be most pertinent and trenchant in any given case. For Dewey (writing well before digital technologies opened the sluice gates for our current info-flood), the quintessential person suited to the task of such sense-making is the artist who brings news to the public. "Artists," he writes, "have always been the real purveyors of news, for it is not the outward happening itself which is new, but the kindling of it by emotion, perception, and appreciation."[35] Artists, in other words, don't just produce our cultural wealth. Through their cultivated critical faculty, they bring the news to the public in ways that show what among the info-flood tends to be valued—and what is merely flotsam.[36]

Nevertheless, it would be a mistake to read the relationship Dewey maps between artists and the public as modeled on a relationship of expert to layperson. In *The Public and Its Problems*, Dewey suggests that publics are groups of people who have been affected by other human actions, yet because they've had no direct influence on those actions, they have needed to organize as a public in order to address the problems those actions created.[37] Clearly, artists are part of such publics because they're just as susceptible as anyone else to the consequences of policies and techno-corporate machinations beyond their control. Whatever else Dewey may mean by "artist," then, it is not a figure superior to or separate from the public and its problems. Indeed, one legacy of American pragmatism's insistence on the inseparability of art from everyday life has been to define art in the perceiving subject whom art affects, not in the art object itself.[38] In this sense, we are all artists, if not on the creative end, certainly on the receiving one, validating anyone as a legitimate purveyor and critic of cultural value. This is why democratizing creativity leads to creative democracy: in good faith, it calls on all of us to be purveyors of the news, to curate culture—to be citizen critics.

In 2009, the *New York Times* ran a short piece about curating. If it had appeared in the Arts and Leisure section, it would have been unexceptional: just another article about the curating that goes on in art museums or archives. But this story ran in the Fashion and Style pages; it treated curation as an emergent *social phenomenon*. Citing cases of flea markets with "personally curated" food stands, nightclubs promising to "curate a night of Curious Burlesque," and a sneaker store that "curates" its inventory, the article observed the oddity that the verb "curate" had become what its author deemed "a fashionable code word among the aesthetically minded, who seem to paste it onto any activity that involves culling and selecting."[39] And so it is: everyday examples of what might be called *vernacular curation* are now so abundant that even by citing the *Times'* own examples I have effectively "curated" illustrative instances to make the point.

Curation has become a vernacular art that plays an integral role in the associative relations of public life today. Vernacular curation is the counterpart of creativity's democratization. Given the growing abundance of aesthetic texts, increasing access to them, and the diminishing traction of old distinctions between such categories as professional and amateur, author and audience, fact and fake, the need arises to sort and classify the array of cultural output in different, interested ways. Vernacular curation involves "curating culture" in order to publicly exhibit aesthetic tastes, to produce a presence to aesthetic experience, or to make a case for aesthetic value or meaning. Coinciding in part with the spread of new media technologies that make such curatorial acts easy and commonplace, the precipitous growth in acts of curatorship by nonprofessional citizen critics now gives them powerful rhetorical influence in organizing the public salience of nearly all forms of aesthetic mediation.[40]

To curate is to cull and select, to arrange and order, to classify and rank, to preserve and safeguard, all with the tacit assumption that what one selects for display or safekeeping, and how one displays or keeps it, might have some rhetorical impact. But there is an important difference between the culling and selecting that goes into any list-making process and the culling and selecting that we think of as curatorial. The difference exceeds *what* is curated and pertains rather to the audience for whom curatorial acts are performed. When you go to the store for beans and rice, you're not curating your pantry; and the to-do lists people make aren't curated either, even as there's always more to be done. What makes curatorship distinct is its addressivity toward others.

Vernacular curation is an important form of engagement in cultural public spheres today because it circulates ineffable moods that orient strangers toward their encounters with the inevitable alterity of public life. To survey the cultural field and re-present a selection of it as an expression of preferential tastes and styles is also to put forward a particular case for what matters, or ought to matter, to others. In that sense, all curating is inherently rhetorical: an expressive force that might generate meaning, produce presence, or inspire action, however "distant" it may seem as a mode of civic engagement. But the cultural milieu and technologies that encourage citizens to curate culture also downplay the symbolic message of these acts in favor of more affective contributions that operate in more expressive ways. To make this case—exploring the genesis of vernacular curation and its repercussions for the affective order that saturates all experience—I offer a (condensed) rhetorical history of curation as a social practice with six major phases, beginning in ancient Rome and leading to our present day, when communication media have capacitated ordinary citizens to perform curatorial acts as a stand-in for more deliberative modes of public engagement.

I. Public

The English verb "curate" comes from the Latin *curare*, meaning "to take care." The first curators were appointed Roman public officials known as *curatores rei publicae*—roughly, "those who take care of the common good." The position was also sometimes called a *curator civitatis*, indicating that this official was responsible for seeing to a city's orderly functioning and maintenance. The Roman emperor Domitian appointed the first known *curatores* in the last third of the first century CE. These positions held high social status and found their holders sent to foreign provinces throughout the empire, including in Africa and Asia. One of the foremost duties of *curatores rei publicae* was to supervise the finances of these provincial cities or civic communities, investigating instances of corruption and embezzlement, and ensuring that resources were spent prudently for the maintenance of shared public works and the "common good."[41] It was the *curator rei publicae*, for instance, who restored and cared for the public baths where citizens of different sorts bathed and conversed.[42] That this role belonged to someone in an appointed position attests to how much "the common" was nevertheless determined from a privileged vantage that excluded the "idiots" who might have hesitated over the limitations of a single, powerful decision-maker who came from outside the community.

By the fourth century CE, likely as a result of Diocletian reforms or the ubiquity of foreign *curatores* throughout the empire, *curatores rei publicae* were no longer appointed directly by emperors and sent far afield to care for the Roman provinces. Instead, local councils began electing *curatores* to serve as senior magistrates within the community in which they were already established.[43] This meant that high social standing or foreign origin no longer held the same weight, and the *curator* became a public figure less associated with the maintenance of Roman power abroad than with civic-mindedness toward a more familiar community at home. It remains unclear just how much autonomous discretion the *curatores* at this time had, but evidence supports at least some instances of their acting *cum amore populi*—that is, with the enthusiasm of the people, or out of love for the people—when it came to restoring public baths.[44]

The takeaway here is twofold. First, the very first curators (at least, the first to go by that name) served a distinctly *public* purpose. They saw to the responsible delegation of finances directed to the maintenance and smooth operation of shared public spaces. Inevitably, these duties required a process of selection. Funds were never unlimited, and choosing to attend to certain civic needs would have meant choosing not to address others. But the curator's unique responsibility was to execute these choices (whether autonomously, in response to the people's will, or at the behest of a more central authority seems to have varied), and to do so with the recognition that they were choices of consequence for the civic life and well-being of a public that shared some needs—the need to bathe, for instance—they could not fulfill without the government's help.

Second, the evolving administrative procedures that saw curators initially appointed directly by the emperor and later elected more democratically reveals the first of several historical contingencies that divested curators of some of their elite status and brought them closer to the people themselves. Though it has taken thousands of years, an ongoing trend in this general direction has culminated today with the production of ordinary citizens as vernacular curators whose quotidian acts of sorting and classifying serve to care for the civic good the way only those vouchsafed that authority had been privileged to do in the past. But curatorship that involved caring for the public commons, as in ancient Rome, is only part of the story that gets us to where things are today.

2. Spiritual

By the Middle Ages, the role of the curator had shifted from a public office to an ecclesiastical one. In Medieval Latin, the word *curatus* meant something like "one responsible for the care of souls," and the *curator rei publicae* had been reincarnated as a "curate": a parish priest or clergy member who assisted the priests and vicars in assuring the well-being of a congregation. As Paul Kolbet has shown in his study of Augustine's sermons, taking responsibility for the care of souls (sometimes translated as the "cure of souls") was closely aligned with the rhetorical arts dating back to Plato.[45] In the *Phaedrus*, Plato characterizes rhetoric as a *psychogogia*, or a guiding of the soul through words.[46] The role of the curate followed a more Christian form of this psychogogy, which Kolbet regards as a philosophical form of therapy "pertaining to how a mature person leads the less mature to perceive and internalize wisdom for themselves."[47] The curing of souls, which would become the central duty of pastoral curates, thus involved enchanting the congregation through words designed to lead them away from temptation and toward the path of salvation.

No longer a public office intended to safeguard the literal "common wealth" of public funds, or to care for the public commons to which these funds might be put to use, the curate now was a shepherd of the people, guiding them toward piety. Taming the all-too-human beast, though, called for different techniques than guarding public resources and selecting the civic ends to which they would be directed. Foucault has suggested that these new techniques indicated a new kind of power, one he called "pastoral power."[48] Pastoral power had an individualized nature in that its agents—pastors or curates—sought to assure individual salvation by knowing people's minds and directing them onto the righteous path. In practice, the work involved was more classically rhetorical because it was performed principally in sermons, which (though a genre unto itself post-Augustine) an Aristotelian frame would regard as epideictic public speeches. The assimilation of curatorial curing or caring by the religious establishment, no doubt with different responsibilities accorded to curates of different faiths or denominations, meant that the original concern with civic space and public wealth shifted to a concern with the public itself: with its people, who themselves, under God, could care for society and assure its collective virtue by saving their own souls from damnation.

In this way, like the shift to an elected *curator rei publicae*, the spread of religious curates in an increasingly pastoral and feudal context brought curation a step closer to the people. In the same way that the imperial state offered no buffer between one's identity as a citizen and the rhetoric of the state, the church offered no buffer between one's identity as a Christian and its own salvific rhetoric. Post-Reformation, that is, church rhetoric fell outside the civic realm; its concern was salvation, a different end than citizenship. The people, the congregations, were still directed to act according to God's will, a will expressed by a clergy who, before the spread of literacy, claimed special authority to relay God's voice. But with the Protestant revolution and the printing press, the curatorial onus to "take care" shifted: through their behaviors and habituations, the people were now entreated to ensure the care of their own souls. By doing so they could contribute to the greater good, even though guiding people in that direction was an official curate's responsibility. Over time, as print technology and the spread of literacy enabled more people to read and interpret Scripture on their own—and, crucially, as these changes gradually increased the spread of more secular forms of cultural production—the social function of the curator changed again.

3. Scientific

By the seventeenth century, the role of a curator began to assume the form we are more familiar with today: someone who selects and organizes artifacts, performances, or events for public display and safekeeping. In 1662, for instance, the Royal Society of London named the polymath Robert Hooke its "Curator of Experiments."[49] But the appointment was merely a job, not a public office, not a conferral of spiritual authority, not even an entrée into the elite fellowship of the Society itself. Hooke's duties were simply to demonstrate scientific experiments for the Royal Society's regular meetings. These duties were premised as much on Hooke's scientific expertise as his unrelenting inquisitiveness. The job seems to have been less experimental in ways generative for advancing science than performative in ways that promoted scientific exploration as its own reward. Although Hooke's curatorship may have served only the Royal Society's insular audience, it marked a subtle turning point for the role of curators in knowledge acquisition to the extent that publicly staged demonstrations of scientific experiments went on to become commonplace during the height of the eighteenth-century Enlightenment. In that light, Hooke's official position as Curator of Experiments can be seen in retrospect to mark a distinct shift in the social role of curators.

Figure 3.2. Ole Worm, *Museum Wormianum* (Leiden, 1655).

Here was a curator whose curatorial authority now derived from his own *curiosity*—a word evolved from the same Latin root *cura* to mean, by Hooke's day, both an object of interest and the inquisitive interestedness itself. The curator accordingly now played the part of an exhibitor, showing off the natural curiosities of the world and the reasoning human's capacity to attain mastery over their mysteries. Even so, that Hooke's particular curiosity and scientific aptitude were rewarded with a job that expected him to showcase them attests to curatorship having not yet become a vernacular art of nonexpert laypersons. Which is not to say there weren't people who performed acts of curatorship on their own. Already by this time, gentleman collectors had been keeping "cabinets of curiosities" gathered from all over the world.[50] One of the first such collectors, predating Hooke, was the Danish antiquary Olaus Wormius ("Ole Worm"), whose collection of oddities became Denmark's first museum, the Wormium. Its inventory included both human artifacts and other-than-human objects tending toward the bizarre, wondrous, and mythical: musical instruments, taxidermied sea creatures, unicorn horns, and so on (fig. 3.2). Often collected in the name of natural science, but also to showcase artworks and other artifacts of foreign origin, these curiosity cabinets now have an unpleasant air of colonial spoils and exoticization.[51] But it was the display of these curiosities for an audience—and, eventually, a *public* audience—that brought curators into the realm of museums with which they are still largely associated today. To understand this transition to curation's more cultural phase requires recognizing the convergence of curiosity collectors and those who saw to the caretaking and display of curiosities.

4. Cultural

The German tradition of *Galeriewerke* is one example of curation's cultural turn. *Galeriewerke* were collections of prints in high-quality albums displaying impressive collections of art, the first known example being Archduke Leopold Wilhelm of Austria's *Theatrum Pictorium*, published in 1660.[52] A precursor of the modern exhibition catalog, the portability of these albums exposed people far afield (still mostly elites) to works of art well outside their local provenance or physical location, the purpose being mainly to demonstrate the exquisite taste and largesse of those who owned the collections that each *Galeriewerk* reproduced.[53] Collectors would hire artists to draw their collections, either by directly representing the private gallery walls where they were displayed or by drawing fictive "walls" that portrayed the most exceptional and representative work from the larger holdings. David Teniers, for instance, produced such representations to be distributed as albums and as paintings to be hung for aesthetic value in their own right (fig. 3.3). Although this process entailed a curatorial practice in itself, the emergence of the museum curator as such was still not much apparent. Not until the *Galeriewerk* tradition of representing collections gave way to public galleries that displayed the collections did the museum curator become more commonplace.

An illustration of this can be seen in the case of what would become the Düsseldorf Gallery. Between 1709 and 1714, the German prince Johann Wilhelm II von der Pfalz built a structure adjacent to his palace to house his considerable collection of art.[54] Initially, the space was accessible only privately, at royal social functions and for friends and elites given special entrée as guests. Its method of display reflected this purpose: with paintings hung from floor to ceiling, one flush against the other, the close proximity of each artwork had the effect of highlighting the impressive wealth and size of the collection as a whole, making each work's beauty or significance only subsidiary. This crammed style of display may have been commonplace in the baroque period also in part because it accommodated the more efficient creation of print albums.

Figure 3.3. David Teniers the Younger, *The Archduke Leopold Wilhelm in His Picture Gallery in Brussels* (1641–57).

In 1756, Prince Wilhelm opened the gallery to the public and hired Lambert Krahe to oversee its organization and display.[55] Krahe made substantial changes. By reducing the number of paintings displayed on any one wall, he gave each artwork more room to stand out (fig. 3.4). Deemphasizing the grandeur of the collection as a whole, Krahe's new arrangement had a more pedagogical and art-historical aim. It both drew more attention to individual artworks, inviting each to be appreciated on its own, and more deliberately juxtaposed each painting relative to works from different schools, educating viewers about the comparative principles of Flemish, Dutch, and Italian styles, for instance. Though Krahe was technically the gallery's director, the success of his model helped make the curator, for the next two centuries, a role associated largely with cultural institutions such as art museums.

5. Commercial

As curators organized artworks and curiosities in ways that were instructive for public audiences, these audiences soon became interested in owning such artifacts themselves. An untapped market emerged. The age of rampant

Figure 3.4. M. G. E. Eichler (after P. P. Rubens), *The Electoral Picture Gallery at Düsseldorf: Fifth Room, Third Façade* (1776).

colonialism—and the subsequent rise of museums to showcase its spoils—had made public exposure to other cultures more accessible. While the artifacts of other cultures and places were principally acquired by the travel or conquest of a privileged class, the industrial revolution was beginning to change that. Nothing better exemplifies this phenomenon than the birth of the department store. At the onset of the eighteenth century, with the rise in free trade, the abundance of cheap (and expendable) labor, and an inventive, industrial spirit powered by technological innovations in production and transportation, early department stores such as Harding Howell and Co., Au Bon Marché, and Marshall Field's (among others) appealed to a rising middle class in England, France, and America. These department stores showcased—and sold—goods from all over the world, some exotic and decadent, others domestic and practical. To make this possible, the new departmentalized stores needed buyers to select their inventory and stock their many departments with those goods believed to be the most desirable and profitable. Although these buyers did not go by the title of curators, we can certainly understand them in that tradition.

Curation accordingly entered its commercial phase when the consolidation of vastly different products—from kitchen supplies to perfume, millinery to rugs—came under one roof of an individual business enterprise. Not only were these stores curated at the level of their design, with different rooms and halls devoted to different categories of products; the need to select which products to stock and how best to display them made the department store a kind of commercial museum. For the first time in history, goods were sold at fixed prices, stocked at high volume, and displayed accessibly to encourage browsing and touching. There's a clever circularity to department stores initially being modeled on the curatorial principles of museums, and museums later incorporating gift shops, modeled on the curatorial principles of department stores. But, as the fashion buyers for such stores changed the role of curation from the cultural to the commercial, they also shifted the curator's role from teacher to tastemaker. In the decision to stock certain kinds of products, and certain variations of these kinds—by choosing to sell hats, and then more particularly, hats of a feathery style, for example—the buyers inculcated a set of tastes and fashions that, at least for the privileged set of the population able to shop at these stores, came to be associated in the broader public with being *au courant* or having cultural capital. Shopping became a rite or ritual, and the department store a new sort of church.[56] Pastoral power had become purchasing power. While this made a store's curator both master of, and slave to, the consumer, it gave people shopping at such stores, particularly in metropolitan cities, an unprecedented opportunity to flaunt their individual style and idiosyncratic tastes for a public audience on the streets. And it is this practice of publicly displaying personal style and taste for strangers that set the precedent for what, with the eventual advent of networked digital technologies many decades later, would become curation's current technological phase.

6. Technological

The modern legacy of the curator as gatekeeper to both cultural and commercial life lingers still. Certainly, the postmillennial emergence of a more participatory, mobile, and networked media environment has seen curation enter a technological phase in which the cultural and commercial have more or less converged. One example of such convergence sometimes falls under the aegis of "content curation," which concerns how to select, organize, and distribute digital content pertaining to particular themes or topics, usually for the purpose of targeting a capitalizable market.[57] But digital media companies, both start-ups and behemoths alike, do not alone perform acts of curatorship. Their tack has rather been to enable and enlist their "users" to become curators themselves. Thanks to the growing ubiquity of media technologies that make this possible, curatorship has become a widely practiced vernacular art. We can call these media technologies "curatorial media."

Curatorial media are more than just "social" as their more common appellation suggests. These technologies don't only connect people; they connect people with the things with which they identify—usually aesthetically mediated things at that. Pinterest, for instance, allows its 100 million monthly active members to collect images and pin them onto virtual boards that publicly display one's tastes, preferences, and styles for anyone to see. So the fashion maven can have his board of stylish socks and short-hemmed pants, just as the lover of typefaces can have her page of favorite fonts. From microblogging services like Tumblr or Twitter to photo-sharing communities like Instagram or Flickr, social media have inherently curatorial properties insofar as they give people a chance to express their tastes and predilections by identifying with some cultural artifacts and not others.

These terministic acts of identification, which sometimes merely take the form of clicking a like or share icon, do not always have much rhetorical salience, at least not the kind that resembles public discussion of important issues. But that does not make them irrelevant to public participation that we should still recognize as capable of contributing to social change. It merely makes this participation more *gestural*—a more "pure persuasion," in Burke's sense. Networked technologies now mediate public sociality, not just in the hands of a media elite, but through mobile devices in our own. When people share, post, comment, rate, review, like, pin, recommend, livestream (etc.) something for others, they articulate a set of relations between the intimate realm of their own lifeworld and what they take to be of interest to others. As these curated relations circulate and recur, an affective ecology develops as a kind of petri dish that "cultures" our orientation to strangers and their common concerns. Today, this orientation is circumscribed by the wider algorithmic culture in which it takes form.

Despite the tendency to enlist "users" as content creators and arbiters of taste, the underlying reason for doing so is the widespread privileging of algorithmic logics, big data, and crowdsourced knowledge as the most valid sources of expertise. This has led to major cultural configurations—search engines, recommendation systems—built around automating what are essentially curatorial processes. Many of these systems and techniques now operate through neural nets capable of learning and adapting as they are trained on more data, so that even the people who wrote the algorithms can't always know or predict their results. The more data Netflix collects on its members' viewing preferences and tendencies, for example, the larger the set of information from which its algorithms can learn. The larger the data set, the likelier it is that the patterns found in it would otherwise have been indiscernible to human computation. The deeper the patterns the machines learn, the greater the system's claim to make recommendations of superior accuracy and validity. The more impervious the system, the less we need the human curator. In the technological phase of curation, the role of most people is to produce the data for the algorithms to curate; it's not to do the curating themselves.[58]

In a way, Dewey's creative democracy foretold this moment: the artist bringing news to the public was, in the same act, both contributing to the cultural field and suggesting ways that the field should be appreciated—both citizen artist and critic at once. Today, whether it's writing and uploading a song recorded at home or streaming someone else's music on Spotify, whether it's the slow-food recipes someone created and shared online or the restaurant review they posted to Yelp, if various algorithms are now organizing and curating the readable "content" that people both produce and consume, then *all* of our actions can have some drop of consequence as our data trails lead to subsequent algorithmic decisions that sort what supposedly has most importance, relevance, or worth. If the democratization of creativity and the curation of culture have helped to engender subject formations I've called citizen artists and citizen critics, that does not mean the same person can't perform both these subjectivities. But, as we'll see in chapter 4, neither does it mean that citizen artists and critics always play nice.

CITIZEN ARTISTS,
CITIZEN CRITICS

Near the end of 2018, the CEO of Google, Sundar Pichai, appeared before the U.S. House Judiciary Committee and was asked on record to tell Congress why a Google search for "idiot" pulled up an image of Donald Trump. Managing to suppress any sniggers, Pichai explained that no one at Google "manually intervenes" on any search. Rather, search results are an automated process of crawling billions of web pages to look for matching keywords and then of ranking them using over two hundred signals meant to reflect what's happening across the web at any given time.[1] Meaning, Google didn't deliberately frame Trump as an idiot; the people did by posting such content online. Of course, this also means that prior to any specific search, the signals Google uses in its search algorithm (e.g., freshness, relevance, popularity, etc.) are chosen and weighted by Google engineers, and inevitably these choices lead to search results that would be different if the algorithm had privileged different signals and weights. The free ability of people to post creative and critical content online, in other words, always exists in tension with the ways that a platform's policies or technical decisions invariably advantage some types of content over others. This chapter is about that tension—and the antagonisms it can inspire.

The example of Google's search engine is just one of many in which it's possible to see how the parallel trends traced in the last chapter—of creativity's democratization and culture's curation—are coming into conflict. At least tacitly, the democratization of creativity that has made aesthetic expression an ordinary part of social life today has depended on a supposition that everyone's creative self-expression or critical opinion has immanent value, hence an equivalent legitimacy. In practice, though, the need to curate all these contributions inevitably imposes some hierarchy on them that undermines their equivalency by "ranking" some above others. Having explored some of the wider historical trajectory that brought us here, I now focus on some of the stakes involved when concerned gestures by citizen artists and critics can converge more in conflict than in conciliation.

Stakes are high in a post-truth time when world leaders are frequently likened to idiots and anyone can be an artist or critic (or, for that matter, a world leader). In such a context, recuperating "the idiot" can be a dangerous project. To be clear: Trump and his counterparts across continents and political views are not the kind of idiots that I've argued it's important to validate. The figure of the idiot that deserves to be taken more seriously is someone recessed relative to more didactic modes of public subjectivity, someone engaged but tentative: hesitant to speak for others, undisposed toward being dogmatic, given to concerned gestures more than outright exhortation. That figure bears little resemblance to Trump. The claim is not that there's no time or place for strong words, raised fists, or street-storming. But when the capacitation of everyone to "participate" in public life from an online distance can also lead to election meddling, direct-marketed propaganda, and generally to frauds, fakes, fibs, forgeries, and "facts" of all kinds, it becomes necessary to rethink the relationship between participants in communication technologies and the ways these technologies enable and validate some modes of participating more than others.

In cultural studies, and to some degree across the theoretical humanities at large, attempts to theorize the possibility of social change have made it necessary to raise questions about agency. Whose voice can be heard? What does it take to achieve legitimacy in the sphere of public affairs? Who gets a seat at democracy's proverbial table? Whether in reference to the subaltern, the disenfranchised, the counterpublic, the undercommons, or something else, these questions ask about how people can make themselves heard by the state and be equally recognized for their immanent value in the gauntlet of public life. Alternatively, from a rhetorical standpoint, agency is not just about one's authority to speak and represent, but more specifically about "the act of effecting change through discourse."[2] It is a matter of *how* change happens through rhetorical means.

Eliding both these formulations (the *who* and the *how*), a shift in emphasis from agency to capacity might offer a way to identify the affective forces within concatenated relations whose complexity precludes their being isolable to any particular agent.[3] When the very technologies that afford people the capacity to express themselves for strangers and friends are also constraining the values attributed to different ways of doing so, agency is hard to identify. As Nate Stormer and Bridie McGreavy have observed, "Agency identifies force by its application, whereas capacity imagines force in its relations."[4] Agency is what you see when an encounter wants something from you.[5] Capacity operates the conditions of encounter itself. How, then, should we think about those human/digital relations that capacitate new creative adventures in how we get on together—or apart? By exploring the case of a public conflict that took place in 2013 on Goodreads.com between a self-published author and her amateur book reviewers, we might hope to better understand not just how different individual agents have interacted in agonistic ways, but also how their actions can be understood relative to the capacities—emergent, material, mediated, and affective—specific to those conditions in which their interactions occurred.

Though the high-profile controversies surrounding national politics are the sorts that garner the news reports and prompt congressional hearings, we miss out on the importance of "the idiot" and the affectability of concerned gestures if we neglect the everyday engagement with the arts that gets toward the political by way of the aesthetic. In other words, if we take seriously the emergence of a new class of citizen artists and citizen critics, then we are left to explore in more detail how the public work of citizenship is being enacted through creative and critical engagement with the arts. As citizen artists, we are potential makers, hackers, culture jammers, DIYers, street artists, photographers, writers, filmmakers, musicians. As citizen critics, we are a new kind of gatekeeper, all of us potential curators, tastemakers, reviewers, reporters, bloggers, experts-on-demand. It is a question of shifting sensibilities about what it means and feels like to be a citizen in a transnational age of social media and networked technologies. Naturally, there are many answers to this question, and they'll differ depending on whom you ask and under what circumstances. It is not my interest either to make grandiose claims about how citizenship "feels" or to address the "is" of citizenship as such.[6] What is important about citizen artists and critics is the way they shift the bar of civic engagement in a more gestural direction.

Without necessarily engaging the state or "the political" at all, these modes of citizenship nevertheless express concern in a way that has a bearing on how we structure and navigate the everyday venture of our social interdependence. Citizen artists are those who create and share their personal experience and feeling with strangers through an aesthetically mediated form. Though they sometimes act as self-avowed artists, their essential attribute is not their artistic identity but the proclivity to share their own creativity in the presumed belief that the human right to self-expression offers an intrinsic contribution to the benefit of the social fabric (though it's sometimes just for kicks). Citizen critics, meanwhile, are those whose critical opinions, tastes, and conversations about art constitute the enactment of their very citizenship. Rosa Eberly, who coined the term, defines the citizen critic as "a person who produces discourses about issues of common concern from an *ethos* of citizen first and foremost—not as expert or spokesperson for a workplace or as member of a club or organization."[7] If there is anywhere it makes sense to go looking for citizen artists and critics interacting in cultural public spheres, that place is online.

CURATORIAL MEDIA

All social media are curatorial media. They allow people to sort and to choose, to organize and to classify their personal preferences, be they friends or skinny jeans or playlists. Curatorial media platforms such as Goodreads and Amazon reveal the tension inherent in the deeper cultural ethos that would supplant more traditionally deliberative forms of public engagement with the forms of participation undertaken by citizen artists and critics. The trouble is, the likes of Goodreads and Amazon are not just in the business of enabling citizen artists to promote and sell their books, and citizen critics to rate and review them. Despite appearing to provide a free and open discursive space, as the emergent field of platform studies can attest, these platforms also put forward strong visions of what public engagement with the arts (among other things) ought to entail.[8] They do so by technologically constraining that engagement and channeling it toward a particular kind of communication. On Amazon and Goodreads, such constraints take numerous forms. Some are hidden in proprietary algorithms; others are overtly stated in site policies. Exploring how some of these constraints impact the affective ecology of participants on these platforms will tell us more about how cultural public spheres operate in a digital context.

Curatorial media rely on human techniques of self-expression and more-than-human technologies governed by algorithmic logic. Such logic involves processing data inputs according to procedural rules and classificatory schemes that spit them out into different outputs. Geoffrey Bowker and Susan Star have shown that all systems of classification are an inextricable part of social relations, a kind of infrastructural *work* with pragmatic consequences for how we perceive the world and interact within it.[9] The tricky part is that, today, classification systems are also almost always invisible, in part because they're automated. Perhaps the biggest rhetorical coup of digital media has been the technological systematization of curatorship through procedural algorithms that categorize, rank, recommend, filter, and spit out search results in automated procedures that conceal their highly contingent nature by tacitly purporting to be inevitable and logically infallible.[10] These automated procedures also discreetly underwrite the forms of digital communication undertaken in the belief that such communication is free and unconstrained by the media that circulate public expressions.

By now it is widely acknowledged that algorithms play an increasing role in human affairs, embedding us within what some have called an algorithmic culture.[11] As Scott Kushner sees it, "The category of algorithmic culture enables an understanding of both how computational logic pervades contemporary culture and how it shapes the possibilities of life itself."[12] For Ted Striphas, algorithmic culture entails "the sorting, classifying, and hierarchizing of people, places, objects, and ideas using computational processes."[13] The automated and binary logic of algorithms, Striphas suggests, has come to replace older forms of cultural criticism and classification.

In the realm of the arts, for instance, it has long been believed that cultural products (indeed, whole genres of aesthetic expression) come to attain what symbolic value they have in the public eye as a result of the classificatory work of trusted experts whose training and critical authority confers on them a modicum of public influence.[14] Striphas worries that this old "elite culture" paradigm is being supplanted by an algorithmic culture directed toward producing "a *statistical determination* of what's culturally relevant."[15] The new model "renders culture" through an aggregate of the data produced by people online, regardless of the context of that data's creation: "In the old cultural paradigm, you could question authorities about their reasons for selecting particular cultural artifacts as worthy, while dismissing or neglecting others. Not so with algorithmic culture, which wraps abstraction inside of secrecy and sells it back to you as, 'the people have spoken.'"[16] The apparent reason for Striphas's concern, then, is not just that the subjectivity of the individual human voice and its context are being subsumed into a contextless crowd of big data, but that the algorithmic procedures whereby classificatory decisions are now made remain hidden from public scrutiny behind the shield of proprietary intellectual property laws.[17]

In that case, it is not unreasonable to say that algorithms do plenty of asserting, but very little arguing. Ostensibly, that is, at least when it comes to the arts, algorithmic culture removes the obligation to offer warrants for the critical claims being made about cultural products. In such a paradigm, the conferral of symbolic value on cultural goods need not be informed by familiarity with the long tradition of similar goods into which new artifacts emerge (as in Bourdieu's system of cultural capital); nor need it be supported by argumentation, rational or otherwise (as in a Habermasian public sphere); nor, for that matter, must claims for symbolic value be refined by discussion, debate, dialogue, or deliberation directed toward achieving consensus (as in Gadamer's hermeneutics). In short, algorithmic culture makes the very discursive components of a public sphere thesis inessential to conferring value on cultural goods that have gained some public attention. Rather than the formation of public opinion, in other words, the cultural public sphere's sorting algorithms privilege the crowdsourced formation of that which is worthy of public attention.

This reconfiguration of the cultural field makes everyone susceptible to, and complicit in entrenching, the taste-making apparatuses and techniques that help the arts inspire public attention. When aesthetic texts enter the cultural field already commodified by the creative industries in which they emerge, our best recourse is to approach them publicly in registers adjacent to what they "mean" so as to leave them impervious to appropriation. Yet, the creative industries and the new media that drive them try to enlist people to articulate the affective registers of artworks by empowering us with more curatorial capabilities. For instance, Rob Gehl gives the name "affective processing" to the idea, promulgated by the web's underlying business model, that users are "expected to process digital objects by sharing content, making connections, ranking cultural artifacts, and producing digital content."[18] Affective processing is a form of immaterial labor, in which humans are given to act more and more like computers. It was once only computers that did the processing; now we also are the processors.[19] Among many who have theorized immaterial labor, Gehl's insights stand out for the way he distinguishes this labor by its techno-affective register.[20] Like affect, computers operate in what Friedrich Kittler has called a "semantics-free space" where all signs are reduced to binary.[21] Technicity is indifferent to signification. If humans labor like machines, though, our intrinsic affectability brings to the machines that which they cannot produce on their own: the impossibility of indifference.

By reviewing, posting, sharing, liking, friending, ranking, pinning—in short, by producing what Alice Marwick labels "status signals"[22]—we participate in a culture of curation that sometimes exhibits merely phatic properties. The content of these digital gestures is ancillary to the gesture itself. Just by taking part, through minor acts of curation intended for a public audience, we build "affective networks" that organize a semblance of community. "Affective networks," Jodi Dean writes, "produce feelings of community, or what we might call 'community without community.' They enable mediated relationships that take a variety of changing, uncertain, and interconnected forms as they feed back each on the other in ways we can never fully account for or predict."[23] For Dean, the process is aggregative, as each Tweet, each post, each review "accrues a tiny affective nugget, a little surplus enjoyment, a smidgen of attention that attaches to it, making it stand out from the larger flow before it blends back in."[24] Because the water always heals over again after the minor splash of these actions, acts of vernacular curation can seem inconsequential to cultural public spheres understood as arenas in which aesthetic texts give rise to, or themselves participate in, developing a shared purpose or public opinion relative to our mutual concerns.

I have been trying to suggest that this impression is a mistake. While the vernacular curation of culture certainly does take traditionally rhetorical forms, it is also enabled by rhetorics that have less interest in symbolicity or meaning than in building the affective predispositions that guide our social interdependence in the first place. This is not just a matter of media behaving rhetorically at the level of their discursive affordances, and thereby tacitly putting forward particular ideological values. Media are powerful in part for reasons that go beyond propositional messages altogether. "Given the ubiquity of affect," Eric Shouse has observed, "it is important to take note that the power of many forms of media lies not so much in their ideological effects, but in their ability to create affective resonances independent of content or meaning."[25] In a time of both computational and vernacularized cultural curation, our engagement in public life is often a matter of creating these affective resonances and leveraging media technologies to that end.

THE ETHOS CONUNDRUM

In August 2013, a public controversy arose over some bookshelves. The fuss wasn't about the bookshelves' design or cost or location; the shelves weren't even tangible. In fact, they were "virtual bookshelves," created by registered members on the literary social media site Goodreads.com. What caused such an uproar was the way the shelves' books had been curated. Goodreads, which at the time had over 20 million members (it now boasts more than 85 million), allows people to curate virtual bookshelves of the books they have read, want to read, or are currently reading, to give those shelves descriptive names, and to share their thoughts about these books in the form of rankings, reviews, and comments. The controversy arose because some members had created bookshelves filled with books they described by giving the shelves such names as "Author Should be Sodomized" and "Should Be Raped in Prison."[26]

Online bullying, if that's not too mild a phrase for what happened on Goodreads, has been around as long as the web itself. Where people interact among strangers, especially under guise of anonymity, there will be conflict. It will get personal, sometimes nasty, and it's not likely to change anytime soon.[27] Goodreads, like many other web forums, already had no shortage of trolls. Their browbeating appeared most often in excoriating book reviews and comments sections. Such reviews, no doubt, were a big part of the larger kerfuffle that crossed a line to something more heinous with the threatening bookshelves. Like book reviews, the shelves are acts of cultural curatorship: attempts to make a case for what's in and what's out, what's good and what's not, by telling a story about how a particular text or collocation of texts should be understood or appreciated.

Goodreads is structured to allow authors and readers alike to interact in the same virtual space. But the site also distinguishes the two. Members who self-designate as authors, whether self-published or best-selling, get a "Goodreads Author" badge at the top of their online profile. In turn, these authors can leverage the cultural capital of their known status to promote their own books, contest their bad reviews, or promote the books of others. The vast majority of members, though, are not designated authors; they are ordinary readers, there (presumably) to share their opinions publicly and to experience the community of others doing the same. But readers on the site carry an ethos of their own: it's harder to dismiss readers' shelves or reviews as promotionally motivated. Whether or not one agrees with their opinions, one at least tends to presume that their efforts are earnest.

Nevertheless, the way this author/reader structure of Goodreads plays out in practice has sometimes pitted readers against authors in an agonistic struggle for control over the site's discursive norms. Such a struggle, in any case, helps to explain the controversy that rose to its fever pitch around the debut of a self-published twenty-two-year-old author named Lauren Howard. Howard, who was new to Goodreads, had promoted her book, *Learning to Love*, on the site in advance of its release. Here's some of the copy: "Innocence personi-fied, Aimee Dalton dreamed of the day she'd meet her Prince Charming . . . but love at first sight isn't always as simple as a fairy tale . . ."[28] Howard was surprised to see the novel already being rated and reviewed before anyone had even read it. She joined a message board to ask how this could happen. Goodreads, she learned, gives readers the chance to rate and review books both based on their *interest* in reading them and, elsewhere, to rate and review based on having already done the reading. After posting her presumably inno-cent inquiry to the message board, though, veteran readers got annoyed. Still before its release, *Learning to Love* began receiving even more one- and two-star reviews. Worse, insults aimed at Howard herself flooded these reviews. Then came the rape threats in the bookshelves.

As curatorial media, platforms such as Goodreads and Amazon promulgate a paradox. To legitimate and include everyone as citizen critics is to devalue the idea that a critic's ethos has a role in the validity of aesthetic judgment. Some critical practices may well be more compelling or persuasive than others, but all are equally valid, these platforms imply, and their validity is guaranteed prior to the critical act regardless of one's supposed expertise or critical deftness. Meanwhile, though, Goodreads and Amazon also hold fast to ethos as an essential measure of a critic's legitimacy, going so far as extrinsically to confer status on some members in the form of name badges and reviewer rankings. The controversy that arose on Goodreads in response to Lauren Howard's promotional efforts for her self-published debut, *Learning to Love*, needs to be understood within this greater affective order of curatorial media's paradoxical denial and delivery of rhetorical ethos. Before returning to how the controversy played out, then, it may help to spend some time discussing the ethos conundrum on Goodreads. Doing so will involve thinking about how the site's operational constraints—and their embeddedness within the larger political economy of curatorial media—influence the affective order from which discursive practices on Goodreads emerge.

In March 2013, Amazon acquired Goodreads for somewhere between $160 and $200 million.[29] The important difference between Amazon and Goodreads is not just that Amazon sells products and Goodreads doesn't. It is hardly the case that one site's communicative sphere is free from the sway of commercial interests and the other is not. After all, even though Goodreads does not inventory or sell products, its discursive space decidedly earns capital through advertising sales and affiliate revenue made possible by the sheer quantity of its members. Both sites, that is, exploit their users for the capitalizable data they can produce through participation that amounts to unpaid digital labor.[30] Where cultural public spheres are concerned, the important distinction between Amazon and Goodreads consists in the different ways each venue has built into its platform structurally encoded constraints on the kinds of critical engagement and expressions of taste that they want their membership communities to practice and privilege.

The ethos conundrum, in other words, is not just limited to Goodreads, but something that more widely orients citizen artists and critics toward their ways of rhetorically engaging with aesthetic texts. In the case of Amazon, the a priori operational constraints take the form of a vertical status hierarchy to rank the credibility of its reviewers. In the case of Goodreads, these constraints involve explicit rules forbidding certain ways of engaging with the books that a given member might wish to review or discuss. While these rules are justified in the site's policies on the basis that they are intended to maintain civility, they also limit one's available means of persuasion. In both cases, the constraints are executed automatically through procedures encoded into the site's functionality. You might not even know they're there.

These constraints, again, are determined by the power of technology to influentially mediate a set of social relations as if from outside those relations. The difficulty of seeing the technicity of digital operating behaviors at work beneath the many communicative freedoms and possibilities that the sites do legitimately enable is one reason it calls for such critical scrutiny. Beyond nearly unenforceable age constraints, for instance, neither Amazon nor Goodreads restricts who can speak on their pages, though both sites do reward and discourage some discursive practices.[31] The welcome inclusion of anyone with a web connection—the more the merrier!—allows these and other platforms to hang above their masthead the flag of "democratic" inclusivity, impartiality, and equality: an ostensible fulfillment of the web's beautiful promise of democratization. Nor do these sites censor tastes. Positive and negative reviews of any text are equally welcome, and no one is held accountable for providing a warrant or justification for their opinion beyond its mere assertion. Ostensibly, anyone is welcome to share any opinion about any text; that act alone is accorded intrinsic value. Yet, the a priori operating constraints encoded into the public communicative spaces on Amazon and Goodreads decidedly do delimit what their members are encouraged or allowed to say, and how they ought to say it. Better understanding the operating constraints on Goodreads is therefore imperative to situating the controversy over the platform's discursive norms. Importantly, doing so is a nonhermeneutic project.

TEXTS, TALK, AND THE NONHERMENEUTIC

When the field of cultural production inspires public attention and discussion, cultural public spheres begin to take shape. In their most classic form, cultural public spheres accordingly consist of texts and talk. The "texts" are cultural (art works, entertainments, aesthetic objects or events) and the "talk" is the discourse these texts inspire (discussions, reviews, interpretations). In at least this elementary sense, cultural public spheres can be seen as the communicative ecology whereby "something approaching public opinion" about works of art takes shape through public conversations about them.[32] The cultural field is uniquely implicated in the formation of a *sensus communis* about such intimate matters as taste, beauty, and art's function, among the various other ways the aesthetic might intervene in our lifeworld, generate experience, and meliorate life.[33] As encounters with the arts raise discussions of intimate lifeworld concerns, and as these discussions gain pertinence for others beyond merely our personal investment so that the products and processes of the cultural field begin to implicate strangers in shared matters of concern, cultural public spheres come into being.

This understanding can be called the texts-and-talk model. Roughly put: an aesthetic text is published or otherwise released; it inspires discussions or interactions between strangers; these interactions take place before audiences in specific contexts; these audiences and contexts delimit the "available means" of effectiveness; the rhetorical arguments thus delimited in turn help to achieve, from amid the antagonisms and contingencies around them, a trend of opinion about that aesthetic text's meaning, value, or implications. Such, anyway, is the model of cultural public spheres that follows from a traditionally rhetorical paradigm. And it has much to recommend it. Certainly, for instance, a texts-and-talk model is the template that Rosa Eberly works from in her seminal study of twentieth-century literary public spheres, when she defines them as "discursive spaces in which private people can come together in public, bracket some of their differences, and invent common interests by arguing in speech or writing about literary and cultural texts."[34] There is nothing obsolete or inaccurate about this conceptualization. It reasonably describes actual communicative practices undertaken by countless people.

Studying cultural public spheres—at root, the way strangers talk about art—lends itself to interpretive analysis of the talk itself. If the aim were to illuminate such a public in situ on Amazon or Goodreads, there would certainly be plenty to draw from. The sheer abundance of reviews on either site, for instance, offers valuable symbolic-discursive data from which to identify a host of rhetorical features of critical discourse surrounding a particular book. It would certainly be possible to cross-reference different reviews of a single book and develop a sense for the rhetorical topoi most commonly mobilized on its behalf. Isolating the recurrent topics mentioned across multiple reviews of the same book (e.g., repeated references to its disappointing ending, to the difficulty of its vocabulary, or to the richness of its characters) would reveal the issues that hold the most rhetorical salience relative to that particular book, and in doing so would begin to sketch the contours of its public significance.

This sort of rhetorical criticism would be valuable and worth pursuing if the goal were to identify the nature of a particular book's traction in public opinion, or to gain a sense for how, as a whole, the critical arguments surrounding a literary text most commonly warrant the claims made for its symbolic value. There is also, undoubtedly, important work that could be done on a still larger scale to find the most commonplace rhetorical maneuvers and modes of argumentation that recur across reviews or comments about different books. Doing so might lead to a better understanding of the rhetorics driving the reviews of citizen critics as a discursive genre. These projects and others, in short, would root us in a symbolic order and invite hermeneutic approaches intent on ascertaining what all this discourse means and tells us about a public's engagement with literature.

But if we want to see how concerned public activity today is more than just rhetorical in the symbolic-discursive sense of talking about cultural goods and the issues they raise, then a texts-and-talk model and its hermeneutic inclinations won't show us all there is to see. After all, in a meme-ified time of scrolling and swiping, people often "encounter" or "interface with" cultural texts more than they "read" them.[35] As I have argued, public activity around the arts also involves asignifying, affective moods that dispose us to new encounters and experiences in ways that hold open the possibility of a commons built from shared concern. As we saw with TED Talks in chapter 1, identifying the influence of factors that dispose people to certain ways of listening (or reading, or feeling, or many other things) requires a nonhermeneutic method with different objects of critical attention. In the same way that studying the TED Commandments offers a different set of insights than studying the TED Talks themselves, examining the rhetorics of particular reviews or analyzing as a case study the public discussion of an especially inspiriting book will not get us to our mark. What we need instead are ways to scrutinize how gestures of concern by citizen artists and critics operate within an affective order that is delimited, adjacent to any symbolic action, by the media through which they circulate. Because these media are both technical, at the level of a platform's operational constraints, and social, at the level of the wider cultural environment hospitable to them, it is difficult to pinpoint a precise locus of critical attention when affective orders are our object.

What's more, the distinction between affective and symbolic orders is in some ways a misdirection, ontologically false but conceptually true. We can't actually parse affectivity here and symbolicity there, as if never the twain shall meet, because the two are intra-actively entangled, one reinforcing the other. The distinction is conceptually useful, however, for its invitation to become attuned to different registers of our rhetorical sociality: that is, to the "pervasiveness of persuasiveness"[36] in all aspects of lived experience, some of which is signifying and representational, much of which isn't. While abundant interpretive attention is already given to the symbolic-discursive aspects of the social, the affective orders that capacitate what the social can do are more urgently in need of critical attention.

To this end, the best way to understand the affective order may be through the German concept of *Stimmung*. Originally used to designate the tuning of a musical instrument (but also the instrument being in tune *and* its being ready to be played), *Stimmung* is notoriously untranslatable.[37] In English renderings of Heidegger, who used the term regularly, *Stimmung* is often translated as "attunement," which in his thought is a kind of mood or atmosphere that is always with people and around them. What I call the affective order is that realm of being-with that, Heidegger would say, "sets the tone for such being."[38] By identifying an affective order of social life that's coextensive with a symbolic order, I mean to indicate the ways that moods, by enveloping people within their atmosphere, set the tone for how people respond to the symbolic actions they encounter within it. Affective orders are where mood conditions persuadability. They involve those material, technical, and asignifying processes that, like tuning or not tuning an instrument, create the set of preconditions that dispose people to be affected and influenced in particular ways.

Traditionally, the aesthetic has been the realm of human creation most associated with creating a mood. Just think of how common it is to imagine music putting us "in the mood" (as countless R&B songs testify). But such moods, or *Stimmungen*, are not on/off propositions. Though our moods may change, we are *always* within some sort of affective atmosphere, an ambient mood or comportment from which our behaviors, outlooks, choices, and judgments emerge.[39] Most often, though, we only become aware of the affective order when we experience, in everyday life, a change in intensity or felt valence of an encounter—with a book, maybe, or with another person, with a song, or just with the puddle seen through a window that tells you it's raining. When it comes to Goodreads, the question becomes how the platform generates moods through cultural techniques that dispose people to interact on it the way that they do.

THE CULTURAL TECHNIQUES OF GOODREADS

The original impetus for Goodreads, founded by Otis and Elizabeth Chandler in 2007, was the couple's realization that their favorite way to find a new book was to browse the bookshelf of a friend. The premise underwriting this realization is one that pervades digital culture and its algorithmic architecture: if people share some known and established aesthetic preferences—for the same book, the same musician, the same TV shows—then they will also share some unknown preferences, at least within a given aesthetic medium. Sharing one's tastes publicly therefore builds associative relations that help people deduce their probable preference for texts with which they are unfamiliar or about which they would otherwise be less certain. The more information we have about the preferences of more people, the easier it is to identify statistically viable correlations and predict tastes.

Framed in social media's ubiquitous idiom of preferential allegiance (the site abounds with "friends," "likes," "followers," and "fans"), to be a Goodreads member is to be interpellated as part of a bibliophilic community expected to value the sanctity of individual taste equally alongside the sharing of such taste. Of course, the site enables the expression of one's tastes in different ways, not all of which endeavor the rhetorical nuance of critically argued judgments or reviews. Merely adding a book to one's virtual shelf is, in the language of Kenneth Burke, an act of identification that both serves tacitly to demonstrate an affinity with those who have added the same book to theirs and implicitly demonstrates one's distinction from those who have not.[40] This rhetorical act of dis/identification is encoded in the site's architecture as adding a book to one's shelf automatically groups one within a linked network of others who have added the book as well.

Here, a bookshelf becomes a cultural technique for the earlier practice of organizing one's taste preferences for display to others. People have organized their aesthetic preferences for others well before doing so through a technique like the bookshelf, let alone its digital variation. Yet, unlike their physical counterparts, digital bookshelves have the unique attribute of acting as mere inscriptions. These shelves maintain a kind of proxy materiality insofar as they stand apart from the symbolic registers of discourse that the site's members might activate through rankings, reviews, comments, and the like. Rate the book (on a scale of five stars) or review it, or comment on someone else's review, and these encoded acts of dis/identification embed one further within the site's network of others with similarly aligned preferences. Literature itself is less vital as "equipment for living" than is the bookshelf that enframes its importance.[41] Yet members on Goodreads do more than curate bookshelves. They also review books in ways that exceed the rhetorical sufficiency of curation's mere inscription.

Reviewers on Goodreads are permitted to give their reviews whichever form best suits what they want to express. For instance, for several years the site's top two "all-time most popular reviews" included video clips—each a GIF showing a few seconds of looped footage culled from the web—followed by short captions or longer paragraphs of exegesis (fig. 4.1). The third most

Fifty Shades of Grey (Fifty Shades, #1)
by E.L. James (Goodreads Author)

Katrina Passick Lumsden's review

★☆☆☆☆

What in the hell just happened? Did I really read that? Oh, my god, I did. I did read that.

Figure 4.1. Screenshot of the "All-Time Most Popular Review" on Goodreads.com.

popular review was written in satirical dialogue. The site's openness to reviews of different forms pushes the conventional "book review" genre into unconventional modes (the video content in reviews that use video, for instance, is original only insofar as it's been remixed or repurposed). There is, in other words, a strong sense in which Goodreads expands the available means of persuasion for this entire genre of cultural criticism, not just by legitimating the visual, for instance, as equally viable as language, but also by legitimating what amounts to gestures as discursive acts with an affective force.[42] The popularity of reviews, measured in likes, page views, and other status signals, is accordingly conferred from an ethos generated from rhetorical choices internal to the review itself, rather than credibility conferred extrinsically.

Yet Goodreads also compiles a ranking hierarchy of its members, regularly publishing periodic and all-time rankings of its Top Users, Top Readers, Top Reviewers, and Most Popular Reviewers broken down both by country and overall. All categories are assessed on a strictly quantitative basis. So, the Top Users are those who have added the most books to their shelves; the Top Readers are those whose profiles claim they have read the most books; the Top Reviewers have posted the most book reviews; and the Most Popular Reviewers have written reviews that have received the most likes. These calculations are unambiguous. The quantitative basis of Goodreads's ranking system acts rhetorically as an institutional disinterest supported by an apparent "just the facts" neutrality. In other words, cultivating ethos as an achievement of discursive quality (through eloquence, for instance, or the inventional creativity of posting videos instead of text) is not the only way Goodreads allows its members to attain status.

It would seem that the more fundamental tactic of Goodreads is to promote a participatory ethos, whereby merely contributing to the site, and thereby establishing a more publicly visible profile, suffices to confer on its members a modicum of credibility. Yet, despite its quantified basis, the measure of extrinsically conferred status is not a material requisite of the technology: hence the rhetorical nature of the site's operational structure, which situates its visitors within a particular affective horizon of possibility. The point is not just that Goodreads is not disinterested when encoding its choices about member ethos, but that it *can't not* make nonarbitrary choices that give rise to the site's unique affective ecology. In short, the material or algorithmic rhetorics on Goodreads emerge in the ways that its technological back-end deals with those factors in a mediated environment that materially *must* be controlled, though they can be controlled in any number of ways. For example, not all reviews of a book can possibly appear on a single page simultaneously, which means some appear more prominently than others. If some books inspire hundreds of reviews, how to decide which ones get buried?

In a word, algorithms. But that hardly tells the whole story, because algorithms can be made to follow nearly any set of rules to the end of achieving nearly any range of effects. Goodreads is not unique in protecting the sorting procedure it uses, the site explains, "to determine the most interesting reviews." As site administrators elaborate, "The recipe for our special sauce is a closely guarded trade secret, but the ingredients are: length of the review, number of people who liked it, recency of the review, popularity of the review (i.e., number of people who have liked reviews by that person across all books)."[43] Algorithms—the closely guarded recipe—require disambiguated data in order to operate. Though the data, the ingredients, are all quantifiable, which data to cook with is a rhetorical decision that could well have gone otherwise.[44] Despite apparent attempts to promote a participatory ethos in which every reviewer is equally validated just for participating, even at the level of the site's interface, a predetermined measure of status orients visitors to the site in a particular way. In view of larger Western and historical roles around critical engagement with the arts, it's easier to see how this cultivated orientation could lead to the sorts of rancor that festered on Goodreads.

The engagement of ordinary citizens as critics of cultural goods is nothing new. Though newer media technologies have made it easier and more common for the ordinary person to act as a socially validated critic, the role of literary criticism in the public sphere has a longer history. Peter Uwe Hohendahl traces some of this story in his important book *The Institution of Criticism*. Whereas Habermas shows that during the Age of Enlightenment literary discussion in aristocratic salons eventually came to empower the bourgeois middle class to discuss political opinions, Hohendahl brings into focus the ways that subsequent and ongoing public conversations about literature have danced carefully between a general reading public and an elite one—their respective critical statuses sometimes on equal footing, at other times not.[45] Although written in a specifically German context in the early 1980s, Hohendahl's account of literary criticism in ever-changing literary public spheres certainly has relevance for the globally networked cultural field we face today. What we continue to see is the private subjectivity of "idiot" readers and experts alike interacting rhetorically with public audiences to invent a literary text's prevailing value and meaning. As readers become rhetors, literary texts begin to live a public life.

Distinguishing the separate claims to authority of these reader-rhetors, however, becomes a difficult problem, and it's made manifest in the terminology used to describe readers of different status.[46] The tendency through the twentieth century has been to classify literary criticism and literary theory (including the innumerable methods and philosophies thereof) as the kind of literary assessment made by experts, usually scholars whose professional work consists in developing and sharpening a broad but penetrating critical understanding of literature. Literary critics and theorists thus are reader-rhetors whose voice is accorded cultural authority because it conforms to the academic, intellectual, and aesthetic expectations of scholarly journals and their audience. Their literary assessments, however, tend neither to reach the general public nor (to the extent possible) to admit popular literary consensus into their own sphere of influence, thus reifying their own status through the insularity of the public that circumscribes them.

Distinct from literary critics or theorists, meanwhile, professional book reviewers are another class of reader-rhetor in more reticulated public spheres. In America, such reviewers publish in the popular press (*Time*, *Esquire*, etc.), industry review magazines (*Publishers Weekly*, *Kirkus Reviews*, etc.), and periodicals with elite status that are nevertheless not academic (the *New York Review of Books*, the *New Inquiry*, *N+1*, etc.). Reviewers are accorded status and cultural authority by virtue of their role as journalists for popular media outlets—with some outlets according more status than others—and their assessment of a literary text is more likely than the literary critic's or theorist's to reach the general public. Still, though, a book review carries a connotation of inferiority, certainly of difference, compared to the work of the critic, perhaps largely because book reviews are a late capitalist phenomenon tied to the commercial publicity of recently published books.[47] In both discursive modes, a specialized language with particular vocabularies and discursive norms contributes to the exclusionary status of those able to perform it.

Finally, the vast majority of reader-rhetors are neither critics nor professional reviewers, but everyday people of various professional backgrounds, whose subjectivity acquires a public orientation whenever they engage in conversation or debate about a book's merits or common social significance. Because such reader-rhetors have no institutionally conferred public status when it comes to discussing books (save, perhaps, what's implied by the advertising revenue that follows from garnering enough page hits on a personal blog or website), their judgments and critiques of literary texts rely on rhetorical inventions in a vernacular and distinctly personal mode. It's these nonexpert readers—citizen critics—who stimulated the controversy on Goodreads. While it goes without saying that for academics and professional critics rape threats wouldn't fly as part of their critical practice, a vociferous set of readers on Goodreads believed the norms for citizen critics should be different.

If the exacerbated personal attacks and sexist truculence that pervaded a segment of the Goodreads community over Lauren Howard's self-promotion of *Learning to Love* in 2013 are any indication, we can certainly say that the site's affective ecology had diverged from equilibrium. In this case, the juxtaposition of authors (citizen artists) and readers (citizen critics) fomented a struggle between two sides that occurred in part because of the ways Goodreads addressed the ethos conundrum that its very operational constraints helped to create. When Lauren Howard queried a message board about promoting her book, she spoke with a conflicting ethos of her own: on the one hand, with the cachet of being a "Goodreads Author" and, on the other, with the inexperience of being a newcomer. Veteran readers on the site, having the exact inverse ethos conflict, expressed their annoyance toward Howard as an aggressive manifestation of the "authority" they could claim based on their experience in the Goodreads community, but also in a territorial agonism that announced an orientation toward the site as a place to discuss books, not to promote them.

Within its symbolic order a boilerplate case, among many, of web trolls going too far, the controversy tells us something more interesting about cultural public spheres and the role that acts of curation play in their discursive associations. What made the bullying on Goodreads gain wider attention, that is, was more than outrage at such vindictive behavior. The unique expression of such vitriol by curating and naming personal bookshelves also gained attention because it worked against the ethos parameters that Goodreads encodes into the site's operational affordances. Based on the presumed utility of bibliophilic acts of identification, Goodreads allows its members only to distinguish those books they have read, are currently reading, or would like to read. There is no corresponding option encoded into the site that allows readers to indicate books they do *not* want to read. By curating shelves on that basis, however, and on the more particular basis that their authors were reprehensible, the offending Goodreads members—and again, we are talking about an extremely small but influential minority of the whole—undermined the affective orientations that the site endeavored to promote through its presumption of bibliophilic identificatory benefits.

The suggestion that bibliophobia and disidentificatory orientations were legitimate ways to engage publicly with literature was not something the site was designed or prepared to accommodate.[48] In turn, the controversy that ensued also came to concern what kinds of critical discourse were legitimate in the discussion of books, given that the site did endeavor to legitimate the free expression of opinions whose validity the site's disavowals of critical ethos endorsed. More particularly, the controversy came to concern the extent to which highly invective, often irrational personal attacks—what we'd more formally call ad hominem arguments—are a legitimate basis for expressing one's aesthetic judgments. Does not liking an author justify disapproval of her work?

The question exceeded the one long raised by philosophers of art, who have asked if we should discredit works of aesthetic ingenuity either if their creators undertook unethical means in their creation (Should Gauguin's paintings be dismissed because he abandoned his family to create them?) or if their creators exhibited reprehensible behaviors in their personal lives (Should we ignore Heidegger's philosophy because of his anti-Semitism?).[49] The bullying controversy on Goodreads was about the rhetorical norms of discourse surrounding how citizen critics support the aesthetic judgments they make in a public context. Are ad hominem arguments justifiable? That these arguments get malicious, that they often have no empirical basis (most readers on Goodreads don't personally know the authors whose books they review), and that they might be relevant for some readers but not others, no one questioned. The right to free speech in this context carried only minor relevance as well: yes, yes, free speech. But *rape threats*?

In his *Rhetoric of Fiction*, Wayne Booth recognized the tendency of readers to conflate the author implied by a text's narrator with the living author who wrote that text, as if both were the same. To distinguish the two, he introduced the idea of an "implied author" and a "flesh-and-blood author," his assumption being that readers typically only "know" the implied author; the living one is inaccessible, off the page.[50] Because Goodreads allows the flesh-and-blood author to participate in the site's discussions, however, this distinction is more easily forgotten. In fact, the logic flips: in this context, living authors become metonyms for their books, instead of the other way around.

In short, the cultural techniques that Goodreads builds into its platform's parameters for participation, specifically its ways of organizing taste for public display and assigning ethos accordingly, can explain why ad hominem attacks verging on outright character assassination might to some members seem pertinent to their aesthetic judgments. The stakes of the site's discursive norms were therefore not just territorial, the authors vs. readers narrative that was promulgated in most blog discourse about the controversy. More than that, the stakes concerned a tension between the freedom of a public, consisting in this case of both authors and readers, each of whom, after all, are global citizens entitled to enact their citizenship through the expression of their opinions to strangers, and the operational constraints of the medium—Goodreads—which, on one hand, facilitates this discussion in the first place but, on the other, constrains the game board on which such discussion can transpire. On Goodreads, to read is to enter into social relations structured by the automated networks formed from identifying with particular books: from reviewing them, writing commentaries about them, or just adding them to one of your virtual shelves. To visit your profile page is to be furnished a real-time list of feeds associated with the books you've indicated an interest in, so as to enable discussion with those who are writing and thinking about those books themselves or those who have merely identified with certain books in one way or another. This access to social input and output about books operates on the tacit belief that reading common texts can democratically bring people together in the formation of a community. Although the site, with millions of books in its database, accommodates a plurality of interests and opinions, it gets entangled in status judgments that are a joint consequence of the stickiness of citizen critics and citizen authors on the site, as well as the ethos conundrum manifest in the legitimation of all individual critical judgments, provided they are not explicitly disidentificatory judgments.

To form identifications based on disidentification—following a sort of Machiavellian "the enemy of your enemy is your friend" model—makes for an asocial kind of reading (or at least, a sociality via asociality, via agonism), which threatens the community of members who have fallen in line with the site's attempts to model a networked cultural public sphere. What this points to conceptually is an affective ecology enacting a double paradox. The first comes from privileging both the autonomous ethos of those who express their individual aesthetic judgment and the attributed ethos of those aesthetic judgments formed socially.[51] The second paradox comes from simultaneously assuming that no critical judgments can be wrong and that only those reached collectively are truly legitimate. These two paradoxes are manifest in how the controversy over Lauren Howard's debut book played out on Goodreads.

PREFIGURING THE POLITICAL

Here's what happened. In her personal blog, Howard announced that she had decided not to release her book at all, the "main reason" being "the recent occurrences on the website Goodreads."[52] On Goodreads itself, she posted a review of the book that just said, "NO LONGER BEING RELEASED."[53] Howard contacted Goodreads to complain and, eventually, the site removed the reviews, commentary, and bookshelves that its staff deemed too hostile. Some online petitions emerged and received a couple thousand signatures from Goodreads members worldwide (from America to England to New Zealand), asking Goodreads to curtail bullying on the site.[54] The *Huffington Post* published an editorial about the petitions, which generated such an impassioned response that the *Post* subsequently issued a disclaimer, followed by an exculpatory article from Andrew Losowsky, the senior books editor of the online journal.[55] Meanwhile, citizen critics began posting more reviews and comments to Goodreads, now directing their ire to the site itself on the grounds that their contributions to the discussion were no longer publicly visible—for instance, "BECAUSE GOODREADS FUCKING DELETED IT WITHOUT GIVING THE AUTHOR OF SAID REVIEW ANY WARNING."[56]

Indeed, on September 20, 2013, Goodreads announced a new policy for its reviews and virtual bookshelves. "There is," a site moderator explained in the announcement, "a line between relevant criticism and unhelpful ad hominem attacks or off-topic reviews that single out individual readers or authors. Reviews—or shelves—that cross this line are not allowed."[57] Some predictable disapprobation followed immediately in various blogs and forums,[58] but the policy had now been fixed. The site reserved the right to determine—without being accountable to share its warrants—where that "line" would be drawn and to delete infractions without notice. The free exchanges of at least this particular incarnation of a literary public sphere were no longer quite as free. *Learning to Love* is still findable on Goodreads, misty cover image and all, under the nom de plume Lauren Pippa. Though the announcement "NO LONGER WILL BE RELEASED" thwarts any hope of reading it, that has not stopped the book from receiving some sixty reviews and nearly two hundred ratings, now approaching a rather adulatory 4.5 out of 5-star average.

The case of Goodreads instructs us that discursive norms, those rhetorical means that people are expected to follow and accept as necessary, are a product of the affective ecology in which they might emerge. Yet, that affective ecology is itself partly determined by the material technicities that constrain its possibilities. These operational constraints can claim the power to decide in advance, as if from some hypothetical "outside" position, that social engagement should honor certain norms. Doing so, however, curtails possibilities for social action that are seldom potentialized until the actual moment of an exigence. This is as true of discussions around aesthetic texts as it is of more overtly political discourse. Setting political norms in advance, as Judith Butler puts it, "is to prefigure the kinds of practices which will qualify as the political and it is to seek to negotiate politics outside of a history which is always to a certain extent opaque to us in the moment of action."[59] The desire to deny or delay such preestablishing of the political is what an idiot rhetoric offers. Instead of emphatically plowing onward according to norms taken to be obvious and already determined, an idiot rhetoric would rather ask, as Lauren Howard did, *What's going on here?*

Howard's willingness to pause and to question, along with her refusal to release her book, shows how idiot rhetorics can sometimes involve gestures of refusal. Nothing better exemplifies the act than Herman Melville's Bartleby intoning, "I would prefer not to." Gestures of refusal happen regularly and across the political spectrum. Think of ethical vegetarians, refusing to eat animals. Think of those who refuse birth control on fundamentalist grounds. Think of conscientious objectors, abstainers, boycotters, strikers. It's important to note that such gestures are unescapably ethical. As Giorgio Agamben understands in his discussion of gestures, "What characterizes gesture is that in it nothing is being produced or acted, but rather something is being endured and supported. The gesture, in other words, opens the sphere of *ethos* as the more proper sphere of that which is human."[60] Silence need not mean stupidity, nor hesitation mean hampering. But the idiot's gesture of refusal is different than the "spiral of silence" that sometimes gives people the tendency to remain silent when they perceive their views as in opposition to those of the majority. The idiot's reticence, this Bartleby-like *preference not to*, is not necessarily driven by a fear of the isolation or reprisal that might result from speaking or acting against the grain.[61] The refusal posed by an idiot rhetoric is the audacity to not play by someone else's rules.

In its insistence on communicative action, its prizing of openness and inclusivity, its privileging of the rational over, say, the intuitive, the public sphere thesis from Habermas onward curtails the range of alternative actions, behaviors, and modes of sociality that might conceivably count as political for any given crisis. This, anyway, was a point that Jodi Dean made in her early attempts to think about communicative capitalism in the networked context of transnational technoculture.[62] Her move to privilege civil society over the public sphere can be read as a desire to identify the political as a process, not just as a fixed site, a set of communicative norms, or a variety of standards to ensure the opportunity for equal participation of all. By supplanting the public sphere thesis with a civil society model predicated on difference, that is, she effectively takes the side of an idiot rhetoric.

Certainly, that was the side that Lauren Howard took, whether she realized it or not, in her gesture of refusal to release her novel. But the affective force of that gesture, its relative uniqueness as a more passive idiot rhetoric, is made most evident against the brutal counterpoint of another conflict on Goodreads, also between a citizen artist and a citizen critic. In 2014, with the Howard controversy still smoldering, a Goodreads Author named Kathleen Hale received a bad review of her own. But Hale's response was nearly the opposite. Outraged at the bad review, Hale stalked the reviewer online. She even paid money to run a background check on the reviewer, then rented a car to find her, and staked out her home. Though she ultimately left without a confrontation, Hale did publish an essay in the *Guardian* of London about stalking the reviewer.[63] Unapologetic and domineering, this was anything but an idiot rhetoric. Its insistence on having a moral high ground, its utter disbelief in a truth other than her own, could hardly have been more antithetical to the "idiot's" hesitance to feel authorized to speak for another. Holding open a space for situationally emergent norms was precisely not the point. Closing that space down was.

In the same way that an a priori privileging of the rhetor over the *idiotes* constitutively denies the legitimacy of an idiot rhetoric, predetermined conditions delimiting "the political" foreclose the generative process of determining what counts as political in any given circumstance. A rhetorical model of publics attentive to the idiot as a valid rhetor of a more recessed or questioning kind is a processual model, rhetoric in its multiplicity being quintessentially pliable and adaptable to the emergent contingency of all situated action.[64] In this sense, theorizing norms for public communication, as if to develop best practices for resolving the inevitable (indeed the necessary) conflict arising from our social interdependence, misses the point of what an idiot rhetoric can give us. Such an understanding is processual insofar as no fixed best practices exist. An idiot rhetoric offers an insistence on not predetermining which practices best fit a particular event. Indeed, if the study of rhetoric teaches us anything, it is the wisdom of only ever abiding by "rules of thumb"—rules there may well be cause to abandon outright depending on the constraints of an emerging exigence.

And still norms are just what we get in so much of public sphere scholarship, that with a rhetorical bent included.[65] While normative theory is not itself suspicious, any one-size-fits-all model of discursive norms will inevitably fail to account for situations whose appropriate forms of discursivity emerge only in the context of unfurling experience, not in advance. Certainly, at the level of experience, there are times when being uncooperative, irrational, partial, uncharitable, and unreasonable is what a situation calls for—or better yet, calls forth. This tendency of experience to call forth certain affective orientations tends to go missing from most thinking about public spheres as a construct used to describe political action that falls outside private settings but is free from state or corporate control. The problem with the Goodreads quarrels—both Lauren Howard's and Kathleen Hunt's—is not only that their autonomy from institutional influence is not at all clear. It's that despite the real-time responsivity and customization offered by the "If, then . . ." logic of algorithms, platforms like Goodreads can't help but prefigure the political in advance of whatever ways people might find it exigent (or merely advantageous) to use such platforms in practice.

In the Lauren Howard case, it was probably not lost on anyone involved that Goodreads (only since owned by Amazon) was part of a larger algorithmic culture whose curatorial media are designed to make money for their hosts. The controversy that arose around the ad hominem criticism on the site, however, was less about bullies going too far than about the extent to which Goodreads was or should have been regulating the discursive norms of its platform. If the commercial motivations and influences of authors were permitted alongside the critical and socially generative motivations of citizen critics, what would become of the possibility for a disinterested critical practice around the arts to contribute some wider social purpose? Was the ethos conundrum really a conflict between algorithmic culture's tacit embrace of an omnivore model of aesthetic taste, as opposed to an elite/mass model that, while meant to sustain entrenched hierarchies of privilege and status, nevertheless allows a space for genuine critique?[66]

To the contrary, if the rewards of Kathleen Hale's stalking exploits are any indication, curatorial media and the creative industries with which they're aligned are more favorable to the domineering likes of Hale than the idiot rhetorics of Howard. As it turns out, the popularity of Hale's *Guardian* article soon earned her a book contract to tell the story for a larger audience in a collection of essays eventually published in 2019 and titled *Kathleen Hale Is a Crazy Stalker*. That Howard's book has languished, while Hale got a new one, only sets up a cycle of further tension between citizen artists and citizen critics. But maybe that's what curatorial media want: the valor of both sides being right despite their knotted tension, and the theater of a fight.

5

UNCOMMONWEALTH

Wealth is uncommon. Despite all the abundance of the historical present—our age of dog parks and food porn, our bounteous access to information everywhere—we have not succeeded in making wealth any less consolidated. But the problem is not just monetary. In the introduction, I mentioned Muhammad Ali's not counting his sit-ups until they started to hurt. Uncommonwealth is what results from our different kinds of social accounting, from different estimates about what matters and when and for whom. We are differently attuned. People get left behind; we lose our resilience in the face of an incorrigibly plural world when we overlook those heavy burdens one endures without being counted. Most of the time, as Ali seemed to realize, our burdens can't quite be counted at all. They're ineffable, ambient, the moods that wear us through the ever-onwardness of our days. But if our affective commonwealth provides the resilience that we do share, there is too much of our lives that doesn't count, too much uncommonwealth attuning our interdependence. Nowhere is this more apparent than in the micro-activist and distinctly local ways that some communities work to build a commonwealth that can't be taken away because the very gesture of building it satisfies the concern inflecting its character.

While the first two chapters of this book began proffering a case that concerned gestures matter, and the middle two speculated that they matter most in the everyday cultural field where citizen artists and critics do their work, the final two chapters explore how the building of affective commonwealths can refine a shared attunement and response-ability to one another. If the postulate that concerned gestures matter is to be believed, then it is important to see how, despite their frequent failure to produce instrumental effects, concerned gestures nevertheless can build affective commonwealths that orient people toward a being-in-common on the basis of shared concerns—and not on the basis of overdetermined notions about any "common" that could ever be all-encompassing. The conceptual persona of the idiot that has made appearances throughout these pages now comes to stand as emblematic of those who are excluded from—and concerned to slow down—processes of determining what counts and what doesn't. From such exclusion, there sometimes emerges a creative and critical process of building the sort of worlds that are worthy of being shared.

Take the bookshelf. Having seen how citizen artists and critics can clash over virtual bookshelves, let's now take a look at how citizen artists and critics can build and replenish a community through physical bookshelves, the kind hammered together in the world of wood and nails. The most widespread example is what are sometimes called public bookcase projects. A public bookcase is what the name suggests: a publicly available case with shelves designed to hold books free for anyone to take. Such shelves function differently in each community of practice, here like a small lending library (take a book, read it, return it), there through an economy of trade (take a book, leave a book), but generally as a repository for anyone to leave books they don't want, or to find ones that they do.[1]

The first public bookcases were conceived in 1990 as an artistic project by an artist duo named Clegg and Guttman. Their Open Library Project involved installing shelves of books outdoors in such unseemly public spaces as vacant lots, cemeteries, street corners, and so forth. Sometimes abandoned electrical utility boxes were outfitted with shelves and stocked with books; other times the shelves were built from scratch, cemented to the ground, and weatherproofed but left unlocked. For Clegg and Guttman, modern capitalist society provided few institutions that served as truly shared public property in the way that libraries did, yet public libraries were helplessly bound to the bureaucratic system of a society with consumerist values. A more direct form of participatory democracy would require the infrastructure necessary for people to sidestep that bureaucracy and create public resources themselves. The Open Library Project enabled them to do so.

In some ways an off-line precursor of the internet and the wikinomics model of social knowledge that networked technologies would soon cultivate, the public bookcases gave people a chance to build a community with their own resources.[2] Because they were located physically at fixed locations, sustained anonymously, and unregulated in terms of which books or types of books they contained, the bookshelves created communities that were based more on geographical proximity than particular shared interests. Their "user-generated content," to use a phrase more familiar now than it would have been in 1990, literally built a commonwealth for strangers to share or abuse. Since the initial Clegg and Guttman shelves, variants have cropped up across continents everywhere from rural outposts to suburban neighborhoods to city centers. Expanding from a professional art-world project to an everyday one, public bookcases of all shapes and sizes have become do-it-yourself techniques for citizens to foster community and shared wealth in highly local contexts without bothering to address the state on a larger scale. These DIY bookcases aren't there to communicate a statement or to deliver any particular message. They exist as resources to stave off the uncommonwealth that can result from relying on the presumption of equally distributed democratic welfare instead of building it locally oneself.

Let us recall that *communication* has not always been conceived of as something people do with language. In the late seventeenth century, when John Locke first suggested communication was something we do with language, his model was the principle of making private property into a commons.[3] The experience people had in their minds, for Locke, was a private and individual affair, a kind of property. He believed, however, that through the skilled use of language people could express their private experience and, in doing so, build a common realm shared by all.[4] Public bookcase projects illustrate a contemporary and material iteration of this proto-communicative process of making private property common. In this case, however, what is being shared aren't the ideas someone has as a metaphorical or intellectual private property, but rather the books that someone privately owns. Because books themselves are often mediums used for communicating their authors' otherwise private ideas, the act of sharing books in public bookcases enacts a double structure: on the one hand, making actual private property common and, on the other, making available for the commons a metaphorical private property, expressed in the metonymic "communication" of a book's ideas to someone else via the book's owner.

What we have here is analogous to the fundamental double structure of a gesture: what Giorgio Agamben calls "the communication of a communicability."[5] If gestures are the communication of a communicability, then leaving a book in a public bookcase is an exemplary gesture. Yet the mere act of leaving or taking a book depends on a host of other material and mediated factors such as the bookcase being functional, unlocked, and in a convenient and accessible location to begin with. A gesture is never just a gesture; it is always a gesture by virtue of exhibiting its own mediality. As Agamben says, *"It is the process of making a means visible as such."*[6] In this sense, Lauren Berlant is right when she reads Agamben to be saying that a "gesture is thus only a potential event, the initiation of something present that could accrue density, whether dramatic or not."[7] Public bookcases and other variants of DIY libraries exemplify the communicative power of concerned gestures by showing that, even if they don't suffice to bring about larger changes in cultural policy, they can nevertheless build an affective commonwealth that has value for those who participate in cultivating its resources.

The importance of these micro-activist gestures has become particularly heightened a couple decades into the twenty-first century, when libraries worldwide are increasingly imperiled. While the field of library and information science has bemoaned the crisis facing public libraries much longer than that,[8] it is only recently that the public has become so vigorously involved in the issue. Reasons for the public library crisis are as manifold as the claims from some camps contesting the idea that a "crisis" even exists. Short of exploring these arguments here, suffice it to say that the predicament arises in part from the entrenchment of free market logic; in part from top-down austerity measures that rendered precarious those already in compromised positions relative to their survival, emotional and otherwise; and partly, too, from the advent of digital technologies that are complicating the nature of books, reading, and what it means to have access to cultural capital. A long and evolving relationship between libraries and their publics has existed through history, and it has been marked by changing rhetorical arguments about what libraries ought to provide for the people they serve.[9] What I hope to show in this chapter is rather how one public's engagement in defense of its libraries reveals some ways that gestures of concern operate as vernacular rhetorics to resist the uncommonwealth and to affirm a more positive, shared affective commonwealth instead.

VERNACULAR RHETORIC AND BRENT'S LIBRARIES

Critical studies of culture have repeatedly shown a commitment to identify and challenge the obstacles preventing the empowerment or liberation of certain groups or interests. Out of concern for the excluded, the disenfranchised, and the powerless, much of this work supposes that functioning democracies depend on public modalities of communication that are capable of including those whose voices are not often heard or heeded, and that the governmentalization of communication techniques and technologies deserves critical scrutiny to the extent that it delimits the available means and media of public communication.[10] Given these commitments, attention to vernacular rhetoric—rhetorical measures undertaken within the local context of otherwise disempowered citizens' everyday experiences and means—has offered scholars a valuable way to imagine an inclusive democratic practice more worthy of our heterogeneous sociality.

Yet theories of the vernacular take widely divergent approaches. Sometimes the vernacular is understood as a demotic or enchorial mode of expression, other times as a medium; here it's a demographic category or marker of status, there a form of resistance.[11] I venture that understanding vernacular rhetoric's most salient role in public affairs requires recognizing the vernacular's affective register. Three characteristics of vernacularity's affective register are particularly worthy of attention. These can be expressed as maxims about the "affective vernacular." First, the affective vernacular is a precondition of the rhetorical; whither affectability, whither rhetoric. Second, the affective vernacular is not directed toward the telos of civic judgment; expressivity and circulation alone are its necessary and sufficient conditions. Third, the affective vernacular cannot be refuted; it can only be denied the chance for emergence or counterbalanced with more affectivity.

To try these maxims on, I explore the case of some concerned publics first emergent in late 2010 around some proposed library closures across England, and specifically in the London Borough of Brent. The diversity and disenfranchisement of Brent's populace make its public involvement in defending its libraries an especially trenchant illustration of vernacular rhetoric. In particular, Brent's library controversy, and the cultural policy paradigm in which it took place, found ordinary people frustrated by officially sanctioned channels of public deliberation and left to pursue their own vernacular rhetorics in a less discursive and more material way. These extra-discursive rhetorics illustrate the powerful potential for gestures of concern to build an affective commonwealth even when the goal of demonstrable social change remains far off.

Brent didn't become a London borough until 1965, created by the consolidating of the municipal boroughs of Wembley and Willesden, which were divided by the River Brent. Libraries existed in the area well before that time, and Brent absorbed them when it became a borough of its own. These libraries, among the most cherished of which included Willesden Green and Kensal Rise, had a long history in the area that became threatened, in 2010, when they faced permanent and total closure. Tracing some of this history will help to underscore why the people of Brent became so actively and emotionally involved when the shutdown of their local libraries became a looming reality.

In 1891, residents of Willesden Parish voted by a margin of two to one in favor of a measure to establish a library commission and build three public libraries in the area.[12] This measure would not have been possible if the British Parliament had not, some forty years earlier, passed the Public Libraries Act of 1850, giving local boroughs throughout England the authority to establish public libraries in their communities using local taxes. The Public Libraries Act institutionally codified the importance of free public libraries for the first time in British history, taking a clear stand on the value that libraries have in ensuring a free and civil society for all. The act initiated a "public library movement" that swept England for the rest of that century and, after the 1891 vote in Willesden, resulted in the libraries at Kilburn, Harlesden, and Willesden Green, which remain among Brent's major libraries to this day.[13]

Kensal Rise Library, however, may have been the area's most beloved. Opened in 1900 in a ceremony conducted by Mark Twain, the site was donated by Oxford's All Souls College, which stipulated in an explicit covenant that the gift was contingent on the site being used continuously as a free public reading room and library; otherwise, the property would revert to the college. Like Willesden Green before it, Kensal Rise Library was an immediate success, and soon it had a hard time keeping up with the growing needs of the community. According to some figures, "80 people per day used the Reading Room in its first week, and this figure rose to 150 after six months."[14] By 1904 the building had already been extended, in part with funds from Andrew Carnegie. Indeed, Kensal Rise has continuously changed with the times to better serve its community. In 1922, it was the first library in the area to move to a circulation system that enabled visitors to take books from the shelves directly rather than have staff librarians mediate.[15] With the Princess Frederica Primary School only a block away, the library also became a haven for schoolchildren and their parents. The library responded by enlarging the reading room again in 1928, and in 1934 it built a separate children's library and children's reading room upstairs.

By 1965, when Brent became a borough, England at large was undergoing some major changes in its library policies. Just the year before, Parliament had passed the Public Libraries and Museums Act of 1964, a monumental piece of legislation requiring all local councils to make public library services a statutory duty. With the act of 1850 having been pushed even further, in effect, public libraries were no longer just options for taxpayers who voted them in. They were now among the fundamental services that all local governments were mandated to provide for their citizens, and failure to make such provisions would lead to oversight by the secretary of state. The act of 1964 calls for local councils and library authorities to establish or sustain a "comprehensive and efficient" library service for all people "whose residence or place of work is within the library area or who are undergoing full-time education within that area."[16] Moreover, the act requires that these services be free of charge and promoted publicly. In Brent, this meant the new borough's council would be responsible for sustaining the Kensal Rise and Willesden Green libraries, among the others that it had inherited after consolidation.

Within these responsibilities, however, the Brent Council (like local councils all over England) had considerable wiggle room to interpret what "comprehensive and efficient" library services entail. As the story of Kensal Rise and other area libraries attests, since their inception around the turn of the last century, the immediate communities they served had been influencing their expansion and evolution to meet the needs of local exigencies. In other words, before local councils were on the hook to provide and sustain library services, libraries in what became Brent were already treated as valued and robust community centers. They played an integral role in the everyday lives of local citizens, and the citizens responded by participating civically in ways that ensured their libraries would continue to be relevant centers of local value. These discursive responses reached special urgency in the public sphere that emerged around some startling threats to Brent's libraries in 2010.

SOCIAL EXCLUSION AND LIBRARIES

In November 2010, a council overseeing cultural affairs for the London Borough of Brent invited public proposals for the consultation of its Libraries Transformation Project (henceforth LTP). The transformation would be radical: to the great dismay of local library-goers, the project planned to permanently close half of Brent's twelve libraries and devote its resources to enhancing the six that remained.[17] Despite the shock of the news, the plan's foundation had been planted in 2008, when the council began discussing a long-term agenda for Brent's libraries after similar stock-taking had taken place on the national scale in the first years of the new millennium. The Department for Culture, Media and Sport, which oversees all British libraries, had held a full-scale investigation of public libraries in 2000;[18] it released a similarly comprehensive *Framework for the Future* report in 2003, detailing its outlook for "libraries, learning and information in the next decade";[19] and it has researched and published intermittent reports on libraries since then as well. In 2008, UNISON, a public service union, published an independent report called *Taking Stock: The Future of Our Library Service*.[20] Given all this attention on a national level, by the time the Brent Council issued its November 2010 LTP proposal, what to do about England's public libraries was already a major issue of contention nationwide.

Almost immediately, in any case, thousands of Brent's citizens publicly expressed their concerns in an effort to defend the importance of libraries to their daily lives. Although these conversations and protests were overshadowed in the international media by the contemporaneous Arab Spring and Occupy movements, the public activity over Brent's library closures nevertheless came to form the burning center of a veritable national crisis. By 2011, six hundred libraries across England—20 percent of the total—were threatened with closure.[21] The Brent case was hardly the start of this trend, but it became the emblem.

To understand the significance of the LTP in the context of Brent, however, it helps to know more about Brent's demographics. The Greater London area contains thirty-two boroughs, twelve inner and twenty outer, plus the City of London at the hub, though the City is not itself a borough. Brent is an outer borough in northwest London, geographically the fifteenth largest of London's boroughs, with Wembley as its major town. Brent has one of the highest population densities in outer London, with an estimated 282,672 residents, 59 percent of whom are black, Asian, or members of minority ethnic groups—a figure that is double the outer London average. With 71 percent of its residents from an ethnic group other than white British, 48 percent of its population born outside the United Kingdom, and 130 different languages spoken in Brent schools, a strong claim can be made that Brent is among the most diverse areas in all of the British Isles. Despite this, or perhaps as a corollary of it, Brent is also among the most deprived. The Index of Multiple Deprivation—which measures income, employment, health, education, crime and living environment, and barriers to housing and services—found in late 2010 (not the most recent report, but the one most contemporaneous with the LTP) that Brent had been steadily growing more deprived and was then among the 15 percent most deprived of the 354 boroughs in all of England.[22]

Around the time that Brent's libraries were under peril, in what would seem to have been a boon for areas like Brent, cultural policy in the European Union had codified an interest in treating "social exclusion" as a key index for the health of democratic life. For years, at least in England, the policy paradigm regulating cultural affairs had linked poverty and deprivation to disadvantage, suggesting that some people just lacked the resources necessary for civic and social engagement, though they would presumably be happier and more participatory if only they had the means.[23] Such a model neglected to take into account that many people were in fact trying to participate in public life—through organizations, clubs, social movements, and so forth—but they weren't afforded the influence or the forum necessary to bring about visible change because the status quo relegated them to a fate of being ignored or easily dismissed. In effect, many were treated as "idiots," given an ostensible chance to speak, but not the chance to be heard.

The turn to social exclusion policy emphasized a more multidimensional approach to such problems by attributing them, as Dave Muddiman suggests, "not simply to a lack of material resources, but also to matters like inadequate social participation, lack of cultural and educational capital, inadequate access to services and lack of power. In other words, the idea of social exclusion attempts to capture the complexity of *powerlessness* in modern society rather than simply focusing on one of its outcomes."[24] While such an outlook may seem standard from the standpoint of critical theory, it did not become prominent in European policy until relatively recently, and it remains absent in any explicit sense from American policy still.[25] Today, an emphasis on social exclusion, even without more explicit task forces bearing that name, remains in policy conversations about the social and economic disparities among different communities in democratic European societies. Although the concept has a variety of definitions and uses, in a general sense policies guided by social exclusion attend to the ways *inclusion* can be achieved so as to ensure all citizens the opportunity to participate civically in their communities. As the Commission of the European Communities reports, "Social exclusion refers to the multiple and changing factors resulting in people being excluded from the normal exchanges, practices and rights of modern society."[26] Accordingly, policies made under the social exclusion model respond to those circumstances necessary to ensure that all corners of a society have the rights, resources, and opportunities needed to exercise the full measure of their communicative citizenship.

Given the adoption of social exclusion as the public policy model in England, the controversy over Brent's libraries demands to be understood along the axis of inclusion and exclusion. In this view, the extent to which libraries foster the social inclusion of the citizens they serve corresponds directly to the extent to which a state intent on eradicating social exclusion must provide libraries for its citizens. But a critical cultural approach to the library closures thus faces a problem: if recognizing "the complexity of powerlessness" is an aim of both the critical cultural project and of the policies such a project might endeavor to critique, then what is the justifiable basis for a critical response? In other words, how can a project fundamentally grounded in critiques of inequality challenge a state policy that is itself committed to critiquing the conditions of social life that create inequality? Here's where the complexity of an affective commonwealth comes to the fore.

If public libraries are a shared resource for all, then they are part of the commonwealth of those societies that support them. But the ideal nature of a commonwealth's various resources is not always agreed upon by all who might share in its wealth. Since the first libraries in ancient Egypt, there has never been shared agreement about what libraries ought to be and do. Competing arguments, what the pre-Socratic philosopher Protagoras called *dissoi logoi*, have always surrounded libraries and their expected function. In his history of the library's evolution as a concept, Matthew Battles describes two such conflicting visions of early libraries. These *dissoi logoi* pitted Parnassan libraries, invested in preserving "the essence of all that is Good and Beautiful (in the classical formulation) or Holy (in the medieval)" against Universal libraries, which were "not to be praised for particular influences or qualities" of specific volumes, but for the sheer breadth of the collection as a whole.[27] In their respective models of quality and quantity, Parnassan and Universal libraries indicate a conflict between privileging the rarefied status of a canon or privileging the notion that all information is important to preserve and catalog.[28]

Today the spread of networked technologies, including born-digital texts, high-speed scanning devices, and optical character recognition (OCR) software, has brought about a new set of competing arguments about libraries, which can be summarized as "Needs or Reads."[29] Should libraries deemphasize tangible books and buildings, focusing instead on providing the technological resources that match a community's needs for engagement and development? Or should libraries emphasize their traditional service of book lending, and accordingly prioritize the acquisition of new books and the building space necessary to accommodate them? Rhetorically, the *dissoi logoi* of Needs or Reads leverage opposing attitudes toward which issues are salient in the function of contemporary libraries. The Needs argument is about the "transformation of libraries into needs-based services," while the Reads argument promotes "the modernization of the traditional library service."[30]

In part, each model derives from interpretation of statistical evidence about trends in library usage over the past decades. These data, usually generated from surveys, vary widely across contexts. For instance, a 2013 British survey, undertaken by the Department for Culture, Media, and Sport, found that only 36 percent of people surveyed said they had visited a library during the previous year.[31] A similar survey in America, undertaken by the Pew

Research Center during the same period, found that 53 percent of surveyed Americans reported visiting a library in the year prior to being interviewed.[32] Similar comparative analyses reveal that the reasons patrons give for using libraries are the same as the reasons others give for not using them: library-goers increasingly use libraries for access to technology, and non-goers ascribe their lack of interest to the internet's having made visiting libraries unnecessary. Technology, in this case, plays a rhetorical double duty. To concede that libraries are unnecessary because the web offers similar affordances available from home is at once to concede that libraries offering web services are valuable to the extent they provide services not available elsewhere. Conversely, to identify a library's value in the access it affords to technology is to find libraries without value if they neglect to provide such access when it is needed.

Diminished funding from the state, alongside the senescence of the benefactor model, has meant that (in England especially) a "Private Finance Initiative" has increasingly been regarded as a helpful way to support the survival of public libraries.[33] Noting that public libraries today are surrounded by a "discourse continually advocating a more commercial approach to service design and delivery," David McMenemy suggests that because the "citizen-consumer" now expects "the same levels of service from their public services as they do from any commercial service they deal with," the burden of policy-makers rests on making libraries attractive choices for a public who can choose to use them or not.[34] In this view, the *dissoi logoi* of Needs or Reads may function as normative arguments supporting different ideals, but what matters is creating libraries that people choose to use.

From a rhetorical perspective, though, policies that privilege the public's choice can be said to promulgate "choice" merely as an ideograph—the sum of a whole affective orientation distilled into a single word.[35] Communicative capitalism may blithely assure us of our liberty to choose—and, in principle, who could disagree with such a liberty?—but the reality is that not everyone has alternative options for access to the kinds of services and resources that public libraries can provide. Practical wisdom thus suggests that the way to make libraries more appealing depends largely on which people one hopes to make them more appealing to. Given the public's heterogeneity, however, contrasting policy arguments about Needs or Reads can seem rather limited by their respective one-size-fits-all programs. At issue, then, is not just whether libraries become internet cafés or large free bookstores. The tacit but more crucial stakes are how libraries interpellate the publics they purportedly serve, and how publics resistant to being accordingly subjected endeavor instead to shape library policy in their collective self-image.

In short, when potential changes in library services bring forth public spheres intent on resisting these changes, the salient emphasis in library rhetorics shifts from defining public libraries to defining a library's publics. When public spheres emerge around issues related to public libraries, however, something peculiar happens: the public sphere becomes a kind of meta-public sphere, whereby the key issue of public discourse is not just the libraries, but also the importance of the public sphere in their sustenance. One reason this might happen is because libraries enable and enact the ideal of a Habermasian public sphere. As John Buschman has argued, libraries are essential to thriving democracies because they are "a place where the ideal of unfettered communication and investigation exists in rudimentary form, allowing for critical and rational discussion of the issues of the day."[36] When these issues happen to concern the degradation of public library services, they also concern the imperilment of the public sphere that libraries help make possible. In turn, public spheres attending to public library issues fight vigorously for state recognition of the public sphere ideal when determining the future of library services for local communities. In that case, it is possible to identify a third pair of *dissoi logoi* emergent in library rhetorics, namely, competing arguments about whether a library's public consists in citizen-consumers or public citizens. As Buschman suggests, the purpose of libraries may well be the cultivation of citizens equipped to participate in the public sphere; but, if libraries "have had their purposes recast in economic terms in this era of economics as the basis of our public reasoning," then "we have rhetorically transformed library users into 'customers.'"[37] The *dissoi logoi* of citizen-consumers or public citizens capture this problematic.

Both positions show how understanding a library's public in a certain way is tacitly to define their libraries similarly. Citizen-consumers constitute the version of the public envisioned in a free market model of public libraries. Such a public performs its citizenship effectively by consuming: in this case, by going to libraries and partaking of their services, whatever those happen to be. The logic holds that if people are not using their libraries, then libraries are not fulfilling the market's demand; underused libraries thus need to be shut down or consolidated or transformed. The opposing position, which treats library-goers as public citizens, works differently. Public citizens enact their citizenship not by consuming, but by participating in civil society in order to identify and advocate for the diverse needs of their social interdependence so that the state might act accordingly. The reasoning here follows the deliberative path of a rhetorically modeled public sphere, in which public consensus, achieved through the vernacular discussions of informed and reasonable citizens, forms a signpost for state action.[38] The question in both arguments is what role ordinary citizens play in shaping the libraries that are meant to facilitate the fulfillment of their citizenship in the first place.

Cultural policy, with its imperative to make decisions that rule out other alternatives, seldom has the luxury of playing both sides. Libraries materialize, or don't. If they do, they do so in particular forms and not others, becoming a literal part of the commonwealth. But what I've called the *affective* commonwealth accounts for something more ephemeral and primary: that is, in this case, a socially dispersed attitude about the function of libraries that characterizes the public mood through which libraries elicit or don't elicit the concern of those attentive to them. We can say that an affective commonwealth is that shared resource of public feeling that contributes to (by reminding us of) our capacities for being-in-common. But that does not mean that we all feel the same way or occupy the same mood. It means that our commonness often consists in our shared ability to rehabituate a collective mood in ways that affirm more positive orientations toward our inevitable differences, accentuating that any commonwealth is not just shared but made—that if we aren't careful, our uncommonwealth will replace any sense of being-in-common.[39] Gestures of concern build affective commonwealths not by advancing reasoned arguments and mobilizing in their defense, but through the idiot rhetorics that spread an unfinished orientation to being-in-common as a creative and collective process—a process always in flux, subject to further change. Looking closer at the Brent case shows how this can play out rhetorically through a community's vernacular gestures of concern.

VERNACULAR RHETORICS IN THE PEOPLE'S PROTEST

It is hard to emphasize enough the vigorous *concern* of the Brent protests. After announcing the impending closures in its LTP report, the Brent Council agreed to a three-month period of "extensive public consultation" about the report.[40] It was during this time that the first public outcries began: in part, for the obvious reason that the LTP's plan to overhaul library services had just been made public, but also because the council had agreed to entertain public opinion about the proposal only during this three-month time of consultation. Such consultation periods are not unique to the library controversy, but are part of the Brent Council's "have your say" custom, whereby the council opens its policies to public deliberation for various lengths of time. In this case, the three-month consultation phase included several officially sanctioned opportunities for the participation of ordinary citizens in the public sphere.

These included five "Area Consultative Forums" hosted regionally throughout Brent for a neighborhood's residents to give spoken testimony about the LTP's local impact; six "Service User Consultative Forums" for such testimony to be made by interest groups such as pensioners, minorities, youth, the disabled, and others; two "Public Meetings" for Q&A with council members; an "Open Day" for general public discussion at Willesden Green Library; a paper, postal, and digital questionnaire freely available online and at libraries throughout the borough; and open opportunities for written correspondence with, and requests for information from, the Brent Council.[41] In addition, and perhaps most substantially, the consultation window also marked the deadline for community interest groups to submit full-scale proposals of their own as alternatives to the LTP. For three urgent months, it seemed, the people of Brent still had a chance—within the system—to save their libraries.

And the people responded. By March, nine groups had submitted as many alternative proposals. Attendance at the consultative forums and public meetings spiked compared to meetings before the LTP release. By the end of the consultation period, according to the council's records, the council had responded to at least 101 emails challenging or questioning the LTP;[42] it had answered numerous queries about the council's statistical information and methodology;[43] and it had received eight official petitions calling for retention of the libraries, with signatures that ranged on a given petition from 1 to 6,071 residents.[44] Of course, merely quantifying the public's involvement isn't the point. Close inspection of the forum minutes, meeting transcripts, email correspondence, and other Q&A evidence reveals a discursive public keen to express their concerns about the status of their libraries and what libraries mean to them.

What emerges in reading these records is not only the public's clear and earnest investment in its libraries, an investment made evident in a wide range of opinions about what libraries should offer to their communities and how. These are striking, certainly. More striking still is a recurrent theme in the public meetings, forums, and inquiries: namely, claims that the consultation process had itself been unfairly limited, marred by flawed evidence, and provided an inadequate scope for citizens to participate civically in debates about decisions affecting their communities (for a sampling, see fig. 5.1). In other words, despite the numerous sanctioned public forums for addressing the library problem, the engaged public responded in ways that critiqued the LTP's efforts as a Potemkin Village that destroyed an already existing public sphere with the farce that its consensus might have some bearing on public policy.

The meetings designed for the public to question members of the council were particularly rife with such critiques. Many challenged the council's

"The arrogance and autonomy of the way the Council has handled this process has been staggering. A local library is a community hub."

"It's very disappointing to realize that the local council care absolutely nothing about local opinion on this matter."

"Brent is not listening and our councillors' behaviour is scandalous...the library is the most important community building in our area."

"The Council have a duty to the whole community, not just those near selected high street locations."

"I was born in this area and still live here after twenty-six years. It is an integral part of our community—it would be like losing a limb."

"I am deeply disappointed with Brent Council. We do not have any community spaces in Kensal Rise which cater for all ages, cultures, and faiths which do not discriminate."

Figure 5.1. Selected "vernacular voices" from the Brent protests. Friends of Kensal Rise Library, Written Evidence.

figures about library usage and accused the council of engaging in a rigged game. One attendee said the council was "disguising from people what [was] going on," and another asked outright, "What [was] the point of a consultation" if the outcome was already predetermined.[45] Indeed, the indignant feelings recurred at the Willesden Green "Open Day," where one attendee complained that the public meetings had been a sham: "Councilor Powney ignored us in the public meeting; therefore it wasn't a public consultation."[46] Others likewise bemoaned the inadequate publicizing of the meetings and what one person called the council's "deliberately misleading" published information about the consultation period at large. Some also derided the council's questionnaire as "appalling" and full of "leading question[s]."[47] In written evidence later submitted to the House of Commons, a feeling of injustice and unfairness becomes clear in an assortment of comments (fig. 5.1).

While the problem of social exclusion was thus central to the public's concern, it remained curiously sidelined by the council whose policies presumably operated under such a paradigm. Meeting minutes from the public Q&A sessions, emails to interested citizens, and the original LTP proposal all point to a council motivated as much by an economic exigence as by the model of social exclusion. At one public meeting, Councilor Powney told the audience, "This is not a referendum. We have to make changes. . . . The key thing I want everyone to understand is that we're in a position where saying let's carry on spending money is not an option."[48] In email correspondence, the council repeatedly responded to public inquiries by emphasizing that the council was in an "extremely difficult" or "very difficult financial situation" so "a rationalization strategy [was] necessary."[49] The original report had also listed seven reasons for the LTP's existence in the first place. Several issues more or less related to social exclusion appeared on the list, but on top was "the current economic situation and impending public sector spending reductions."[50] The council had pointed to statistics comparing the annual cost of maintaining libraries with annual library usage in order to arrive at a cost per visit for each of Brent's libraries.[51] According to these figures, those libraries threatened with closure accounted for six of the eight highest cost-per-visit numbers because they had seen the least traffic in relation to their operation expense.

Such evidence allowed the council to take the clever position of treating economic needs and social exclusion as inextricable considerations. Effectively, the council could make its case on either basis: not enough people use these libraries, so we can't justify their cost; or, if these libraries cost so much to run, then they need to attract more people. The voices emergent from the public during the consultation phase, however, were notably concerned with social exclusion alone, albeit in a twofold sense: first, to ensure their libraries be saved because libraries are important community hubs where social inclusion is made possible in an everyday, local context; and, second, to ensure the public's fair discursive inclusion in the conversations that would determine the fate of such libraries.

After the consultation period, the council moved quickly. Only a month later, by April 11, 2011, they published their final LTP executive report.[52] While ostensibly having taken into account the results of the public consultation, the final report nevertheless remained obstinate on the major point of contestation, the issue of branch closures. It also rejected every alternative proposal submitted by public interest groups. In response, that July three Brent residents filed a High Court suit against the Brent Council, claiming the council had "adopted a fundamentally flawed approach to the objective of making savings in its budget" and instead "started from the false premise that library closures were an inevitability, thereby closing its mind to alternative means."[53] Above all, the claimants said, the council "acted unfairly by failing properly to consult the public on the proposals generally, by withholding relevant information from consultees and by failing to undertake adequate inquiry and consultation in relation to the needs of those groups protected by equality legislation."[54]

The British press billed the lawsuit as a "landmark" case that would establish a precedent for how library closures would be treated across the country. What rights did Brent's public have to participate in determining how to fulfill, in a local context, the 1964 Public Libraries and Museums Act's mandate that municipalities provide "comprehensive and efficient" library services to their residents? With rampant library closures imminent throughout England, this topic was very much national news. And at this stage, the peoples' cause gained even more momentum.

Several high-profile British celebrities put their weight behind the struggle in Brent, giving it all the more attention. Prominent authors Zadie Smith, Philip Pullman, Alan Bennett, and others, along with musical celebrities Nick Cave, Depeche Mode, and the Pet Shop Boys, each publicly expressed their allegiance to the goal of saving Brent's libraries, some with speeches and others with fundraising efforts. A group called Brent SOS (i.e., "Save Our Six") Libraries formed to organize a more cohesive public opposition. Websites and blogs cropped up like clover overnight. All these voices in the cause expressed vernacular rhetorics positioned deliberately in opposition to the council and the state's official, institutional rhetorics. So websites like Voices for the Library showcased first-person testimonies submitted by hundreds of regular people expressing through personal stories the value of local libraries in their daily lives.[55] And groups like Friends of Kensal Rise Library, the Cricklewood Homeless Concern, and Keep Willesden Green, among others, formed or redoubled their efforts to fight the closures in Brent. While these groups were autonomous and discrete in their particular interests, together the conversations they joined attested to the robustness of the public sphere emergent around Brent's libraries.

Ultimately, though, these efforts were unsuccessful. On October 13, 2011, the High Court ruled in favor of the Brent Council. That morning, all twelve of Brent's libraries were closed in anticipation of the ruling. After the verdict, six were immediately reopened—and the ill-fated six were at once boarded up.

Brent's library controversy illustrates the difficulty that precarious subjects can have in making their voices heard against the obdurate will of authority when the authorities both hold ownership of the problem and the sanctioned means by which it might be articulated otherwise. While the public that participated in these sanctioned channels can clearly be regarded as "vernacular" along any of the concept's established matrices, the essential vernacularity of this public did not attain its greatest salience until it responded to the consultative period's shortcomings with—as we'll soon see—rhetorical means of its own. I aim to conclude the chapter by suggesting that the affective register of these means gives occasion to rethink how we conceptualize vernacular rhetoric as an idiot rhetoric.

Throughout this book I have treated affect as a way to think about those subtle energetics of communication and sociality that maneuver at registers adjacent to the regime of meaning or signification, and accordingly align more with idiot rhetorics in their recessiveness than outspoken rhetorics in their persuasive patriarchies.[56] The affective is hard to identify, let alone trace, because it can neither be affixed to an individual on the basis of being personal, the way feelings can, nor be semanticized socially, in the way of emotions. As Brian Massumi writes, "The problem is that there is no cultural-theoretical vocabulary specific to affect," and "in the absence of an asignifying philosophy of affect," we default to supposing that affect is rather the same as emotion.[57] Although today we'd have to admit that the lexicon wrought by the surge in affect theory has vastly improved since Massumi bemoaned it in 2002, his general emphasis on affect's likeness to *intensity* remains. Affect's intensity derives from being decentered from any individual and instead mobilized through the dynamic relations that pass between people and between people and things (and, more controversially to some, between things and things) in the form of language, bodies, images, sounds, movements, energies, and so forth. "Affect," in this sense, is not "in" the symbolic exchanges that make our relationality manifest; rather, it is always manifesting anew through the relationality itself: the invisible vectors of mood that pass between and around us with the potential stickiness to connect all the subjects, memories, material influences, and sensations of our social field without which symbolic exchange would be impossible.

In Brent, after a public consultation and subsequent lawsuit that by all empirical measures made official channels of public dissent appear to have failed, the stickiness that took hold locally around the threatened libraries can help to account for more vernacular efforts to keep the struggle alive. Unquestionably, threats to Brent's libraries inspired great passion, vitriol, and even desperation among those citizens who expressed such feelings because they counted on these libraries as part of the routine and habits of their everyday lives. But in keeping with the distinction between feeling, emotion, and affect, all the fraught feelings and emotions expressed in public discourse around the issue and its politics were different from the emergent affective tonality that the controversy began making manifest. Affect arises (and is readable) most of all from within the ordinary, the everyday, as distinguished from "the political" realms that encroach upon it.

The everyday, for Henri Lefebvre, is a "residual" space outside of politics and economics, and it is defined by "what is left over after all distinct, superior, specialized, structured activities have been singled out by analysis."[58] In this telling, the everyday and affect share important similarities that implicate one in the production of the other. Nearly all theories of affect, as Ruth Leys rightly (if suspiciously) assesses, "suggest that the affects must be viewed as independent of, and in an important sense prior to, ideology—that is, prior to intentions, meanings, reasons, and beliefs—because they are nonsignifying, autonomic processes that take place below the threshold of conscious awareness and meaning."[59] In Lefebvre's designation of the everyday as a residual space distinct from institutional politics, in his identification of the everyday as what falls outside of what institutional structures and systems can commodify and determine, he gestures toward a space similarly independent of ideology, that is, independent of attempts to pass off a social order as a natural order of benefit to all. The social order of the everyday is rather formed outside the cone of top-down order as such. In brief, although affective orders influence all places where there are people or things existing in relation to one another, which is to say everywhere, social practice usually accumulates its greatest affectability in quotidian ways.

The everyday's deep affectability, coupled with vernacular rhetoric's rootedness within the everyday, makes the vernacular an intrinsically affective register. This carries at least three important implications. First, the affective register of the vernacular is a *precondition* of its rhetorical potentiality and not just a manifestation of its emotional symbolicity.[60] The everyday contexts and background assumptions that give rise to the vernacular are produced through the affective orientations that precede them, not just "always already" but also "always not yet." As a precondition that continues evolving, affect is not merely functional— that which serves to capacitate the rhetorical. It is also self-sufficient in that its processual manifesting is always ongoing, perpetual. Second, then, we might say that the salience of the vernacular's affective register to the public sphere is to embody a public testament of belief without exclusively being directed toward a civic judgment that its disempowered status often cannot sway anyway. The affective vernacular fulfills its needs by being there. Finally, its adjacency to ideological intent or signifying content makes the affective vernacular unsusceptible to critique. To phrase it as a principle: third, the vernacular's affective registers cannot be refuted. The struggle in Brent makes these points clear.

After the libraries closed, Brent SOS Libraries appealed for a judicial review. People took to the streets. A round-the-clock vigil began outside the libraries at Preston Road and Kensal Rise, hoping to stop the boarded-up libraries from being emptied of their books and computers. Residents erected a "Brent Council Wall of Shame" outside Preston Road Library, where children, artists, and others wrote comments, drew pictures, posted signs, and generally railed against the council or expressed their allegiance to the cause of saving Brent's libraries (fig. 5.2). While the Wall of Shame falls decidedly in the camp of vernacular rhetoric, its affective register can all too easily be conflated with its emotional one. For that reason, it makes a particularly good way to illustrate the key distinction between affect and emotion.

The Wall of Shame was a rickety affair, made of plywood and nails, and serving none of a wall's typical purposes: the division of space by walling in or walling out. "Something there is that doesn't love a wall," Robert Frost reminds us in his poem "Mending Wall." The Brent Council was such a something. The wall's sole apparent purpose was not to separate the people physically from the council that had closed its libraries, but to separate them symbolically. The wall existed to accommodate the writing on it. This writing, along with the photos or drawings it accumulated, expressed deep emotion from the people whom the library closures affected. "I can't read," someone wrote. Another: "Education is the key of life, and your [sic] taking it away! Pleass [sic] save our library!" The pathos of these appeals is self-evident, and the bald confessions and solecisms are all the more heart-wrenching for not being performances.

But for all its emotionality, for all the pathos it elicits, the writing on the wall is not affective in the way I've been suggesting we should understand affect. The text and photos belong squarely within the symbolic order of a public sphere fighting to save one of its most prized access points for culture and the capital it might confer. This communication is vernacular through and through. But to call it *affective* (even though an encounter with the wall undoubtedly has some stickiness in the complex ecology of orientations toward the issue) is not a claim that can be warranted on the basis that the comments and images posted

Figure 5.2. The "Brent Council Wall of Shame" and local protesters, circa October 2011.

on the wall might have an emotional impact. Perhaps writing on the wall served a sort of cathartic "venting" function for a clearly frustrated populace; but that is the only sense in which we could say it was self-sufficient. The wall served, instead, as a concerned gesture, a vernacular rhetoric operating outside officially sanctioned means, to continue the struggle by striving for the goal of saving libraries that, with each new day, seemed more incontrovertibly doomed.[61]

As the protest continued, however, it took on a new and curious set of vernacular practices, which I think better illustrate the vernacular's distinctly affective register. Immediately after Kensal Rise Library closed down, protestors erected a fully functional "pop-up library" on its grounds, using wood, metal poles, and tarpaulin (fig. 5.3). This was a more elaborate affair than the public bookcases that have cropped up around the world on front lawns and street corners on smaller scales since Clegg and Guttman's 1990 art project. Local residents donated the books and staffed the Kensal Rise Pop-Up Library's regular hours. Though of the same essential character as public bookcase projects, the Kensal Rise Pop-Up did something more in the context of its broader political exigence. It gestured with concern—that is, it did not merely *symbolize* or *represent*—the people's need for a library.[62] It communicated communicability. Since opening a century before, the original library at Kensal Rise had always been a haven for the neighborhood's children. In an area of such deprivation as Brent, at the time of its closure in 2011, Kensal Rise Library had long been a

Figure 5.3. The Kensal Rise Pop-Up Library.

stand-in day-care facility for Princess Frederica pupils after school; it was a place they could go until their parents came home from their work shifts. Expressing this locally habituated need at public meetings and consultations had not made any apparent impact. But by building a library all their own, if not quite the haven local children really needed, the people could demonstrate that the library truly was essential to their community and its habitus—so important, it turns out, that they would even build and staff the library themselves as "coalitional subjects" whose struggles were bound up with one another's.[63]

Moreover, the Pop-Up Library fulfilled a legal technicality. Because of the covenant stipulating that if the site of Kensal Rise did not remain a library at all times it would revert back to All Souls College, residents knew that maintaining even a makeshift library on the grounds was necessary in order to retain their claim to that space for a library of one kind or another. Although the Pop-Up accordingly served as an extension of the people's protest, in other ways it was not a protest directed toward the telos of change because, by satisfying the need for a means to borrow books and gather communally, it might well have succeeded by never ending.

Unlike the bodily self-sufficiency of a hunger strike, for instance, which acts primarily as a symbolic but all too material performance of one's commitment to literally embody a cause, the Pop-Up library can be understood outside a symbolic frame altogether. Certainly, by erecting a makeshift library on the grounds of the contested site, the people mobilized a material symbol of their need for libraries. To take away the Pop-Up library would at once take away the symbolic expression of the public will. But the Pop-Up's primary function was not symbolic at all: it didn't *represent* the public's need for a library; it *fulfilled* that need. It served as the library that local residents would miss if it weren't sustained by their own efforts. Accordingly, there was no essential difference between keeping the Pop-Up operational and whatever objective they might have hoped to reach by doing so. Yes, to take down the Pop-Up would be to concede defeat in the political cause against the Brent Council's ruling. But to leave it up was not, at least not in its first order, a means to fight for a victory that would or would not one day be achieved. Precisely because the Pop-Up fulfilled their need for a library, it attained as a second order the demonstrative capacity of a symbolic action able to represent that need.

To think of the Pop-Up as rhetorically directed toward the goal of a decisive judgment in their cause's favor, then, can only make sense after recognizing that its being there alone was also self-sufficient. This asymbolic, pragmatic sufficiency is the affective register that makes some vernacular rhetorics so potent. By endeavoring not to breach the All Souls covenant, the hybrid vernacularity of the Pop-Up operated within a legal apparatus that gave its cause legitimacy. But it also operated wholly outside any institutional logic's ability to counter the vernacular's affective claim for a legitimacy so self-evident that it needs no symbolic expression. Taken to its limits, a hunger strike can end in one of several ways: abandonment of the strike, death by starvation, forced feeding, or submission to the will of one's oppressors. Such strikes are not designed to be sustainable but signify a condition of unacceptability that will not last. In their affective registers, all that vernacular rhetorics have to do (in very British fashion) is keep calm and carry on.[64]

And so they did. The Pop-Up library remained operational for over two more years. The children may not have had their after-school hub, the elderly may not have had their access to the web, but the Pop-Up does seem to have established its own everyday place within the community as their brick-and-mortar library remained shut down. There were still other libraries not too far away. All of Brent is only 16.7 square miles. Undoubtedly, the remaining branches in the borough had larger inventories, more services, and actual facilities. But the Pop-Up demonstrated the power of an idiot rhetoric mobilized through concerned gestures. The elderly and children, after all, are near analogs of the "idiots" in the old Greek sense—neglected voices in the political scene who don't, unfortunately, count in the same way as everyone else. Yet, in the Brent case, these "idiots" were just the ones whose concerned gesture of the Pop-Up gave pause to ask what should count and for whom. The gesture was clear. The "official consultation" had been a sham, the lawsuit to that effect failed to convince, and now, through vernacular means, an affective commonwealth that formed by cohering around deep concernedness assured the public of the legitimacy of its participatory publicness *and* a version of the library they had wanted to save all along.

Until it didn't. On January 31, 2014, after over two years of relatively unimpeded operation, someone going by the handle @DJHarryLove posted this Tweet at 3:16 a.m.: "KENSAL RISE POP UP LIBRARY HAS BEEN TORN DOWN IN THE MIDDLE OF THE NIGHT BY HIRED HEAVIES—KENSAL RESIDENTS WE HAVE TO RESPOND!!" (fig. 5.4). Sure enough, come daybreak, residents woke to find the library taken apart, the books left in the rain to molder. Shortly thereafter, the bursar of All Souls College, Thomas Seaman, announced that the old Kensal Rise Library had been sold to a developer named Andrew Gillick, with full awareness that he intended to convert the space into gentrified residential units.

Figure 5.4. Tweet announcing the Pop-Up's destruction, January 31, 2014.

REPLENISHMENT

When I visited Brent to do some of this research in July 2017, the old Kensal Rise Library had been refurbished, but the ground floor was sitting empty. By the entrance, an intercom system with an illuminated keypad and small video camera had been mounted beneath a brushed-metal placard that read, "Library Apartments 1–4." Since 2010, some 478 libraries have been closed across the

United Kingdom.[65] More closures are likely ahead. Library funding is down by the millions. And Brexit—both the 2016 vote to separate Britain from the European Union and the subsequent debacle of enacting that separation—has only imperiled British libraries more.[66] Against this grim outlook for libraries, how can the Brent case, which was a failure by all measures of appeal to the state, nevertheless inspire resilience and affirm an uncruel optimism? Much as on Goodreads these days most of the reviews and comments about Lauren Howard's *Learning to Love* are positive and encouraging, the aftermath of the Brent protests indicates some ways that the concerned efforts of those involved have been replenishing.

In September 2013, four years before I visited Brent, and four months before the Pop-Up was razed under cover of night, claims emerged in the press that the plan submitted by developer Andrew Gillick to All Souls College, proposing to turn Kensal Rise Library into flats, had included fraudulent emails of support. Some emails were outright fabrications. Others used the real names and email addresses of actual Brent residents, despite being written without their knowledge. A police investigation followed. No one doubted that the emails were fraudulent, as some of the victims were identified and not amused. But the investigation concluded in late December 2013 that no court action would realistically lead to any convictions, and hence the case was dropped. All Souls College proceeded to sell the former library to Andrew Gillick's group, and that was the context, only a few weeks later, when the Pop-Up was secretly destroyed.

By this stage, a lot had been taken from the people of Brent while they were trying to build the sort of world they wanted to be at home in. Given defeat after defeat by official channels of the state—local consultations, national court proceedings, police force investigations—it was not just their library and their homemade substitute for it that they'd lost; an immeasurable affective toll had been taken as well. And yet what they gained as recompense was an undeniable affective commonwealth that they'd built by identifying their shared concern. Official channels of pursuing their cause may have been exhausted, but vernacular ones had not been, precisely because they replenished that commonwealth which would otherwise have been taken from them except in the effort to create it (even as that effort seemed to have "failed" by instrumental logics of objective measures). The concerned people of Brent re-sited the Pop-Up, phoenix-like, at a nearby café where would-be library patrons, young and old, could borrow books or sit and read or talk. The café replacement of the razed replacement may have broken the All Souls covenant stipulating that the site had to be used continuously as a library or else be lost, but it affirmed and replenished the affective commonwealth that gives any community its resolve and semblance of cohesion.

What had at times been a rather public and vociferous protest in this way became more recessed as the invested citizens found their own ways to continue fulfilling a modicum of their needs while refusing to let them be determined by those intent on circumscribing a "common good" on their behalf. Their resilience was not just a matter of renewal and persistence; it was the subtle work of an idiot rhetoric seeking to raise the question of what it meant to pursue the "common" or the "good" in the first place. The evidence of fraudulence could not have better exemplified how others had deigned to speak for them, literally taking unspeaking citizens and putting words in their name—the "idiot" made "rhetor" in order to count at all. Insofar as a successful conviction of fraud would probably not have saved their library in any case (a conviction would likely only have given the property bid to a different developer), the failed fraudulence investigation revealed the ways the concerned citizens had been operating in an affective register all along. While developers started work on converting the old library into apartments, inside the new café Pop-Up down the road things slowed down enough for the Friends of Kensal Rise Library to work directly with All Souls College—and to see if a less burdensome uncommonwealth could be achieved.

Against the odds, it was. On November 30, 2017 (Mark Twain's birthday), after three more years of keeping calm and carrying on, the Friends of Kensal Rise Library officially signed a lease to use the ground floor of the old library building, rent-free, for the purposes of operating a new Kensal Rise Library and Community Centre. The lease was good for the next thousand years. Though the group received some grants to make this feasible, much of the endgame of making it happen involved the grassroots grind of raising the money. Fortunately, the affective commonwealth they'd been building for the last seven years gave them what they needed: neighbors and friends and a community already attuned to the work of sustaining itself. Christmas markets, craft fairs, readings, lectures, author talks, dance concerts, symphonies, art exhibitions, auctions, actors' nights, pasta dinners, triathlons, marathons, you name it, the people came together, creating the very community they envisioned by the gestures of trying to create it. Today, the new facility is open and thriving, offering free internet access, ESOL classes, employment training, yoga, other events, and plenty of books. Local volunteers are its primary staff, and if it has an emphasis other than being a force for good in the community at large, it's to serve the needs of children and the elderly in particular.

The Brent case adds complexity to the thesis that affect is a preoriginary rhetoric and that persuadability is primed by affective vectors of towardness or awayness—vectors that may give rise to symbolic actions once their latency gets personalized as feelings or their ineffability gets semanticized as emotions. Here, an affective orientation toward libraries, laminated by the highly local context of the attachments libraries brought forth among Brent's youth and aging populations especially, can be said to have given rise to the highly emotional rhetorics of protest and frustration. But the rhetorics performed through official channels and subsequently denied in a Kafkaesque attempt to navigate official channels of late liberal life were rhetorics that themselves gave rise to new affective orientations toward the problem. The gesturally produced emergence of these new orientations in turn changed the affective commonwealth, orienting the people around a new exigence, one premised on the delayed duration—the return to the previously unfulfilled promise of the All Souls Covenant—and the new situation, now "understood" affectively, again became subsumed into rhetorical acts, this time of a vernacular register shot through with affectivity.

In this light, vernacular rhetorics are more than just the voices of "everyday" people, and more too than such voices expressed in opposition to more official positions of authority. Vernacularity attains its greatest salience as a rhetoric when, by registering its incommensurability with those channels of activism sanctioned by institutional power brokers, it turns instead to an affective mode that does not take critical judgment as its only telos. By abandoning the instrumentality implicit in actions directed toward an endpoint, the affective vernacular evades the refutations of those who would be disposed to disagree with a particular cause or judgment if one were endeavored. Affects cannot be refuted. Like the conceptual figure of the idiot, they refuse judgment or interpretation, operating beyond anything with which one could viably disagree. To disagree with affects would be absurd, no less than trying to refute the wagging tail of a puppy.

By building and staffing a DIY library, citizens of Brent literally built their community's commonwealth. Affirming a *sense* of community in this way is what creates, again and again, an actual community. As Jean-Luc Nancy has shown, all communities are formed through a communicative process that is always incomplete because to complete it, to institute "a community" as such, is to shut off the ongoing process of performing and affirming its inclusivity.[67] This is one reason the figure of the idiot is so important: by refusing to foreclose this process, by holding open a space to consider the incomplete as endurable, so as not to overdetermine a fixed account of what matters and what doesn't, the idiot allows a community to replenish itself again and again, even against what's lost in the process of building it. In the service of a struggle to protect their access to a library's cultural capital, its literature, its technology, the people of Brent created their own accessibility.

As citizen artists, in their effort to gain access to culture, they created the cultural wealth they wanted access to. As citizen critics, the people of Brent engaged in a long struggle to bring public opinion before the state to challenge its authority. Though the state couldn't make sense of its symbolic methods, the affective means with which the people pursued their cause also made them citizen artists, building and sustaining the very thing they were fighting to protect: not just a library, but also an affective commonwealth built collectively for one another.

AFFECTIVE
COMMONWEALTHS

The English artist and critic John Berger once observed, "If everything that existed were continually being photographed, every photograph would become meaningless."[1] It can be easy to feel as if we're approaching that extreme today. A company called Planet—which has launched several hundred imaging satellites into space and now operates the SkySat satellites that Google uses for mapping— claims to collect over 300 million square kilometers of high-resolution Earth imagery every day. Meanwhile, the Chinese government's Social Credit System explicitly aims to "leave no dark corner" across the People's Republic by using 200 million CCTV cameras to record every square inch of its public space.[2] All of which is separate from the trillion-plus new photographs taken annually by ordinary people worldwide. Given all this "exposure" from corporate, national, and individual sources alike, with so much of the planet being photographed in any given instant, the conditions to evaluate Berger's observation are now upon us. While it's hard to see photographs as meaningless in a world so ensorcelled by imaging, it is certainly possible to see photographs becoming meaning-able in new ways, one of which involves visualizing the commons.

Throughout this book, by validating the idiot rhetoric of concerned gestures that subtly configure shared dispositions toward public life, I have tried to think about the creative and critical ways people produce the kinds of worlds they would like to imagine as worthy of being shared at all. The argument has not been that concerned gestures produce such worlds full stop. Rather, I have proposed that for such worlds to be relied upon, they need to be created again and again through performed enactments of their creative sustenance. The bumper-sticker wisdom to "be the change" requires being it over and over again, because to accomplish a change, to make a change manifest, is to arrest the ongoing manifesting of it that nourishes its ability to flourish. Gestures of concern, similarly, build affect worlds as replenishable commonwealths consisting in the activity of sharing concerns that may be too great to resolve, though the ongoing activity of holding open a space for raising the common as a question fortifies a feeling that things are good enough for now (if only just). In the previous chapter, I framed this process as a collective way of enacting less of an uncommonwealth. Now it's time to look at concerned gestures that, by disclosing the commons already hidden in plain sight, build a commonwealth as an affirmative affective resource.

As might be expected, academics and the general public evoke the commons in different ways. Both do so with such variability and inconsistency as to suggest that the very idea of a commons is one that resists being made common. A partial inventory: local, physical commons (e.g., water management, forests); global, physical commons (e.g., the atmosphere, biodiversity); knowledge commons (e.g., the internet, open-source software); ambient commons (e.g., architecture, interfaces); public commons (e.g., urban parks, sidewalks); service commons (e.g., health care, law enforcement); not to mention all the more metaphorical or theoretically inflected notions of "commons" that my own treatment of the subject could be characterized as following.[3] The commons, the common, commonplaces, commonwealths, common sense, *sensus communis*—these are not all the same, and each has its own history with its own political and cultural extensions. What all evocations of commonness share, however, is an affective tone that appeals rhetorically to an ideal of togetherness and familiarity that could—as if from a vantage of seeing everything— deign to account for an all-inclusive world.

There is no such vantage. There is no neutral position, no "objectivity" that does not leave some excluded "outside." Nevertheless, what Donna Haraway once called "the god trick of seeing everything from nowhere"[4] does seem to have become a trick accessible to just about anyone in a time when the photographic image has captured so much of those public spaces that humans do or don't share on a planet that we can't help but occupy together. There may be no more accessible illustration of this than Google Street View (GSV). When Google introduced its Street View feature in 2007, its stated aim was "to share a virtual reflection of the real world to enable armchair exploration."[5] By sending vehicles into the streets, each mounted with up to nine automated cameras positioned around a sphere propped a few feet above each vehicle's roof, the company sought to photograph every street scene on earth across a 360-degree field of vision. Now, from the privacy of one's home, anyone can access a seamless map of digitally stitched photographs taken from street level on all seven continents.

What follows presently is an exploration of some kinds of imaginable commons that such technology makes visible. Many of the examples considered in previous chapters have been drawn from that part of the cultural field invested in reading literature. From stickers about the importance of reading, to online arguments about a self-published book, to DIY libraries as aestheticized gestures of concern, these examples have been enlisted in part to tug on the invisible thread that connects the literary public sphere Jürgen Habermas traced to eighteenth-century Europe with the more expanded cultural public spheres we know today. One fruit this effort has borne, I hope, has been to show that even in just the segment of cultural affairs devoted to literature, the ordinary citizen's concerns about public affairs are taking a gestural mode of expression that can't adequately be explained by attending to measurable impacts or propositional messages alone. Moving beyond examples from the literary arts, this final chapter is about how artistic efforts to hack, curate, or disrupt GSV images are reconfiguring affective commonwealths.

To make sense of this process, I have from the outset identified symbolic and affective orders as coexisting attributes of any communicative phenomenon. If affectability involves the coming together and apart of socially dispersed attitudes and moods that dispose people to be influenced by symbolic actions, then it is often through the ordinary person's everyday gestures of creative and critical participation in public life that this happens. These concerned gestures, however, often tend to contribute more to sense experience than to promoting a strong propositional message. To fixate on their meaning or impact is to miss their more asignifying dynamism and power. The idea of an affective commonwealth built through such gestures offers a way to think about the historical present and the "conditioning conditions" that give our aesthetic and rhetorical practices, such as a sticker or a speech (among a slew of other things), their capacities to influence, mean, and attain some socially legible momentum.

With the tacit approval of the state, but through a transnational reach, Google makes visible the everyday coexistence of people, animals, plants, buildings, and so on in their ordinary emplacement in the world. When citizen artists call attention to this making visible (what by another name gets called "sousveillance"), they question how *seeing* can be the operative way whereby citizens otherwise unknown to one another come to share some things in common. This orientation is decidedly a vernacular one, allegiant to zestful moments emergent from the mundane, uneventful, and quotidian aspects of everyday life on the fringes. The best way to understand how various artistic practices around GSV do so, I propose, is through a homophonic triad: they sight, cite, and site the commons. More than just clever, the tropes of sighting, citing, and siting are key elements of the affective commonwealths that concerned gestures create in actual practice today. This book began by considering the "idiot" citizens who listened instead of being heard in the *ecclesia* of antiquity. I bring it to a close by trying to see the commons that are going unseen on public streets today.

THE COMMONS IMAGINARY

If affect isn't nameable or representable, what is it that an "affective commonwealth" seeks to name? Are such commonwealths something we can see? Is there something to point to and say, "There, that's an affective commonwealth"? If gestures of concern teach us anything, it's that the very gesture of such pointing can sometimes be what activates the force-effects of that ineffable "sense of something" being gestured to. Attuning to concerned gestures, in this sense, is somewhat equivalent to doing as the dog does when it looks at a pointing finger instead of at what the finger is directing its attention toward. Recalling Giorgio Agamben's sense of gesture as the "*communication of a communicability*" and "*the process of making a means visible as such*," it is not the meaning or goal of gestures that matters, so much as their expressive force. The gesture of disclosing a commons evinces the possibility of creating a commonwealth from what is already around us.[6] An idiot rhetoric of concerned gestures accordingly clears space for the manifesting of a commons that never arrives already manifested, never appears as conclusive or circumscribed. Such gestures can help to spark coalitional subjects that, as Karma Chavez writes, "believe in the vitality of broadening imaginaries that will open possibilities for livable life."[7] What passes for "seeing" an affective commonwealth, in other words, is rather the identification of a commons imaginary.[8]

Thinking in terms of a commons imaginary is a way to identify the failure of social and political structures to configure a commons as an institutional arrangement adequate to the felt experience of those excluded from its privileges. A commons imaginary is akin to what a number of scholars have called a social imaginary, less a concrete place or thing than a prospective idea of what it might mean and feel like to imagine a world in which the common is not elsewhere and for somebody else. Social imaginaries, Charles Taylor explains, refer to "the ways people imagine their social existence, how they fit together with others, how things go on between them and their fellows, the expectations that are normally met, and the deeper normative notions and images that underlie these expectations."[9] Similarly, a commons imaginary is one of the ways people imagine what they do share with others, or could. It's a fantasy of a commons that isn't already circumscribed, but always open and available, because the very circumscription involved in naming any commons as such is enough to foreclose the open-endedness necessary for it to be truly common.

One of Taylor's insights is that modernity gave rise to a particular version of the social imaginary, and that this modern social imaginary is what has enabled (by making conceivable) the very possibility of the public sphere's historical emergence. In this sense, there's something of a "you can't achieve it until you can dream it" mythopoetics to Taylor's thinking, though he's careful to separate the social imaginary from more identifiably explicit beliefs or ideas. It is "not in the realm of explicit beliefs, but through shifts in background understanding and the social imaginary," he's clarified, that "the understanding which constitutes the public sphere can arise."[10] Nor, for Taylor, does change come about through new ideas, even when they're executed in the realm of actual social practice (sorry, TED Talks). Before beliefs or ideas can even potentially actuate change—before they can attain their persuadability—a transformation in the background understanding that constitutes the social imaginary must occur.

Certainly, GSV has brought new forms of imagination into being, and not as ideas to act on or not, but rather in the form of images of what public space actually looks like. By making visible common public spaces around the planet, Google has made the commons imaginary about how we fit in among others much less imaginary. For Taylor, social imaginaries are representable in that they are "carried in images, stories, and legends."[11] Today we can say that GSV provides the table service of a commons imaginary precisely through its images: we don't need to imagine it anymore; it's already delivered to us. Society evolves, Taylor has argued, "not through conceiving new ideas and then acting on them, but through the coming to be of new forms which are partly constituted by, and hence help to spread, new background understandings and a new social imaginary."[12] Yet if GSV and the ubiquitous imagining of our time have contributed to new social and commons imaginaries, it would be futile to approach any image on GSV hoping *through interpretation* to derive an insight into the commons imaginary that somehow represents an actually existing affective commonwealth. We just can't access affect as a ready-made deliverable because it changes according to the dynamism of our encounters (far better to think of it as "experienceable"). That is why, more than through a texts-and-talk model of public life that would jam us within the "bottleneck of the signifier,"[13] identifying an affective commonwealth may better be accomplished by exploring how creative interventions on GSV bring new sets of relations into public life.

When it comes to incorporating GSV into an artistic practice, such gestures sometimes take the form of a category of social intervention called "tactical media." Tactical media are attempts to disturb the symbolic order of a dominant regime through pliable interventions, usually in the context of digital media technologies.[14] Melding art and activism, tactical media, according to Geert Lovink, are "tool[s] for creating 'temporary consensus zones' based on unexpected alliances."[15] If such practices build temporary consensus zones, though, the consensus is operationalized not only symbolically through reason and language, but also affectively through the creation of a dispersed mood oriented around particular encounters. In line with the thinking-feeling I've been doing throughout these pages, then, I suggest here that an assortment of artistic practices around GSV reveals how gestures of concern can build an affective commonwealth held together by concern for the conditions whereby strangers are brought into a kind of relation in the first place—in this case, a visual relation.

STREET PHOTOGRAPHY AND THE PHOTOGRAPHIC VERNACULAR

The genre of street photography has existed at least since the late nineteenth century, when Eugène Atget began taking pictures of Parisian street scenes. Using surreal long exposures and wide angles, Atget captured everyday Paris: not its landmarks, but the more quotidian or unnoticed of its buildings and its working class at the onset of industrial modernization. In doing so, he legitimated the ordinary details of public street scenes as a photographic subject, expanding the range of photography beyond portraiture and forensic science, and establishing a precedent for professional and amateur photographers ever since. Without Atget, there might have been no Henri Cartier-Bresson to issue candid photographic reports from the everyday life of the streets; no Diane Arbus to show the humanity of freaks and carnies; no Walker Evans; no JR, and so on—not to mention a very different visual culture on Instagram.

There are, of course, many versions of street photography's history to be told, but what's important here is to recognize that GSV belongs within this long history of street photography and its vernacular idioms. Though circulation might make certain exemplars of the genre into icons, in the main, street photography is distinguished by producing distinctly *non*-iconic images of public spaces. This is especially true in the case of GSV. Google's fleet of camera-equipped cars, tricycles, people, and camels indiscriminately photo-graph everything they pass.[16] GSV images, then, resist iconicity in part by virtue of being arbitrary: the cameras look in all directions and catholically capture what they see. The indiscriminating nature of these photos divests them of their iconicity. The goal is to photograph the entire public world. Just as curation cannot be comprehensive, the all-inclusive cannot be iconic.

The images displayed on GSV don't really even circulate for the public's attention. Just the opposite: one needs to go looking for them. In this sense, GSV images count as what are sometimes called pull media, defined by Henry Jenkins as "media in which consumers must seek out information" (as opposed to push media, "in which the content comes to the consumer").[17] Accessing the GSV archive is simple enough, and Google's suite of mapping apps makes the photographs searchable and navigable in a variety of ways. But the images, ostensibly at least, neither deliver any ideological message nor purport to have any substantive civic or artistic purpose. The images are, in a way, invisible, at least in the sense of seeming inconsequential; they're so ordinary as to go unnoticed. Better yet, they are nested, hidden, embedded, virtually in the GSV interface and materially in the streets the images represent.

The GSV archive has a virtual and physical presence in that its images, beyond facilitating the novelty of "armchair exploration," are also geotagged to actual sites and spaces, and therefore serve an identificatory utility as an existen-tial wayfinding mechanism: *You are here*. Or *You could be here*. Or *Here*. Or *Here*. The embedment of these images in the GSV interface is especially important in that no automated buttons allow you to share or like GSV images. In a digital realm so otherwise given to enable sharability, the omission is unusual. The interface facilitates no easy extrapolation. As a result, GSV photos do not tend to spark widespread conversation. And how could they, when the photos are not even discrete texts? The images, that is, don't have an edge. They haven't been cropped or framed on-screen because they are digitally stitched together to form a 360-degree panorama on a seamless map. One moves across the photos, over them, up them, down them, astride them. They exist to be passed by.[18]

What's more, GSV images have an innate obsolescence, as it takes months before Google processes and posts the photos taken by its fleet of cars, and much longer before they replace earlier photographs with more up-to-date versions whenever their vehicles are able to revisit and rephotograph street scenes they'd already covered. Like Atget in Paris or Berenice Abbott in New York City, each of whom set about to document the remnants of their great nineteenth-century cities before they were lost to the modernization of the twentieth, GSV has undertaken to document public places, but inevitably does so at fixed moments in time. The replacement of older images, when possible, with newer ones suggests an effort to keep up with the times, but less as a matter of fashion than as a record with a more recognizable empirical referent: look, this is what the world looks like here.

What it looks like, to anyone who has "traveled" through GSV, is almost always mundane. Roads, buildings, medians. Shoulders, sidewalks, shadows. Trees. Cars. More cars. Pedestrians and peopleless expanses. Corners and construction. Wilds. Wastelands. These photos operate, that is, in a vernacular idiom. They depict everyday scenes that are even more mundane than the latent vernacularity of other street photography. Because GSV pictures are taken indiscriminately, they capture public space in its organic process; the pictures aren't "about" that process. The vernacular nature of GSV images, then, is not just their ordinariness, but how they make ordinariness visible *as* ordinary. Put differently, GSV images don't only make the everyday visible; they make visible *that* they are making the everyday visible. And because GSV pictures are stitched together to form a panorama, no rhetorical framing or curatorial calculus of inclusion/exclusion lends GSV images any intrinsic salience. These images may "argue," but their primary impact is to inform.

STREET VIEW'S AFFECTIVE ORDER

Scholars of visual culture and photography have long noted the affective quality of images. Walter Benjamin, for instance, noticed in 1931 (and citing Atget in particular) that photographs elicit responses not because of their formal or aesthetic properties, but because the ordinariness of their referents enchant.[19] Susan Sontag likewise emphasized the emotional power of photographs in her influential writing about photography.[20] And Roland Barthes, in *Camera Lucida*, one of the seminal texts in the field of visual studies, premised his whole phenomenological approach to photographs on the inability to escape a photograph's affective power.

Barthes is particularly insightful about *how* photographs affect, offering us a way to extrapolate a sense of the affective order through which photographs traffic. "Affect," Barthes reflects, "was what I didn't want to reduce; being irreducible, it was thereby what I wanted, what I ought to reduce the Photograph *to*."[21] Central to Barthes's whole theory of photography, in other words, is what he calls the photograph's "affective intentionality," the eclipse of meaning by a photo's affective force.[22] Except Barthes did not write of an eclipse. Famously, he wrote of a photo's *studium* and *punctum*. A photo's *studium* is its nameable meaning, the ways its cultural context draws a spectator to notice and take a modicum of pleasure from it. A photo's *studium* enlists a spectator's passive but conscious cooperation in receiving its cultural meaning, as if being educated by faces, figures, gestures, and settings that are already known in advance. By contrast, a photo's *punctum* punctuates the *studium*; it "rises from the scene, shoots out of it like an arrow, and pierces me."[23] The *punctum* provides a photo's personal poignancy, as if by accident. "It is," Barthes writes, "an addition: it is what I add to the photograph and *what is nonetheless already there*."[24]

Although the concepts of a photo's *studium* and *punctum* have probably been the largest critical legacy of *Camera Lucida*, Barthes's desire to retain the "affective intentionality" of photographs is the more essential point. It is, in a way, what makes the very idea of a *studium* and *punctum* viable. "Indeed," write Elspeth Brown and Thy Phu, "the concept of the punctum is best understood not only as a way of contrasting the subjective dimensions of an image with the objective dimensions associated with the *studium*, a now familiar opposition. Rather, the punctum is a powerful concept because it, in fact, introduces a theory of feeling photography."[25] Theories of "feeling photography," to use Brown and Phu's term, have become still more prevalent as scholars across disciplines have turned to affect in their work.

Not all such work, it must be noted, is careful to distinguish affect, feeling, and emotion in the way I've suggested is fruitful. Barthes doesn't. Sontag doesn't. Benjamin's "aura" comes close, but doesn't. The information theorist Tiziana Terranova, however, tracks especially well with the tradition of affect theory I have been following. Terranova suggests that the power of images for the public masses has very little to do with what images represent or mean: "What is important of an image, in fact, is not simply what it indexes—that is, to what social and cultural processes and significations it refers. What seems to matter is the kind of affect that it packs, the movements that it receives, inhibits and/or transmits."[26] The position jibes well with Jodi Dean's observation that public communication today consists in contributions rather than messages. And it is undoubtedly for that reason that Dean's notion of "affective networks" shows explicit traces of Terranova's thinking.[27] The public sharing of images can act as the visual equivalent of phatic expression: a form of social interaction guided less by the transmission of information or any dialogic process of inquiry than by the performance of autotelic ritual transmissions. Images may well have a message, that is, but what they mostly do is *infect*. They are, Terranova says, "bioweapons," and they infect, or fail to, with vital immediacy.[28]

Of course, the infectious quality of images is what gives them such great power—and potential danger. This is particularly true when thinking about the public as a democratic counterbalance against state authority. The traditional promise of the public sphere, after all, has been the communicative achievement of consensus through enlightenment rationality, so as viably to hold the state accountable to a legitimated public opinion. The totalitarian catastrophes of the twentieth century, however, reveal that the capacity of "old media" to manipulate the masses through spin and propaganda, often in the form of images, proves communication to be susceptible to corruption by private interests or the ideological agendas of the empowered. This corruption has not been limited to totalitarian states, but increasingly can be identified today in rising autocratic and nationalistic impulses, not to mention in liberal capitalism's legal personification of corporate entities, which manifests in similarly despotic, if competing, corporate agendas to control market interests over the social interests of the people.

It was the great millennial hope of "new media" to countervail this corruption by distributing the producers of media content beyond the control of powerful conglomerates and putting it into the hands of the people. If this was not a false hope, it has, at least, yet to be fulfilled. Google's mapping and Street View projects remind us, as Michel Foucault and others have insisted, that the power to see is also a mechanism of disciplinary control. Such power is often wielded by the state and, increasingly, by corporations like Google. In response, the creative and curatorial acts of citizen artists and critics sometimes involve concerned gestures that would hold open the commons as only ever incomplete, as impervious to the "God trick" of supposedly objective control. A robust assortment of such activity surrounds GSV and, more generally, Google's mapping technology. These activities operate in several realms, here under the name of art, there as vernacular performances, sometimes as hybrid operations dissembling a clever admixture of citizen journalism, protest, or civic disruption. Collectively, though, these gestural acts disclose what it might look like to imagine the commons, like publics themselves, as a poetic world making.[29] What I hope then to show are three iterations of commons, each intent on troubling the convergence of publicness and privateness as a consequence of geographical media that, by *sighting, siting,* and *citing* the commons, call attention to their own ocular yet imaginary constitution.

SIGHTING THE COMMONS

In 2011, to widespread disapproval, a German photographer named Michael Wolf received honorable mention for the prestigious World Press Photo Award. It wasn't that Wolf's collection, *A Series of Unfortunate Events*, was aesthetically undeserving, at least not exactly (fig. 6.1). The controversy arose

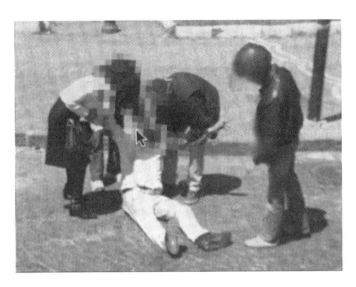

Figure 6.1. Michael Wolf, *A Series of Unfortunate Events*. From *A Series of Unfortunate Events* discovered on Google Street View. Photograph © Michael Wolf.

from its consisting entirely of photos that Wolf had taken of someone else's photos. And not just someone's. The images came from GSV: compelling scenes that Wolf had found in the GSV archive, carefully curated, and then photographed, as the World Press Photo Award site puts it, "by placing a camera on a tripod in front of a computer screen in Paris."[30]

Mishka Henner, a Belgian photographer based in Manchester, England, has received recognition for similar work, with similar controversy. His 2012 exhibition, *No Man's Land*, was a finalist for the 2013 Deutsche Börse Photography Prize and its £30,000 purse. Though he, like Wolf, didn't win the award, being recognized as a finalist for a top international honor brought public attention to questions about the nature of photography and authorship. Henner's photos in *No Man's Land* had also been curated from the GSV archive, but his were taken using screenshots, which only reinforced arguments that he had not authored the photos at all. In interviews, Henner responded to such claims by emphasizing that photos are always *taken*: "I think the verb 'taking pictures' is an interesting one," he said. "If I am walking around with a camera, I am taking pictures. If I am looking at images, I am taking pictures."[31] In this case, the pictures he "took" were pictures that Google had already taken. But from whom, or from what, had Google taken them to begin with?

The cases of Wolf and Henner, as with others doing similar work,[32] call attention to the (in)visibility of people in public spaces. Wolf's work sights people in the context of urban centers, where the crowd makes them invisible; Henner sights people in the context of urban outskirts, where the remoteness makes them visible. Both draw attention to ordinary people being seen in moments when they appear unaware they are being watched. Whether and to what extent the people depicted in Wolf's and Henner's work were aware of the GSV car passing by is impossible to say. What we can say is that the photographs curated from the GSV archive depict people in acts that typically evade the camera's eye: a woman urinating behind a car, a man being dragged across the street, prostitutes waiting along a roadside at midday. By selecting these photographs from among what is almost literally a planet's worth of others, Wolf's and Henner's appropriated images capture the everyday evasions otherwise being evaded.

Theories of the public sphere widely presume that its discursive associations entail relations among strangers, the recognition of the unknown other through conversation, and an intersubjective expression of identity and interest. Without strangers, a public sphere would be something different, a community perhaps, or an interest group, but it wouldn't be a public sphere because it would not exceed one's known associations. The GSV program publishes photographs of people who are almost always strangers to those who look at the images. In fact, GSV algorithms automatically blur the visible faces of those it depicts, making everyone a stranger. Although the photos do not allow for any discursive interaction with the people they capture, by assuring the subjects remain blurred (in what amounts to a feeble conciliation of the right to privacy), GSV photos do nevertheless orient viewers to the potential for a stranger relationality that might, in a different medium, be enacted through associations built around a more common purpose. In this way, as Henner and Wolf show, GSV photos sight a commons more than a public.

A uniform aesthetic characterizes GSV photos: they are all shot at roughly the same height, focused at roughly the same middle distance, and taken with the same slightly washed-out color palette. This uniformity, coupled with the camera's apparent indifference to its subjects, lends an illusion of naturalism to the images—an illusion that has been associated with photography since its outset. Cara Finnegan has argued, for instance, that the illusion of photographic naturalism is so prevalent that it acts as a visual enthymeme in all photography, helping photographs to argue without needing to demonstrate their transparency, their lack of artifice.[33] As Damien Pfister and Carly Woods have compellingly shown, though, this may not be the case much longer, as post-processing through digital editing tools has made visual information so easy to modify and manipulate that instead of assuming the veridicality of photography, we might rather assume the reverse: an "unnaturalistic enthymeme" whereby any digital image's figurative aspects "are continually making an argument about its own unrealism."[34] Because the Street View program endeavors such a ubiquitous range of coverage, and because of the automated nature of its photography (every shot is taken without a human deciding in each instance what to shoot and what not), GSV images elicit a particularly strong faith in their naturalism, which can make it hard to see them as arguments for anything. It's easier to see these photos as surveillance data or documentation than as statements or arguments, and still less as art.

The brilliance of Wolf and Henner is to take these photos outside their context of surveillance and show them as things being surveilled themselves. Sometimes beautiful things. Or just bizarre. Or lonely. Or any number of highly poignant, even haunting scenes. But their work does not turn the camera on the cameras. Their projects are not best read as critiques of surveillance. What they're doing is not something easily read at all; they are sighting public moods, passing moments, what Marnie Ritchie calls the "minor endurance" that more spectacular photographic visualizations are likely to subvert by neglecting the forms of everyday resilience that operate in a more minor key. Although it may appear that Wolf and Henner have the same agenda, or at least are doing things the same way by curating GSV photos and presenting the results as a series for public attention, each achieves his ends through different means, and that difference is important for the kinds of affective commonwealth they cultivate.

The most provocative aspect of Wolf's photos is that they're photos. He actually took pictures, with his camera, of the images pulled up on his computer screen from the GSV archive. In a photojournalistic sense, then, the photographs are documents of a particular time and place, in Paris, when and where Wolf had been using his computer. They are evidence that an image on a computer screen, depicting whatever it is it depicted, had been seen in that time and place.[35] Wolf's photos, in other words, are not indistinguishable from the GSV photos; they are not merely curated appropriations of the GSV photographs, re-presented in a context of his making. In a literal and important way, Wolf's pictures are documentary photographs of an everyday, private world (his own), and what they document is his "sighting" of the GSV interface on a computer monitor as an access point to see virtual images of public space and people going about their quotidian business within it.

Though Henner also culled his photos from GSV, he followed a different method. Unlike Wolf, who browsed the GSV archive casually until finding images of particular resonance for him (privileging their *punctum*), Henner went looking for images of a particular subject matter (privileging their *studium*). His *No Man's Land* collection deliberately seeks to show people in

Figure 6.2. A photo from Mishka Henner's exhibit *No Man's Land* (2012).

interstitial spaces, on the outskirts, literally marginalized (fig. 6.2). And not just any people. His photos specifically show prostitutes that GSV captured while they were waiting at their street-side posts soliciting work. To find the images, Henner visited prurient web forums to learn where sex workers could be found in places other than urban centers. Then Google's maps led him right to them: photographs from GSV depicting the women, usually alone, vulnerable, bored, and suggestive.

And unlike Wolf, Henner didn't photograph the screen of his computer when curating the photos for his series. Because he used his computer to capture a screenshot of the GSV interface, it is more appropriate to call the photos in his collection reproductions of the GSV images, rather than representations of them. As a result, the curated images work differently than Wolf's. They still depict scenes from everyday life, scenes otherwise not typically captured; but, as Henner invites us to see them, the images are institutional. They come from Google's documentary lens, and this is what gives them their power: the Google camera's utter indifference to their plight, and its almost eerie way of capturing these women's bored industriousness, their conspicuous invisibility.

In addition to "sighting" the commons through curatorial acts like Wolf's and Henner's, others are "siting" the commons in creative ways. For his *Map* project, which ran from 2006 through 2013, Aram Bartholl created public installations in cities throughout Europe and Asia. Each consisted in the erection of a towering red "map pin" in the precise geographical location that, by Google's measure, marks a city's center (fig. 6.3). Virtual versions of these pins, 20 pixels in size, are familiar to anyone who has used the Google Map interface. We see them on screens as the teardrop-shaped index used to pinpoint specific places on a virtual map. Bartholl constructed his map pins from wood boards, beams, and paint, with the dimensions calculated carefully, so that, as he explains, "the size of the life size [*sic*] red marker in physical space corresponds to the size of a marker in the web interface in maximal zoom factor of the map."[36] The upshot is what amounts to both a visual allusion and illusion. On the ground, to pedestrians encountering the life-size red marker, it acts as a sculpture alluding to the pins on Google Maps. On Google Maps itself, where Google's cameras captured the pin, the pin creates the illusion of its being a digital signpost, not an artifact in the material world.

The project illustrates one of the more compelling attempts to "culture jam" Google and its mapping enterprise. Culture jamming, as Christine Harold describes the practice, is a strategy of rhetorical protest that "usually implies an interruption, a sabotage, hoax, prank, banditry, or blockage of what are seen as the monolithic power structures governing cultural life."[37] Examples of culture jamming range from changing the text on a corporate logo to modifying street signs and storefronts. Notwithstanding critiques of the practice, culture jamming is a challenge to what Robert Hariman and John Lucaites have noticed as the ability of images to naturalize ideology.[38] In that sense, culture jams complicate the uncomplicated, add friction to the frictionless, bring noise into the signal. Bartholl's *Map* project works as a culture jam because it uses Google's own language of the red pin to play on the ways the images from Google's maps are used as a cultural technique for orienteering through everyday life.

In person, Bartholl's pin sculptures are massive "You Are Here" reminders, a kind of existential wayfinder that, by gesturing toward an absent virtual space with the allusive pin, takes us away from the public screen and drops us back into what W. H. Auden called "the real world of theology and horses."[39] The pin sculptures, however, are not erected in any place of obvious significance. To pedestrians passing by, they therefore mark the location with a salience it wouldn't otherwise have. Yet, by choosing the locations based on

Figure 6.3. From Aram Bartholl's *Map* project, ground-level view.

the precise GPS coordinates that Google identifies as the geographical center of a city, Bartholl transposes the virtual world onto the material. In a virtual interface, where mapping technologies make it possible to pan in and out, in other words, it is easier to gain an overhead perspective that may make such a "center" seem more central than it would in person. By locating and marking the supposed city center in actual space, Bartholl sites a public commons that seems worthy of no special notice. At the same time, however, the pins also bear the letter A in large black print, marking them, in Google's mapping language, as starting positions on a route toward some distant pin B, unseeable from ground level. In turn, the sites Bartholl chooses for his pins both gain salience from being pinned and lose that salience, as the pins mark the place not of a location to reach but a place to leave from.

One feature of a commons imaginary that is particularly important today is its virtuality, not just in the sense that the *idea* of a commons is more make-believe than empirical, or even that the so-called commons has gone online, but in the phenomenological sense that no "commons" can be perceived in toto except as a virtual form often presumed to be constituted elsewhere. Google mapping and Street View technologies visualize the elsewhere of worlds: not a commons as such, but the ambiguity of what it entails and where it resides. The ability in digital interfaces to pan in and out gives perspective on space that isn't possible when immediately embodied on the ground. Bartholl's pins

Figure 6.4. Aram Bartholl's *Map* project, aerial view.

"site" the commons inasmuch as they remind us of its virtuality, its being also elsewhere, an imaginary we cannot see from within it, at least not the way we can when panning out online to get the bigger picture from overhead (fig. 6.4).

But the *Map* project also changes the online encounter, "jamming" the presumed naturalism of Google's maps with a pin endemic not to virtual space, where we're accustomed to supposing it belongs, but to one actually existing in the physical world. In doing so, unknowing users of Google's mapping suite are liable to suppose the program has a glitch; it has planted a pin somewhere you've not commanded one to be. If this raises some skepticism about the naturalism of Google maps, it does so only because Google's mapping satellites and Street View cars actually are able to achieve a kind of naturalism to the extent that they're able to photograph Bartholl's physical pin in its "natural" setting.

To site the commons in this way is to pinpoint a new relationship between public and private, actual and virtual, that our mediated and mobile environments make possible through locative media technologies. Recalling Google's promotion of Street View as a means of armchair tourism, Bartholl's project also accomplishes the real thing, marking places as sites to be seen by the passing flaneur and motorist alike. Considering that the context of our movement through public spaces is now so often mediated through mobile technologies that we carry or wear, some have suggested the flaneur is an obsolete public character, replaced instead by the phoneur, whose passage through public space is traced and mediated by locative technologies that give access to, among other things, Google's mapping services.[40] It is in a world where the phoneur exists that Bartholl is trying to site a public commons as more than a digital overlay of informational and corporate cartography. The idea of toggling between public and private space no longer holds when our private and personal engagement with digital environments (on the screen of a phone, for instance) occurs in public space and acts as an overlay on that space. Adding the "texture" Eve Sedgwick has described as the affective essence of sociality, Bartholl's project resituates the fraught experience of a public/private limbo.[41]

CITING THE COMMONS

In addition to commons sighting and siting, others have "cited" the commons by performing *tableaux vivants* ("living pictures") for passing GSV vehicles. Two men in Edinburgh, for instance, staged a faux murder scene on a street corner, which Google photographed and uploaded to Street View, leading to a tail-chasing police investigation in June 2014.[42] And in Pittsburgh, in 2008, the artists Ben Kinsley and Robin Hewlett organized a whole neighborhood of Northside residents to perform a series of tableaux for a GSV vehicle photographing Sampsonia Way. The resultant *Street with a View* performance included a parade (replete with balcony-tossed confetti and a marching band in full regalia), a pack of marathon runners, a garage band practicing, a cupid figure firing a string "laser" that apparently made anyone it touched fall in love, and a mock seventeenth-century sword fight.[43] Even the Google staff has created similar tableaux, lining the sidewalks outside their Dublin headquarters, for instance, some in costumes, others holding signs for the passing GSV cameras to capture.[44]

The significance of culture jams like the tableaux vivants is to cite public citizens as active producers of their world, not just as passive subjects for the photographic lens. "Citing" is apropos not just as a clever third term in a homonymic trio. "To cite" here means to give credit, to direct attention toward those whose actions are of consequence for others and need recognition accordingly. More than just send-ups or hoaxes, in other words, the projects that "cite" a commons are undertaking the serious business of refusing to let the pictorial representation of everyday life's quotidian public moments give the impression of public inactivity. Though the faked murder scene in Edinburgh and the festival of activities in the Pittsburgh tableaux decidedly were not instances of public activism or overt political purpose, they do seem to involve creating an intensified experience of the fears and joys, kicks and frustrations of being a citizen of the world today.

In noting that "aesthetic" simply means "capable of being experienced," Vilém Flusser has argued that "'habit' implies anaesthetics: that which has become habitual is no longer experienced at all."[45] Conversely, then, for Flusser, art becomes any human activity that, by breaking from the norm and escaping from habit, occasions the fullness of actual experience. As Freud observed when laying out his pleasure principle, "We are so made that we can derive intense enjoyment only from a contrast and very little from a state of things."[46] The habitual state of things is an entropic counterpoint to those experiences that break from it with a glisk. Affective orders operate most influentially when moving us from an unexamined steady state to the experienced event of coming into contrast, into a new mood—even if the mood appears to be a fiction.[47]

Among the more interesting aspects of this third group of GSV hacks is the trope of their fakeness. These were all performances. For the tableaux vivants in Edinburgh and Pittsburgh, this was self-consciously the case. The actors were playing at being public actors before the audience of a passing vehicle they knew in advance would publicize their performance in a context that would pass it off as ordinary, that is, as not a performance at all. There is no need to try forcing some overt political motive onto performances that are, above all, just for fun. To the contrary, the just-for-fun spirit of these performances is what gave them such affective resonance. These performances were not only hoaxes, in other words. They are also gestural actuations of a zest for living and enduring that the performed gesture accomplishes rather than represents. In this sense, they exemplified what Rosi Braidotti might describe as a means of becoming imperceptible; they are examples of an "event for which there is no immediate representation."[48]

Just as becoming imperceptible is "the event for which there is no immediate representation," a tableau vivant unfolds in a way that resists the representable, even as its performance *becomes* representational. This state of becoming delivers its activist power precisely because GSV cameras cannot capture it. It is imperceptible to them. Tableaux vivants may not be meant to last long, but their formation is their essence; it sustains their potentiality. As performances, they take place in nonlinear time; indeed, their "taking place" is entirely that of which they consist. Audiences watch a tableau come to life as actors move into place, assuming their positions, only to dissipate once the actors' positions are held static. The moment when the image most comes to life is the moment it ceases becoming alive. Once formed, when the performers finally hold their pose, coalescing in a materially produced moment of maximum verisimilitude, the living image dies. That's the moment of the Google camera's gunlike click. As Aura Satz puts it, "The *pose* becomes a *pause* in the general process of aging, dying, disintegrating."[49] It is a process, in other words, both of becoming alive and of becoming object, "a mode of slowing down, of enduring, of surviving, of halting the ravages of time."[50] In other words, it's a lot like an idiot rhetoric.

Figure 6.5. From Ben Kinsley's *Street with a View* tableaux, Pittsburgh, 2008.

The nonrepresentational character of the tableaux in Pittsburgh and Edinburgh emerges from different dispositions, each nevertheless expressive of a mood or sensibility vis-à-vis what sort of public image would, to follow Barthes, most rise from the scene and shoot out of it like an arrow. The murder scene in its hard, midday light, the victim laid out flat on the street, the culprit holding a hammer and staring toward the car—the tableau performs a different set of moods than the confetti-strewn parade and marching band do. The former expresses all the attendant despair and desperation of the crime; the latter all the delight and absolution of the revel (fig. 6.5). When photographed and displayed as an image on GSV, however, each can be read as an example of the permeable border between presence- and meaning-effects. The fakeness of the performance, once reified as an image, gives way to the reality of Street View's ostensible naturalism. These performances did happen in that time and place. Displayed on Street View, their status as "fake" performances becomes ambiguous. The performers who staged the tableaux become something other than performers: they get cited as creators of a commons that is not their own except for what is built in their performance of it.

CULTURAL COMMONS, CULTURAL PUBLICS

Though the artistic gestures in each of these examples contributes to a commons imaginary about the kinds of affective commonwealth that might be created from what's already around us, the concern of these gestures have also brought provisional public spheres into being. They may not be robust publics, but there is a texts-and-talk model to be seen here in the discursive attention that has circulated around these assorted creative acts, mostly online, in various "But is it art?" debates about Wolf and Henner, in blogs and art-world literature about Bartholl, and in the popular press, where the tableaux vivants have raised attention for taxing the police force and for their clever novelty. The symbolic order of discussion around these GSV interventions, however, cannot account for how citizen artists and critics have through these projects also cultivated a commons imaginary that sets the tone for an affective commonwealth.

These cases illustrate, yet again, publics whose affectability holds them together as much as their symbolicity. The recessive nature of those involved here makes it harder to identify a public sphere in its traditional form. Here, images rather than words are what accrue the sorts of attention that constitute a mode of publicness, and the curatorial and artistic activity around GSV images is another form of such attention.[51] Indeed, one of the reasons I've argued at such length for the importance of an affective order to our relations among strangers is that affective dispositions clue us in to different varieties of public subjectivity, revealing a commons imaginary in different forms. Doing so compels us to acknowledge that different people have different relationships to publicness and, in turn, different ideas about what it means for them to take part in affairs of "common" import. In each of the three examples—sighting, siting, and citing—the attention being exerted, however, concerns what the banal everydayness of public life actually entails. When we *sight* a commons, we refine our perception of how our sociality holds together rhetorically in a time of radical contingency and pervading uncertainty. When we *site* a commons, we expand the rhetorical by unconcealing what's within it: an affective counterpart that, by capacitating rhetoric's potential for salience, exerts an ambient rhetorical influence. And when we *cite* a commons, we open an unlit trail toward a critical practice of attuning to those gestural and affective influences we are seldom disposed to acknowledge, yet to which we are always susceptible.

The idea of a public sphere offers a way to understand how problems, issues, and identities emerge within public consciousness, how they become significant and on what basis, and how public opinion is formed regarding those matters of shared concern that may be our best bet for a non-appropriative social organization. Public sphere theory, in short, is a way to think about how civil society organizes its desires about the good life relative to the state. Of course, as Pablo Neruda says, the world is full of howevers.[52] There are all kinds of ways we try to organize our desires about the good life that don't endeavor to address the state, that is, that don't meddle with the formation of public opinion. Public opinion is a tendency of opinion against which there are dissenting views. It may not be a majority view at all—it is not the same as consensus—but may rather be the view most deeply held or forcefully expressed so as to create the impression of how opinion is trending. In theory, at least, the expression of public opinion by citizens engaged in its formation is what liberal democratic states have to go by when deciding the course of actions and policies meant to accommodate the people's desires. Public opinion legitimates state action. Yet large parts of our public social relations have nothing to do with bringing public opinion before the state, despite being deeply invested in pursuing the good lives we desire.

Cultural publics, though far from apolitical, differ from more explicitly political publics because attention to the arts is alone sufficient to constitute a kind of public opinion about them. In more overtly political publics, the corresponding circulation of news events and material conditions affecting public life matters only insofar as it enables discussion of the issues that these events and conditions raise.[53] The same structure does not maintain when assessing how GSV art calls attention to the very people and public spaces that form our commonwealth. In such instances, the mere circulation of images modified by the intervention of citizen artists or critics actuates orienting affects that our highly personal engagement with the aesthetic imbues with sufficient force-effects as to render unnecessary any discussion about whatever issues that engagement might elicit. Certainly aesthetic goods *may* give rise to critical discussion of the issues they raise (as when we discuss the relationship between violent video games and school shootings, or the ethics of a best-selling memoir that turns out to have been a fiction), and these critical discussions *may* have a goal with implications for navigating the common interests of our social interdependence (safe schools, honest media); but unless we invalidate the highly subjective force of the aesthetic, we must also recognize the pre-originary and always unfolding affectability that pervades our every encounter. Habermas's historical literary public sphere may have been an exclusionary training ground for the cultivation of critical rationality; today, we are in a better position to recognize that cultural public spheres produce and modify the affective commonwealths from which they emerge in the first place.

The democratization of creativity suggests a model of democracy in which the enactment of one's citizenship is performed through the public work of building a commonwealth. Exceeding the rhetorical ideals of deliberative democracy that Habermas and others have championed, we are instead left to imagine citizens building the commonwealth through their industry and creativity.[54] The talk exchanged between citizens in the public sphere may well offer a way to reach consensus or to form public opinion about matters of shared concern, but then what? There is a difference between talk and work. If we envision ideal citizens as those who participate discursively in public affairs in order to reach a public judgment that state power may or may not then heed, we miss the ways people undertake public work more gesturally, sensuously, and often recessively in ways that create a shared affectability. "Public work," as Harry Boyte has observed, "consists of visible effort by a mix of people that produces things of lasting and general importance to our communities and society; public work adds to and helps to sustain the commonwealth."[55] This commonwealth is also always affective. It draws us toward the political through the cultural by way of experiencing the affectability inherent in our sociality.

RHETORICAL SOCIALITY

Rhetorical sociality is a name for that interminable complex of influences that are an inevitable consequence of being emplaced in a cultured world. In some ways the phrase is redundant. Rhetoric tends always toward the social, and the social is always rhetorical.[56] Pairing the rhetorical with sociality is intended to articulate their irreducible relationship. Constantly, we are producing and responding to ambient influences around us, only the most obvious of which are exerted deliberately by human agents in the form of symbolic action—words, signs, representations, and so forth. Unmistakably, such influences are pervasive: in the clatter of headlines, tickers, podcasts, Tweets, emails, ads, monuments, TV shows, artworks, texts, and talk galore.

These influences need not be strategically waged or motivated by sinister ends, though they certainly can be and often are. Rhetoricity is an intrinsic property of all being, not just all symbolic action. Most often, of course, it is precisely these symbolic influences that we would identify, if we bothered to think about it, as the predominant guides to how we make sense of our world. Whatever we know or feel about the latest act of gun violence, for instance, may derive in part from experience but is likely to derive largely from hearing, reading, or talking about it, whether through the news or entertainment media, intimate or stranger relations, online or otherwise. While people may ultimately follow the guide of their own compass in forming their beliefs and acting, that compass's needle is pulled by the magnetism of these more traditionally rhetorical influences around us. We can't help it.

And yet, alongside the ways that communication symbolically draws us to understand and adapt to aspects of our world in particular ways, we are also susceptible to unrepresentable, affective factors that—no less rhetorically but, I suspect, far less consciously—have influence in ways that dispose us toward those more traditionally rhetorical forms of communicative persuasion. These material, affective factors make meaning possible by delimiting the legible. Their affectivity holds people and things together in vectors of relationality, orientations of towardness and awayness, which are impervious to representation, though we can *experience* them in fleeting tingles, momentary glisks, intensities that encounters with art are particularly successful at making present. When these intensities attain some duration, when the ambient but material conditions of their manifestation serve as a sustained impetus for a collective orientation toward matters of shared concern, then affective commonwealths emerge wielding a unique self-sufficiency.

The self-sufficiency of these affectworlds contributes to making them concerned coalitions: relations among strangers held together by a shared desire to recognize in the present moment a possible "space of transformative investment."[57] This hope for transformation, however, is more than an agenda, presented in the form of public opinion, for those with the power to reify; and it is more, too, than an investment deferred to a future by striving to be in an environment in which our striving could one day be overcome. The space of transformative investments that concerned publics strive to make possible may well be directed toward actuating social change through advocacy for a cause or purpose, but they also build a space for that investment in the present by creating in practice the very world in which it is possible to invest without unreplenishable loss. The former manifests in communication that is meant to persuade and is directed toward an end; the latter involves an ongoing affectability that is always still in process and serves as its own reward. Both are already baked into publics, whether we like it or not.

If the ubiquity of photographs risks divesting them of their salience, then it is worth asking the same about gestures of concern. If gestures of concern are already everywhere but we're just not paying them much attention, might that be because they're too manifold for any to matter? One challenge issued against affect theory is a big *So what?* If affect is already "here" or "happening" and can't be increased or diminished, stopped or started, then what good is identifying its movement or force? But "affect" is not a commodity, like a candy with different flavors and names that comes in different sizes, something to be in or out of stock, eaten and digested. And gestures of concern aren't either. By disclosing a means more than producing an end, what matters so much about concerned gestures is their open-endedness, the way they produce a horizon of interpretability rather than something prefabricated for a particular interpretation. "The gesture," Lauren Berlant writes, "does not mark time, if time is a movement forward, but makes time, holding the present open to attention and unpredicted exchange."[58] Without expiring the moment it's understood, or getting transcoded into a fungible unit for exchange, the idiot rhetoric of concerned gestures slows things down by disorienting habitual ways of being, building an affective commonwealth of conditions more susceptible to change taking hold.

Although an idiot rhetoric would not have been overtly validated in the canonized rhetorical tradition's ancient origins (with at least one unique exception[59]), today such rhetorics are easy enough to see as just another crease of rhetoric's manyfoldedness.[60] One way to do so is to attend more to what rhetoric *does* than to what it *is*. And rhetoric does a lot of things. Most fundamentally, though, certainly as I have been thinking about it here, rhetoric makes things matter in influential ways. A long and fruitful tradition of study has attended, and continues valuably to attend, to how it does so through discourse in just about any imaginable context. Meanwhile, efforts to attend to how rhetoric makes things matter beyond discourse and meaning have been subordinated by more canonized histories.[61] And understandably so—to a degree. Such efforts are all too easily stymied before they even begin by the obdurate problem of affect being unrepresentable. I have tried to surmount that problem by following an inquiry cast as speculative from the start, but this has left me tempted at times to peel the stickers off the Rubik's Cube and re-place them where it would be more convenient for them to belong.

Is affect a condition for rhetoric or is it a rhetoric? I am led to the belief that it is both one and the other provided we are willing to tinker with traditional conceptions of the rhetorical. Symbolic rhetorics are not necessarily born from strategic design, but they are marked by deliberate performance. More gestural idiot rhetorics exhibit different properties, but what they do remains the same. Affect, that is, exercises influence; it makes things matter, maybe not in an artful way, maybe not in a way that's purposive, but it has an influence in a real and consequential fashion. What it doesn't have is a unitary agent, and what it doesn't offer is its own representation. "Affects" are moods that don't belong to us enough to quite be called feelings; they're not our own, but rather the ineffable form of relationality between bodies, orienting one to another so that this relation strives toward becoming something sustainable, something of which sense can be made.

Astronomers tell us that a planet can be weighed only when another planet moves near it. Affectability operates rhetorically in a similar way. As planets are measured by their effect on other objects, what can be known of affective ecologies is known through the coming together of different relations, each of which transmits orientations toward being in the world that "stick" or don't. I have argued that under communicative capitalism, one of the stickiest relations is identifiable in the paired trends of creativity's democratization and culture's curation. We have never been more accountable for building our own commonwealth, yet never labored so much to partition it in service of uncommonwealth. As Jodi Dean has put it, "We are configuring the worlds we inhabit, yet they are ever less what we desire but haven't reached and ever more what we cannot escape yet still enjoy."[62] The trick is to become attuned to the interstitiality of being suspended between such alternatives.

Doing so opens up a critical practice that offers a new vantage on our rhetorical sociality, particularly on our investments in cultural public spheres. These are not just sites for the apolitical engagement of strangers occasioned by art. Conditions are now such that cultural public spheres may rather be the most fecund sites for political action addressed to power, including corporations and the state alike. Though, ultimately, such action may do little to orchestrate perceivable changes in the social fabric, and still less to bring on outright political emancipation, that does not make them unimportant. Until we recognize the unassuming, recessive, and *gestural* quality of such actions, their power to build affective commonwealths will continue to go unseen.

THE POET
AND THE ANTHROPOCENE

In 1962, the same year that Habermas published *Strukturwandel der Öffentlichkeit*, his seminal account of the public sphere, the British-American poet W. H. Auden published an article in the *Massachusetts Review* called "The Poet and the City." There's no indication that Auden was then aware of Habermas, who had just finished graduate school and been appointed to his first professorship in Heidelberg. But Auden's essay shares some affinities with Habermas's thesis about the attenuation of the public sphere under conditions of mid-twentieth-century consumerism and mass media. Whereas Habermas was concerned with those circumstances that inhibited public discourse as a form of political agency, Auden identified those circumstances that inhibited artists from pursuing their vocations. From our vantage, reading Auden as a contemporaneous counterpoint to Habermas can open up the dialectic between art and public discourse that, as we've seen, is so integral to understanding the terrain of cultural politics today. By way of offering some takeaways, then, I'd like to revisit Auden's "Poet and the City" with an updated variation, "The Poet and the Anthropocene."

Throughout this book, I have suggested that concern is an active vector that colors experience and motivates action, even when the "action" takes a more gestural and understated form. Well, so what? Why should you care? Why anyone should care about any of this will naturally depend on their particular concerns, and it's not for me to say what they should be. But, of course, people often do say what ought to concern others; and even when they aren't being exhortatory, all communication offers up at least some *sense* of concern for the measure of those attuned to it. I have tried to think with the premise that one of the more important yet underappreciated ways that people express their sense of concern is through public gestures that disclose the possibility of a more affirmative and inclusive manner of relations. Not all public gestures are affirmative or inclusive, of course. All too many are negative and exclusionary—and often marked by hostility and recalcitrance, the veritable antitheses of idiot rhetorics. But regardless of their substance or vector, the *sense* of concern in play is the same. Though aesthetic expression hardly constitutes the only subject or form of such gestures, the broad realm of the arts makes a particularly fertile site for the ordinary gestures of concern that contribute in building a society's affective commonwealth: the impalpable mood and concern that strangers can share in common as a background resource for navigating their more demonstrable differences.

In Auden's 1962 essay, he wrote about something similar to an affective commonwealth, what he identified as shifts in the modern *Weltanschauung*, or the shared but impalpable worldview that oriented how people viewed their relation to art and public life.[1] Though Auden didn't put it quite in these terms, his interest was in showing that as an affective commonwealth changes, so too do the conditions within which creative participation in public life can occur. By considering several cases, numerous smaller examples, and enlisting the help of some speculative theory, in *Gestures of Concern* I have primarily focused on showing the other side of this dynamic: that the ways we participate creatively and critically in public life are also what build the affective commonwealths that establish the conditions for subsequent public action. Perhaps now is the time to risk speculating more overtly about what shared moods or background beliefs might characterize one configuration of an affective commonwealth today. Auden identified four widespread changes in collective beliefs that, by midcentury, had made it particularly difficult for artists to carry on producing creative work. I'll leave you with these, followed by some modifications that might better account for the well-being of public life now, when the political and aesthetic so often converge.

1. "*The loss of belief in the eternity of the physical universe.*"[2] Auden argued that if developments in science show the universe as a constantly changing process, as something that is not everlasting, then artists who once believed they could make an enduring artistic creation no longer have a natural model of endurance to follow. The search for artistic perfection and permanence hence starts to seem like a waste of time.

Today, in a digital culture of status updates and page refreshes, constant change is a way of life. In such a context, artistic permanence in the vein of *ars longa, vita brevis* is no longer quite as tenable, certainly not on the scale of everyday experience. This hasn't done away with the arts or made aesthetic endeavors pointless, of course, so much as changed the modes of their integration into life. A desire to make a splash now, to get eyeballs, attention, and clicks, has become a guiding principle of the aesthetic. Even in the more institutionally sanctioned art world, when artists undertake participatory, interactive, or relational projects, the permanence of the "artwork" is being supplanted by the fleeting intensity of a new aesthetic encounter. Eternity has little to do with it. Where Auden identified a loss of belief in the physical universe's unending longevity, however, what we now have is a different but related belief.

Modification #1: A growing belief in the physical universe's power to outlast the human. Despite what the naysayers and ignorant might claim, the scientific evidence in support of human-caused climate change is conclusive enough to suggest that it will likely be humans that are gone long before the physical world is destroyed. As a consequence, the set of conditions under which any endeavor to engage the political occurs is vastly different. Most everything we do now happens between the closing hands of a "just in time" or "a dollar short and a day late" way of measuring the expedient.[3] Balancing the urgency to *carpe* our *diems* with the imperative to *do something* to stave off the tragic and to cultivate greater resilience against its encroachment, the high stakes and low investment of concerned gestures begin to seem like an available way forward.

2. "*The loss of belief in the significance and reality of sensory phenomena.*" Auden next observed that people no longer trust the relation between the subjective faith of their senses and the objective reality of the world. We have come to believe that there is no such thing as one real truth about the phenomenal world, only infinite subjective perspectives on it. The traditional notion of art as mimesis thus disappears, Auden said, because the only truth an artist can imitate accurately or inaccurately is his or her own sensory perspective.

Today, in a time when we are so inundated with information that it can be hard to sort through it all, let alone determine which of it to trust, we are in need of more reliable and consistent measures to assess the validity and importance of the many propositions put before us. When the ease of public deception and manipulation is so high, and the repercussions of perpetrating it are so low—Foreign interests meddle in elections! Presidents lie with impunity!—there is no better guide for what to trust than the most elemental media of all: the sensory capacities of our own bodies. Far from engendering a lack of belief in the reality of sensory phenomena, the overly mediated configuration of a networked, information age has revived a tendency to believe that our own direct, embodied perceptions are what can most be trusted. That leads to a second modification.

Modification #2: A revival of trust in the body's senses to disclose a reality beyond representation. I have argued throughout this book, following a pragmatist program championed by John Dewey, that the aesthetic is not separate from everyday experience but organically integrated within it. All too literally, our senses—the very basis of the aesthetic—are the primary means by which we "make sense" of our world. In a time when so much of daily life is mediated through devices that are becoming ever more connected to our bodies, we are reminded again and again just how essential the senses and their perceptual capacities are to how we make our way through our time alive. It can be felt in the interactions with the flat screens of phones and tablets, where the messy depth and texture of touch has been replaced by the smoothness of a glass surface. It can be seen in how easy it's become to post-process digital photographs and create an edited rendition of reality. Media have always been extensions of the senses in ways that determine our perceived reality, but as technical representations of perceived reality become more indistinguishable from organic perceptions of the real thing—whether it's the haptic feedback on an iPhone that feels like you're really pressing a mechanical button, or a deepfake video that falsely puts words into a politician's mouth—the return to what's beyond representation begins to seem like an art in itself.

3. *"The loss of belief in a norm of human nature which will always require the same kind of man-fabricated world to be at home in."* Auden observed that ever since the industrial revolution, technology has changed the world so quickly that it's become impossible to imagine life just a few years into the future. Under such conditions, artists can no longer have any assurance that what they create today will be pleasing, or even comprehensible, to people tomorrow. And the motivation to produce work with integrity will diminish if the very standard of integrity has no stability or endurance.

Today, in a more globalized, exposed, and connected time than Auden's, the idea of a single, fixed "norm of human nature" sounds hopelessly quaint. Or, to put it differently, why would we *want* a fixed norm of human nature? Certainly, it's hard to project the future from within the hyperspeed of networked culture and capitalism, when norms are replaced by whatever's trending, when technologies are designed for built-in obsolescence, and when there's no guarantee that what's newsworthy now won't be forgotten by the time you re-Tweet the hashtag. While Auden was undoubtedly referring to the similar cultural acceleration of his own time, the role of ordinary people in governing that speed has changed since then, as the democratization of creativity has churned out citizens of so many different stripes: citizen journalists, scientists, artists, critics. Under such circumstances, lacking a norm of human nature or a stable "man-fabricated world to be at home in" no longer registers as much of a problem. Why not just create that world oneself?

Modification #3: The belief that we configure the worlds we create. I have suggested in these pages that the democratization of creativity—largely through the affordances of curatorial media and mobile technologies, but also as a new social imaginary about the role of ordinary citizens in building their commonwealth—has empowered people to configure their "world" the way they choose. Though communicative capitalism is only the latest in a long history of dominant regimes that have shown an ability to recapture resistance and fortify the status quo, I have also defended the possibility of configuring better worlds through the gestures of concern that are powerful precisely because their affective register eludes the capture that would fix it as static and therefore manipulable.

4. *"The disappearance of the Public Realm as the sphere of revelatory personal deeds."* For the fourth and final aspect of his argument, Auden contrasted ancient Greek culture with his own. In antiquity, he noted, the public realm was a place for personal deeds and interpersonal interaction. In the modern world, however, public life had become the place for *impersonality*. Consequently, he thought, the arts had lost the human subject as a person of public action.

Today, public life is far from a place for impersonality. Just the opposite: whether on the sidewalks or in cyberspace, public space is a yard sale of everyone's weird tastes and strong opinions out on display. A networked social configuration like the one we now have across the globe knows no precedent in the history of humankind. While that in itself doesn't make it good or bad, one of the consequences has been the blurring of age-old distinctions between public and private, participation and nonparticipation, art and sociality, and between the various social contracts that individuals make with the state and one another relative to the mutual accountability and common resources they share. That leads us to a final modification.

Modification #4: The resurgence of public life as a venue for expressing concern. As I've argued throughout this book, it's not that we've lost the realm of public life as a venue for action of shared consequence, but rather that those actions are taking new forms. If we continue looking for public "participation" or "engagement" according to standards inherited from antiquated notions of what these behaviors involve, we will neglect to see the rich and flourishing diversity of ways people of all types and inclinations are expressing their concerns in aesthetically accessible ways within the vernacular context of the everyday. It would be foolhardy to suppose that all comes up roses, that just by gesturing toward a common purpose, or by expressing a set of knowable concerns, we will somehow all get along and start frolicking through clover. But it would be equally reckless to neglect the power of our concern if we learn to see it in a different light.

The great project of communication would not be necessary if all human experience were not characterized by the fundamental paradox of our being always both separate and together.[4] Every one of us is a solitary being whose singular physiology makes our sensations and feelings uniquely our own. My central nervous system is not yours. Notwithstanding genuine meditative moments of psychedelic or spiritual lucidity, in which people report a deep connection to the universe, and short of some technological singularity yet to arrive, the baseline experience of the human condition is characterized by the felt insulation of individual consciousness. William James once wrote that we all partake in "one great splitting of the whole universe into two halves . . . '*me*' and '*not-me*.'"[5] There are many names for this splitting. Kenneth Burke called our biological estrangement the "*divisiveness* of the individual human organism from birth to death."[6] Martin Buber called it the "I" and "It." There are others. The basic precept is that our enfleshed division from others is so fundamental to all experience that there is no language to mark it from within the experience of separation itself. Indeed, it is precisely our fundamental separation that makes communication necessary to begin with. Our solitary existence is incontrovertible: despite whatever sense of connection we may gain from our communities and kin along the way, each of us is destined to die alone.

And yet—and yet!—the constant sensuous richness of our encounters in and with a more-than-human world reveals that we are also *not* alone. Because nothing is *outside* of experience, because experience is always "experience *of*" and "experience *with*" and "experience *from*," we are invariably embodied and entangled in a concatenation of dynamic energies and processes from which there is no separation. We may be more or less attuned to our entanglement among human and more-than-human things alike, but that does not make it less inescapable. For Vilém Flusser, it is because we are all solitary animals, condemned to die alone, that we *need* communication "to make us forget the brutal meaninglessness of a life condemned to death."[7] Human communication may therefore be "an artificial process," an "artistic technique" that "spins a veil around us in the form of the codified world," but without it we would live in a solitude too unbearable to endure. We would be, Flusser says, idiots, like the "private person" from antiquity.[8] But if by "communication" we recognize only those symbolic codes that we need to forget are artificial in order to carry on without existential despair, then that means we are neglecting the still more fundamental ways of being that those very *idiotes* embodied long ago. Observing, listening, sensing—gesturing with concern.

In my postulate that communication operates in at least two coextensive orders, the symbolic and the affective, we can see the very difference Flusser tries to chart. The symbolic order can be associated with the artificial codes necessary to live among others in the face of an essential separation, and to abide by this artificial codification is *the* hallmark of political activity. In contrast, the affective order can be associated with attributes of communication that are at best adjacent to the political because, unlike symbolic codes, affectability cannot be codified in a way that obscures our essential entanglement with other bodies and things. Affect can't be locked inside a safe and hidden behind a painting. If communication is accordingly both an artificial and natural project of attempting to overcome our separateness and togetherness, then "concern" is the word to describe our fundamental condition of being both separate and together. Concernedness is the background condition for all activity. Even the word's etymology bears this out. The original root of the English word "concern" is the Latin *cernere*, meaning "to sift, to separate." Adding the prefix con- (a variant spelling of the prefix com-, meaning "together") produced *concernere*, which in antiquity seemed to mean something like "to mix together preparatory to sifting." This gives us *con-* (together) + *cernere* (separate): that is, the simultaneous separateness and togetherness that makes communication necessary to begin with.

By celebrating the expressive self-sufficiency of concerned gestures, it may appear that I've extolled the intrinsic value of these gestures *as opposed to* their instrumental value. Instead, I've tried to avoid the unhelpful duality between those human activities that have intrinsic force and those that demonstrably yield instrumental effects. It will do us little service to separate the two when, for any change to "stick," the conditions amenable to it need to emerge. In a contemporary context of rising nationalism, for instance, if we become better attuned to gestures of concern, we will be better able to recognize the ways that fear of outsiders and the pride of belonging and tradition can commingle to cultivate a background mood that tilts unduly toward the insular and enclosed. Without attending to such gestures, we miss the affective force that drives and motivates our more explicit arguments about securing borders or reclaiming some supposed national purity or greatness.

But in a time of near-term ecological collapse, rampant bigotry, bogus skepticism, pandemics, and everyone-for-oneself antagonism, there are plenty of specific concerns to raise our hackles. By inviting us to attend more closely to the ordinary ways people express their concern through gestures whose force-effects are more than representational, I have not meant to suggest that such gestures are a sufficient means for actuating whatever political emancipation or revolutionary impulses one's personal concerns might desire. Indeed, the suggestion has rather been the reverse. Gestures of concern, as idiot rhetorics, are more about creating models of togetherness than they are about circumscribing the common or the good as things that could be determined in advance and on behalf of others. The most ungainly of condescensions is to circumscribe those that refuse to be circumscribed by something else.[9] But we are seeing things wrong, cart-before-the-horsing around about what constitutes the sorts of orientations toward publicness that drive larger sociopolitical shifts. Such shifts are brought about at least as much by the idiot winds of everyday life as by the gales and gusts of revolution. Although our gestures of concern are precisely not grand gestures and decidedly not likely to bring about any radical social or political change, they matter because it is through such gestures that the priming is done for more incremental and imperceptible change to occur.

What are we to *do* with this proposition if we operate as if it were true? Identifying the affective force behind gestures of concern is important, but not because doing so enables us then to level up from "mere" gesture to something more effectual. This isn't a praxis of "heightening" our concerned gestures, or making them more . . . *something*. Gestures of concern have a shelf life with an unknown expiration date. It's impossible to say when they will be "cashed in" or "paid forward," if at all. That open-endedness is the source of their affective power. It opens a space to build in, to identify an affective stasis, the provisional affinities disclosed in the manifesting of a form of relations that strives to be something sustainable.

Though you might receive a grateful acknowledgment in response to the "Get Well" card you've sent to a friend, it's unlikely they'll respond in kind (and absurd to imagine the gesture will cure their cold, let alone something as serious as cancer). The idiot is okay with such absurdity. Indeed, as Deleuze and Guattari observe, the idiot wills it.[10] Social and cultural expectations about the reciprocity of gestures vary widely, but most gestures seem to "end" in a whimper, when they haven't really ended at all (just think of the infinite regress in the "thank you for thanking me" game). It is the incomplete character of concerned gestures, their refusal to escalate to exhortation, that gives them their force.[11] This means that without typically achieving an immediate and demonstrable effect, they can nevertheless *affect* a set of relations in consequential ways—even if those ways are unknown and unrepresentable at the time, and perhaps never actualized at all.

To urge that we become more attuned to gestures of concern is not to endorse feel-good altruism or slacktivist solutions to our social ills. It is rather to stress the importance of creative modes of activity that exceed, and refuse, predetermined parameters delimiting what counts as legitimate engagement with "the political." As Rita Raley has put it, "We need not, and indeed should not, think of political engagement strictly in terms of concrete action, organizational movements, or overt commentary."[12] Lauren Howard's refusal to publish her book on Goodreads; the Friends of Kensal Rise Library's refusal to relinquish their library when they could sustain it themselves; those who "perform imperceptibility" for Google Street View—these and other examples show that there are affirmative ways of being that aren't goal oriented, strong willed, impatient. It is possible to be uncertain without being indecisive or unknowing; it is viable to be active in configuring worlds while being more gestural in the ways we do so.

By pausing or refusing—and by gesturing concern in a way that gives others pause—idiot rhetorics can make the familiar become unfamiliar, creating a susceptibility to change as the manifesting of a new normal, if only for now. Somewhere between J. Alfred Prufrock's "It is impossible to say just what I mean!" and Bartleby the Scrivener's "I would prefer not to," idiot rhetorics express concern without presuming to have all the answers, or even to know quite where a "common" concern might begin and end. Saturated with concern that often isn't attached to anything particular, the idiot daily engages the creative and critical activity of feeling and working through the very question of what sorts of worlds it might be worth feeling and working through in the first place. If an idiot rhetoric insists on anything, it's the commitment to avoid enclosing such worlds by having the last word.

NOTES

INTRODUCTION: THE SHAPE WE'RE IN

1 Part of my project in this book is to underscore the rhetorical nature of such practice. Though I don't discuss it at length, this serial notion of practice is intimately bound with habit. For an extensive treatment of rhetoric as serial practice, see Boyle, *Rhetoric as a Posthuman Practice*, particularly 97–102 on habit. For more on habit as social force, see Pedwell, *Transforming Habit*.

2 W. Brown, *Undoing the Demos*, 17.

3 Stefano Harney and Fred Moten have observed that within a participatory culture, hope is a veritable policy: "Now hope is an orientation toward this participation in change, this participation as change. This is the hope policy rolls like tear gas into the undercommons. Policy not only tries to impose this hope, but also enacts it." See Harney and Moten, *Undercommons*, 80. For the neoliberal logic that enacts this policy, "hope" then becomes an investor's gamble on the free market's ability to bring about the most merited "change."

4 Braidotti, "On Putting the Active Back into Activism," 42.

5 Brian Massumi: "Potential is abstract: never actually present as such" ("Envisioning the Virtual," 56).

6 "Zest" is the word William James sometimes uses to describe the emotional register whereby, despite the inevitable suffering and hardship of living, the human subject can nevertheless be invested with endurance and find meaning in daily life. See especially, James "Is Life Worth Living?," 47; and, James, *Varieties of Religious Experience*, 390.

7 Hans Ulrich Gumbrecht uses the term "presence-effects" to describe a phenomenological layer of encounters with the aesthetic that attains its impact and salience without needing recourse to the interpretive extrapolation of "meaning" from that encounter in order to make sense of it. Gumbrecht, *Production of Presence*, 79.

8 Just one obvious instance of this happens when companies like Google or Facebook capitalize on the data contributed by their users. For Dean's early treatment of communicative capitalism, see *Publicity's Secret* (2002); for her most extended study of the topic, see *Democracy and Other Neoliberal Fantasies* (2009).

9 Berlant, *Cruel Optimism*.

10 Hardt and Negri, *Commonwealth*, 171.

11 Hardt and Negri, *Commonwealth*, 171.

12 Haraway, *Companion Species Manifesto*, 12.

13 Lauren Berlant has already made this connection parenthetically in a published interview, where she refers to a structure of feeling as an "affective commons." My treatment of the affective commonwealth is an extension of this passing remark. See Berlant and Greenwald, "Affect in the End Times," 77.

14 R. Williams, *Marxism and Literature*, 133.

15 R. Williams, *Marxism and Literature*, 132 (emphasis in original).

16 R. Williams, *The Long Revolution*, 65.

17 My language here is Spinozist, alluding particularly to his notion of the *conatus* as the endeavor of all finite things to continue existing within the inherent tendencies of their nature. A finite thing's conatus is its essence (*Ethics*, bk. 3, proposition 7). But this essence is not a set of properties that enables categorization within some taxonomy, so much as it is a form of power that all finite things constantly exercise in their encounters with other finite things and, because each encounter exercises these powers anew, finds them constantly diminishing or expanding. When Deleuze reads Spinoza to show that we don't yet know what a body can do, he is picking up on the conatus as central to Spinozist ontology: the marvel of freedom and possibility even within a world of no free will. See Deleuze, "Sur Spinoza."

18 Kittler, *Gramophone*, xxxix.

19 See Peters, *Marvelous Clouds*, 17, 12. Also note that Alex Galloway and Eugene Thacker turn to the "elemental" on the last page of their book on networks, *The Exploit*, where they describe networks as similarly elemental "in the sense that their dynamics operate at levels 'above' and 'below' that of the human subject" (157).

20 Malinowski, "Problem of Meaning," 315.

21 For more on this argument, see Packer, "Epistemology Not Ideology," 297–98. Packer gives the example of the advertising industry, an ideological criticism of which would focus on the content of ads and the way their material existence rationalizes consumption. Digital culture and its "big data" model, however, make the *content* of ads irrelevant, emphasizing instead such quantifiable measures as how often people click, purchase, or spend time on a site where the ads are present. The indifference of Google, for instance, to an advertisement's message now makes epistemological criticism about the conditions of a message's possibility more urgent than ideological critiques of its content.

22 This sorting produces what Deleuze calls "dividuals." See "Postscript on the Societies of Control," 5, 7. The important point is that networked society operates on a logic of segregation that subjectivizes people as resources for capital. For more on this logic and its racist implications, see Chun, "Queering Homophily."

23 In ordinary usage, "meaningful" has come to denote something salient or rich with importance. In contrast, I use "meaning-full" to draw attention to the fallacy of supposing that some things are *already* full of meaning instead of attaining their meaning by being articulated with and interpreted according to certain contextual and contingent factors.

24 For more on this process, see Gumbrecht, "A Farewell to Interpretation," especially 395–99. Also see David Wellbery's foreword to Kittler's *Discourse Networks*, vii–xxxii.

25 This paradigm is historically quite recent. For more on the term "sharing" and how its salience to morality, economics, interpersonal relations, and mediated communication has changed over time, see John, *Age of Sharing*.

26 This commitment puts *Gestures of Concern* in league with other media-technological inflected treatments of gesture, particularly Vilém Flusser's *Gestures*, André Leroi-Gourhan's *Gesture and Speech*, and Giorgio Agamben's *Means without Ends*.

27 Agamben, *Means without Ends*, 58.

28 Agamben, *Means without Ends*, 59.

29 For more on how communication has been central to the historical tradition of pragmatism and its many doctrines, see Simonson, "Varieties of Pragmatism and Communication."

30 Dewey, "Creative Democracy," 229.

31 Dewey, *Art as Experience*, 4.

32 Here I take a cue from Alain Locke, a radical pragmatist and unsung contributor to the Harlem renaissance, who knew better, in his important 1925 collection, *The New Negro*, than to define art or beauty. Instead he sought to enhance our appreciation of the arts in actual experience—an expansive take, not a constrictive one. Historically, *The New Negro* is the first concerted attempt at a pragmatist aesthetics, though Dewey's major work on art, *Art as Experience* (1934), is often taken as the subfield's starting point despite following *The New Negro* by almost a decade. Richard Shusterman points out that Dewey never mentions Locke's work, yet is likely to have absorbed it indirectly through the art critic Albert C. Barnes, a collaborator with Locke on *The New Negro*, whom Dewey acknowledged as a primary influence on his own aesthetic program. See Shusterman, *Pragmatist Aesthetics*, x. For more on Locke's pragmatist aesthetics, also see Shusterman, "Pragmatist Aesthetics."

33 Auden, "In Memory of W. B. Yeats."

34 This is one way that the processual and pragmatist commitments in *Gestures of Concern* come to the fore, placing it among similar approaches to gesture, such as Erin Manning's *Minor Gesture*, Giovanni Maddalena's *Philosophy of Gesture*, and, more historically, sections of George Herbert Mead's *Mind, Self, and Society*.

35 For an excellent account of "participation" as a keyword of digital culture that has nevertheless had different inflections through history, see Kelty, "Participation."

36 This work was first done in his doctoral dissertation, published in 1962 as *Strukturwandel der Öffentlichkeit*. English-language readers came late to the party, but gave it much fanfare, when the book was finally translated in 1990. See Habermas, *Structural Transformation of the Public Sphere*, 31–56, for his discussion of the literary public sphere's historical origins.

37 For just one historical variation of literary publics beyond the West (and predating Habermas's origin story), see Eiko Ikegami's *Bonds of Civility*, a history of literary and artistic communities in the "aesthetic publics" of Tokugawa Japan between 1600 and 1868. Also see Dillon, *The Gender of Freedom*, for a more feminist reading of historical literary publics.

38 For more on how fan cultures can lead to activist modes of citizenship, see Hinck, *Politics for the Love of Fandom*.

39 McGuigan, *Cultural Analysis*, 15. McGuigan's use of the terms "affective" and "cognitive" are somewhat promiscuous. His notion of affect is not the same as the presymbolic affect I engage with here (his is something closer to emotionality or public feeling). Likewise, what he refers to as a "cognitive mode" indicates something akin to rational sense-making. Generally, the distinction he's making is between emotional-personal discourse and rational-critical discourse—a distinction I would have us trouble.

40 Hauser, *Vernacular Voices*, 61 (emphasis in original).

41 Burke, *Language as Symbolic Action.*

42 Hauser, *Vernacular Voices*, 14 (emphasis in original).

43 Blair, "'We Are All Just Prisoners Here,'" 31. Blair was onto this well before the recent posthuman turn toward nonrepresentational thought. Though symbol use and misuse have long been central to the study of rhetoric, the concerted emphasis on rhetoric's symbolicity is generally thought to have reached a tipping point at the Wingspread Conference in 1970, and has since found rhetoric, Blair says elsewhere, "treated definitively, even exhaustively, as symbolic." See Blair, "Contemporary U.S. Memorial Sites," 18. For more on Wingspread, also see Bitzer and Black, *The Prospect of Rhetoric.*

44 Blair, "'We Are All Just Prisoners Here,'" 32. Blair cautions that it would be unwise "to suggest that it is somehow wrong or incorrect to attend to rhetoric's symbolicity and its capacity to generate meaning." Rather, she says, "it is problematic to treat rhetoric as if it were exclusively symbolic or meaning-ful. There are some things that rhetoric's symbolicity simply cannot account for." See Blair, "Contemporary U.S. Memorial Sites," 19.

45 Rickert, *Ambient Rhetoric*, 9–10.

46 Yeats, "The Scholars," 141.

47 MacNeice, "Snow."

48 See, for instance, Berlant and Stewart's *Hundreds*, which shimmers in a poetics of the noncapturable.

49 I've wrestled in particular with critiques by Ruth Leys. See Leys, "Turn to Affect"; and Leys, "'Both of Us Disgusted in *My* Insula.'" Margaret Wetherell also raises some trenchant critiques in her book *Affect and Emotion.*

50 Another way to frame the project would be to say that scholars across the theoretical humanities have been in the post-representational long enough that it may be time to go back and think about representation from within a post-representational framework. How do representational effects happen in a broader ecological context of distributed agencies and capacities? Thanks to Steve Wiley for this formulation.

51 As Dewey said of the arts, "Art celebrates with peculiar intensity the moments in which the past reinforces the present and in which the future is a quickening of what now is" (*Art as Experience*, 17).

52 This is Rosi Braidotti's description of critical theory that's undertaken as a project of negation instead of affirmation. My project tries to couple a similar commit-

ment to affirmative scholarship with a more materialist interest in the preconditions of interpretation. See Braidotti, *Nomadic Theory*, 292.

53 Heidegger, "Origin of the Work of Art," 22.

54 "Provisional affinity" is my variation of what Bertrand Russell calls a *hypothetical
sympathy*: "In studying a philosopher, the right attitude is neither reverence nor
contempt, but first a kind of hypothetical sympathy, until it is possible to know what
it feels like to believe in his theories, and only then a revival of the critical attitude,
which should resemble, as far as possible, the state of mind of a person abandoning
opinions which he has hitherto held" (Russell, quoted in Manning, *Minor Gesture*, 38).

CHAPTER 1: IDIOT WINDS

1 See Peters, "John Locke, the Individual, and the Origin of Communication."

2 The strange merging of private and public accomplished by digital culture and surveillance capitalism alike attests to some of the difficulty in identifying rifts that once
seemed much starker. This has political ramifications. As Judith Butler has argued,
politics today should not be "defined as taking place exclusively in the public sphere,
distinct from the private one, but it crosses those lines again and again, bringing attention to the way that politics is already in the home, or on the street, or in the neighborhood, or indeed in those virtual spaces that are equally unbound by the architecture of
the house and the square" (Butler, *Notes toward a Performative Theory of Assembly*, 71).

3 Peters, *Speaking into the Air*, 9.

4 The scholarly terrain here is already so well trodden that there are even histories
of various attempts to write communication's various histories. See, e.g., Simonson
et al., "History of Communication History." My personal favorites on the topic
have been Mattelart, *Invention of Communication*, and Peters, *Speaking into the Air*.

5 Peters, "John Locke, the Individual, and the Origin of Communication," 388.

6 For more on being withdrawn from civic life, particularly as a psychological
phenomenon, see Sennett, *Together*, 182–83; and Eliasoph, *Avoiding Politics*.

7 Lauren Berlant has noted the autopoietic character of this process—meaning it
generates and sustains itself. See Berlant, "Commons," 414.

8 In this sense, the figure of "the idiot" I'm interested in has affinities with Lee
Edelman's notion of queerness being efficacious in the same degree as it refuses to
accept a normative social and political order (see Edelman, *No Future*). The idiot's
queerness also resonates with Jack Halberstam's interest in failure being a politics
worth claiming as an alternative to more dominant and exclusionary versions of
what success entails (see Halberstam, *The Queer Art of Failure*). Queerness as willingness to exceed the common, or at least to arrest the impulse toward the common
that's found in the normative order of things—that's the queerness of the idiot.

9 Chen, *Animacies*, 220.

10 Stengers, "Cosmopolitical Proposal," 995.

11 *Rhetores* were, as M. H. Hansen describes, "a small group of citizens who regularly
addressed the *ecclesia*, proposed laws and decrees, and frequented the courts as pros-
ecutors or *synegoroi* [i.e., supporting speakers]." See Hansen, "The Athenian 'Politicians,'" 46. By contrast, according to Josiah Ober, *idiotes* had a common meaning in

the fourth century BCE: "one who was an ordinary citizen and not a political expert." See Ober, *Mass and Elite in Democratic Athens*, 111. *Idiotes* was nevertheless a name used to denote several different kinds of participating citizen: those who avoided all involvement in civic affairs; those who attended public meetings but only to listen; those who merely voted; and those who occasionally spoke at assemblies as *ho boulomenos* (i.e., enacting the ancient right of "anyone who wishes" to propose a law). See Hansen, "The Athenian 'Politicians,'" 46n37; also see 54.

12 I came across Gerdes's work on rhetoricity as radical passivity at the Rhetoric Society of America's 2016 conference in Atlanta, during an exceptional roundtable on the topic "What Rhetoricity Can Do." For more of her work on rhetoricity, particularly as adjacent to vulnerability, see Gerdes, "Trauma, Trigger Warnings, and the Rhetoric of Sensitivity."

13 Berlant, *Cruel Optimism*, 176.

14 With regard to "aspirational ambivalence," see Berlant, "Commons," 414.

15 Kierkegaard, *Sickness unto Death*, 5–6.

16 Heidegger, *Being and Time*, 83.

17 Latour, *What Is the Style of Matters of Concern?*, 39. Also see Latour, "Why Has Critique Run Out of Steam?"

18 The allusion here is to the way concern shares the basic structure of Plato's *chôra*. See *Timaeus*, secs. 16–21. Both serve, paradoxically, as that which makes invention possible and as the invention itself. For more on the *chôra*, particularly relative to the rhetorical, see Rickert, *Ambient Rhetoric*, 41–73; Ott and Keeling, "Cinema and Choric Connection."

19 Whitehead, *Adventures of Ideas*, 180. Brian Massumi notes that Whitehead's notion of affective tonality is akin to what we normally call a "mood" (Massumi, *Semblance and Event*, 65), but I read Whitehead as emphasizing concern as the more pertinent synonym.

20 For more on Whitehead's notion of concern, see Shaviro, *Universe of Things*, 14–26. In Shaviro's reading of Whitehead, concern is "an involuntary experience of being affected by others" (14–15).

21 Thanks to my good friend (and Quaker theologian) Jack Rowan for help with this section.

22 Whitehead, *Modes of Thought*, 153.

23 Though I can't take it on at length, my thinking here again is informed by the Platonic concept of the *chôra*, and particularly Julia Kristeva's use of it in her early theory of semiotics and symbolism. See Plato, *Timaeus*; and Kristeva, *Revolution in Poetic Language*, 19–30.

24 A number of people have made variations of this point. See Glenn and Ratcliffe, *Silence and Listening as Rhetorical Arts*; Ratcliffe, *Rhetorical Listening*; Booth, *The Rhetoric of Rhetoric*, 10; Rood, "'Understanding' Again"; Bodie and Crick, "Listening, Hearing, Sensing"; Lipari, "Listening, Thinking, Being." For an alternative keyed toward rhetorical empathy, see Blankenship, *Changing the Subject*.

25 Gross, "Art of Listening," 75.

26 Gross, "Art of Listening," 75.

27 David Karpf has argued that digital culture makes listening at least as important as speech when it comes to the ability for social movement organizations to develop tactics and strategies in pursuit of their cause. See Karpf, *Analytic Activism.* Similarly, Kate Lacey has argued that the media age has made listening an especially important form of political participation, though it seldom is recognized as such. See Lacey, *Listening Publics.* Also see Richard Sennett's *Together* for a thoughtful argument that listening to others who are different is essential to living together in a more cooperative way.

28 Resmini and Rosati, "Brief History of Information Architecture."

29 Wallace, "Those Fabulous Confabs."

30 Wallace, "Those Fabulous Confabs."

31 Wurman was notorious for turning people away and hand-selecting those people he thought worthy of attending. He made no qualms about assigning status and privilege to those he saw fit. For instance, early conferences included VIPs, who could watch the talks in person, and second-tier guests, who were relegated to watching the talks broadcast live in an adjacent room. Guests were required to wear badges at all times indicating their status for all to see. Wolf, "Wurmanizer."

32 "TED Reaches Its Billionth Video View!" TED Blog, November 13, 2012, http://blog .ted.com/2012/11/13/ted-reaches-its-billionth-video-view/.

33 Heller, "Listen and Learn."

34 Dean, *Democracy and Other Neoliberal Fantasies*, 2.

35 Dean, *Democracy and Other Neoliberal Fantasies*, 32.

36 When Dean wrote *Democracy and Other Neoliberal Fantasies*, she was trying to take the American left to task for failing adequately to challenge the neoliberal status quo that Bill Clinton's presidency only further ensconced and that should have, in her mind, found the left storming the streets ever since the Gore vs. Bush election fiasco of 2000. Her political claim was that the left had lost its symbolic efficiency, succumbed to a pathetic discourse of victimization, ceded ground to fundamentalism, conspiracy theories, and psychotic discourse everywhere, all the while mistakenly supposing communication is timelessly an effective form of democracy, despite its tendency to reinforce the very political-economic rationality that has made it ineffectual to begin with. Prescient at the time, manifestations of her insights have been preponderant post-Trump and in light of more recent swings toward populism and nationalism across the liberal West.

37 See, e.g., Dean, "Why the Net Is Not a Public Sphere." It's worth mentioning that there are clear parallels between Dean's position and one articulated by James Aune in *Selling the Free Market*, which argues that libertarian rhetoric on the political right uses the supposed virtues of a "free market" as a way to justify oppressive inequalities that have "extreme consequences" for the working class.

38 Bratton, "What's Wrong with TED Talks?" The talk's transcript was also published in print. See Bratton, "We Need to Talk about TED."

39 Chris Anderson, interview by Charlie Rose, February 18, 2008, *Charlie Rose* (PBS).

40 I'm hesitant to cite a distinction so widely made in the literature. See, for instance, Massumi, *Parables for the Virtual*, 27; Shouse, "Feeling, Emotion, Affect," para. 1;

Flatley, *Affective Mapping*, 11–19. The distinction between affect, emotion, and feeling is important in part because one of affect theory's contributions to the study of culture is the development of a more refined vocabulary to discuss topics that, while not exactly new, have remained latent in critical discourses for some time, for want of the appropriate language.

41 The point is not that affect should be associated with the pain reflex, but that affectability should be understood as constant and pervasive, even when we don't think we're feeling much at all. The example of the flame is partly an allusion to John Dewey's work on the reflex arc, one of his classic articles staking out his early pragmatist position, though it's seldom cited in more recent affect theory. See Dewey, "Reflex Arc."

42 This time is often identified as a "missing half-second" prior to conscious cognition. See Massumi, "Autonomy of Affect," 89. Tor Norretranders observes that reaction times can be "a lot shorter than 0.5 second. It does not take a half a second to snatch your fingers away when you burn them! So how can it take half a second to move of your own free will? . . . Well, it can because reactions are not conscious. . . . Our reaction time is much shorter than the time it takes to initiate a conscious action" (*User Illusion*, 221). For Norretranders, this gap is what makes possible communication itself. Only through the unconscious process of creating potential worlds by discarding irrelevant information do we access the *exformation* people share as a baseline context for their sociality. Well before Massumi and Norretranders, though, Alfred North Whitehead made a similar observation when he described "a background of feeling" on which all immediate experience depends, one that includes those unconscious observations, ideas, and emotions still lingering from "a quarter of a second ago." Whitehead, *Modes of Thought*, 160, 153.

43 See, for example, Massumi, *Parables for the Virtual* (noting that Massumi is drawing from Deleuze).

44 From the Flaming Lips' song "The Spark That Bled": "I accidentally touched my head / And noticed that I had been bleeding, / For how long I couldn't say. / What was this, I thought, that struck me? / What kind of bullets have they got? / The softest bullet ever shot."

45 Thrift, "Still Life in Nearly Present Time," 34.

46 "Intensity" is the word Brian Massumi uses, as have many others after him, to designate the unrepresentable quality of affections and "the immanent affirmation of a process" in-the-act of experience. See *Semblance and Event*, 84; also see *Parables for the Virtual*, 24–34. "Spark" is the word Eric Jenkins uses for "moments of intense affect" that activate or stimulate some kind of perceptual change in lived experience. See *Special Affects*, 7–9. "Shimmer" is the word that Gregory Seigworth and Melissa Gregg use to evoke the idea of affect in their introduction to *The Affect Theory Reader*, a key text in establishing the study of affect as a quasi-coherent (if interdisciplinary) field. "Glisk" is my own. It's admittedly an obscure word, best described by Charles Harrington Elster as "a subtle sensation: a slight touch of pleasure or twinge of pain that penetrates the soul and passes quickly away." Elster, *There's a Word for It!*, 26.

47 Ong, "Review of *Classical and Christian Ideas of World Harmony*," 245–46.

48 "Symbolic," as I use it, does not refer to Lacan's version of the term, or merely to visual iconography like peace signs and lemniscates. I would call it a *communicative* order if the affective order didn't also involve communicative phenomena. In lieu of a broader "communicative" order, I've settled on "symbolic" to indicate the wide array of referential resources for making meaning—marks, signs, sounds, movements, etc.—that are able to represent something based on social agreement.

49 For more on the TED Talk formula, see Heller, "Listen and Learn."

50 Heller, "Listen and Learn," 74.

51 Peters, "Ten Commandments as Media Theory."

52 Campbell, *Philosophy of Rhetoric*, bk. 1, chap. 5, sect. 1, pt. 3, 53n. Also see Bitzer, "Re-evaluation of Campbell's Doctrine of Evidence."

53 Lanham, *Economics of Attention*, 137–38.

54 Lanham, *Economics of Attention*, 139.

55 For more on the C-B-S model and its critiques from a rhetorical perspective, particularly in light of networked media, see Pfister, *Networked Media*, 24–26.

56 The "mathematical model" I reference here is Claude E. Shannon's seminal theory of communication from 1948, later elaborated with Warren Weaver.

57 Stormer, "Vibrant Matter," 320.

58 A favorite quote: "It is sometimes better to stammer from an excess of emotion than to speak in well-turned phrases" (Milosz, *Captive Mind*, 110).

59 In three dialogues he wrote in 1450 under the title *Idiota*, Cusa's idiot was a layperson, in contrast to the orator or philosopher, and useful for helping Cusa advance his project of refuting both scholasticism and Renaissance humanism with his own mystically inflected doctrine of ignorance, premised on the humility needed before God's wisdom. See Cusa, *Idiota*. For more on Cusa's refutation of scholasticism and humanism, see Fuehrer, "Wisdom and Eloquence."

60 Deleuze and Guattari, *What Is Philosophy?*, 62.

61 Deleuze and Guattari, *What Is Philosophy?*, 62.

62 Deleuze and Guattari, *What Is Philosophy?*, 63.

63 Carey, *Communication as Culture*, especially 12–14. For more on the transmission view and its origins in seventeenth-century Europe, see Peters, *Speaking into the Air*, especially 8, 77–80, and Mattelart, *Invention of Communication*, especially 3–53.

64 Carey, *Communication as Culture*, 15.

65 For more on the latter point, see Biesecker, "Rethinking the Rhetorical Situation."

66 For a starting place about rhetoric beyond representation, see Vivian, *Being Made Strange*.

67 Bakhtin's take on Dostoevsky may help to explain part of Deleuze and Guattari's attraction to Dostoevsky's version of the idiot. See Bakhtin, *Problems of Dostoevsky's Poetics*, 61.

68 Whitehead, *Adventures of Ideas*, 250.

69 See Stengers, "Cosmopolitical Proposal," 1003. For more on equivalency, also see Nancy, *After Fukushima*.

70 Stengers, "Cosmopolitical Proposal," 1003.

CHAPTER 2: STICKINESS

1   Adam Kendon, a standout in contemporary gesture studies, has noted that the most typical understanding of "gesture" refers to "that range of visible bodily actions that are, more or less, generally regarded as part of a person's willing expression." See Kendon, "Language and Gesture: Unity or Duality?," 49.

2   For more on the historical roles of bodily gestures in rhetorical delivery, see Crowley and Hawhee, *Ancient Rhetorics for Contemporary Students*, 330–52; Hawhee, *Bodily Arts*, 153–55; Holding, "Rhetorical Gestures in British Elocutionism"; Holding, "Rhetoric of the Open Fist"; Austin, *Chironomia*.

3   Latour: "We might be more connected to each other by our worries, our matters of concern, the issues we care for, than by any other set of values, opinions, attitudes or principles" (Latour, "From Realpolitik to Dingpolitik," 14).

4   Thanks to Kate Hoyt for pointing me to the case of Vandalina. Most of what I know about the group I've gained from her excellent work. See Hoyt, "Protest beyond Representation," 79–110.

5   Güler, "Vandalina."

6   Stewart, *Ordinary Affects*, 4.

7   Siegert, *Cultural Techniques*, 2.

8   John Durham Peters has noticed the word's translation difficulties and made a useful distinction on this second count: "Techniques are material but are not necessarily durable, while technologies always are. Speech is a technique, but writing is a technology." The essential difference for Peters is that technologies enable us to leave durable marks of our presence in our absence, while techniques involve a handicraft evident only its execution. Peters, *Marvelous Clouds*, 90–91. For more on techniques, with emphasis on embodied knowledge, see Spatz, *What a Body Can Do*, especially 26–38.

9   Winthrop-Young, "Cultural Techniques," 6.

10 Leroi-Gourhan, *Gesture and Speech*, 114.

11 For more on Leroi-Gourhan's importance, see Peters, *Marvelous Clouds*, 16–17, 91, 272–73; and Ingold, "'Tools for the Hand, Language for the Face.'"

12 Winthrop-Young, "Cultural Techniques," 7.

13 Baker, "Populist Conservator," 26.

14 Goldblatt, *Bumper Sticker Liberalism*, 5.

15 Baker, "Populist Conservator," 26.

16 Brinkema, *Forms of the Affects*, 33, 37.

17 Gestures, for Flusser, are media for representing affective states of mind. Or, conversely, as he puts it, "'affect' is the symbolic representation of states of mind through gestures." Flusser, *Gestures*, 4. Note, however, that the word Flusser's translator renders as "affect" is probably closer to "sentiment" than the Spinozist sense of affect as intensive force that I've been using here.

18 Burke, *Rhetoric of Motives*, 269.

19 Gestures in the sense of bodily movements might come closer to absolute pure persuasion because their bare physical movements tend to be interpreted as what

Burke elsewhere calls "nonsymbolic motions," making an interest in advantage-gaining "symbolic actions" less apparent; see Burke, "(Nonsymbolic) Motion / (Symbolic) Action." Readers looking for a difference between "gestures" and "gestures of concern" might begin here. I'd note, though, as a sort of embedded footnote to this footnote, that Burke's differentiation between nonsymbolic motion and symbolic action is easy to overstate. As Debra Hawhee has shown, even if their want of symbolic signification precludes nonsymbolic motions from being meaning-full, material motion by any kind of body is still "sense-full" and "hovers at the edges of language" (Hawhee, *Moving Bodies*, 157).

20 Burke, *Rhetoric of Motives*, 269.

21 I am aware of compelling arguments that assembly democracy well predates its conventionally attributed origin in ancient Athens (see Keane, *Life and Death of Democracy*), but my interest in the mutual blossoming of rhetoric and democracy supersedes my interest in historical comprehensiveness with regard to the latter.

22 Rice, *Distant Publics*, 48.

23 Rice, *Distant Publics*, 56.

24 Rice, *Distant Publics*, 69.

25 Berlant, *Cruel Optimism*, 12.

26 Though Berlant doesn't present it as such, an intimate public sphere is one way to collapse antiquated divides between public and private that do little for the always-on, always-seen nature of surveillance capitalism today. For more on surveillance capitalism and its "disregard for the boundaries of private human experience," see Zuboff, *Age of Surveillance Capitalism*, 19.

27 Berlant, *Cruel Optimism*, 226.

28 Berlant, *Cruel Optimism*, 226.

29 Dean, *Democracy and Other Neoliberal Fantasies*, 26.

30 Foley, "Sound Bites," 619.

31 Foley, "Sound Bites," 619.

32 Freud, "Fetishism," 152.

33 Papacharissi, *Affective Publics*, 68.

34 Rice, "New 'New,'" 211.

35 Rice, "New 'New,'" 211.

36 Dean, *Democracy and Other Neoliberal Fantasies*, 24.

37 McCullough, *Ambient Commons*, 118.

38 O'Sullivan, "Aesthetics of Affect," 126 (emphasis in original).

39 O'Sullivan, "Aesthetics of Affect," 126 (emphasis mine).

40 O'Sullivan, "Aesthetics of Affect," 130.

41 It's for this reason that Deleuze and Guattari theorize art as a "bloc of sensations" (Deleuze and Guattari, *What Is Philosophy?*, 164). For more on sensation and art, see Deleuze, *Logic of Sense.*

42 The story I tell here is not about Fairey's Obama Hope poster, but for an excellent account of that image's origins and subsequent global circulation and repurposing, see Gries, *Still Life with Rhetoric.*

43 I'm getting the details of this history from Fairey's own account. See Fairey, "Sticker Art."

44 Fairey, "Manifesto."

45 Fairey, "Manifesto."

46 Nancy, "Art Today," 97.

47 Nancy, "Art Today," 97.

48 Nancy, "Art Today," 94.

49 Brennan and Lomasky, *Democracy and Decision*, 34.

50 Brennan and Lomasky, *Democracy and Decision*, 34. For more on expressive voting, see Copeland and Laband, "Expressiveness and Voting."

51 Waxman, "This Is the Story behind Your 'I Voted' Sticker."

52 Osborne, *World of Athens*, 206–8.

53 Hauser, *Vernacular Voices*, 60 (emphasis in original).

54 Hauser, *Vernacular Voices*, 13.

55 The term "ecology" is derived from the Greek term *oikos*. A German zoologist named Ernst Haeckel is credited with coining the word (Ökologie) in 1866, when he defined it as "[der] Haushalt der thierischen Organismen"—the household of animals. Etymologically, ecology has from the start been regarded as "the science of the household of organisms, i.e., of their relation to their biotic and abiotic surroundings" (Schwarz and Jax, "Etymology and Original Sources of the Term 'Ecology,'" 147). But if the Greek distinction between the *oikos* (the private realm of the household) and the *polis* (the public realm of political activity) gives us the very basis for theories of the public sphere, even a metaphor for understanding communication itself, "ecology" carries a different set of connotations. Notice here that the concern with the "household" is not with *private* spaces—the bear's den, the bird's nest, the rabbit's burrow, and so forth—but rather with the natural world itself, under whose celestial roof all things coexist. The rehabilitation of the Greek concept of *oikos* at the very advent of ecological thought, in other words, enlists it for a decidedly different purpose than to reinforce the ancient divide between the private sphere, home to the free but essentially hidden interactions of the domestic realm, and the public sphere, which accommodates the open interactions of free citizens in the political. To think about public spheres ecologically in this manner is therefore to broaden their figurative household in a way that troubles traditional notions of a public/private divide and includes both affective and symbolic orders of sociality.

56 Rice's work on rhetorical ecologies is where I first encountered the term "affective ecologies," an analog of what I call an "affective order." Rice (whose surname was Edbauer when she published "Unframing Models") tantalizingly refers to "*affective ecologies*" (her emphasis), but only a sentence later supplants the phrase with "rhetorical ecologies," the former never to return again (Edbauer, "Unframing Models," 9).

57 In his essays on pragmatism, William James makes a similar observation to resist the futility of a rationalism that would deign to answer whether a river makes the banks or the banks make the river—an absurd question for his more humanistic pragmatism, which refuses to separate reality from the flux of human experience. See James, *Pragmatism*, 96–97.

58 Hauser, "Incongruous Bodies," 2.

59 There's a whole library of literature to cite here, but my distillations are in the interest of avoiding its rabbit hole and following a different Mad Hatter. Latour and Deleuze are often associated with flat ontologies, but to my knowledge the first use of the term appears in Manuel DeLanda, *Intensive Science and Virtual Philosophy*, 47.

60 See, e.g., Guattari, "Place of the Signifier in the Institution."

61 Correlationism is a broad and challenging topic that goes back to Immanuel Kant's notion of a transcendental subject. I've found Timothy Morton's overview in his introduction to *Humankind* to be a particularly helpful entry point.

62 Davis, *Inessential Solidarity*, 3.

63 Davis, *Inessential Solidarity*, 2.

64 Rickert, *Ambient Rhetoric*, 159.

65 For more on the visual rhetoric of "Hands Up, Don't Shoot," see Marshall, "Warburgian Maxims for Visual Rhetoric."

66 See Carolyn Pedwell's always brilliant work about how the spread of digital communication technologies has given rise to new affective habits within social movements, protests, and collective efforts to actuate social change. For their manifestation in the Black Lives Matter movement in particular, see Pedwell, "Digital Tendencies."

67 Barad, "On Touching," 209.

68 Commoner, *Closing Circle*, 23.

69 James, *Pragmatism*, Lecture IV, 53.

70 Tuan, *Space and Place*, 11.

71 Massumi, *Semblance and Event*, 1.

72 For more on the concept of solidarity, particularly as an expression of the commonness shared by humans and nonhumans, see Morton, *Humankind*.

73 T. Brennan, *Transmission of Affect*, 1.

74 Ahmed, *Promise of Happiness*, 40.

75 On Ahmed's reference to the "toward" and "away" impact of affects, see Ahmed, *Queer Phenomenology*, 2; Ahmed, *Cultural Politics of Emotion*, 8; and Ahmed, "Happy Objects." For an approach to stickiness from a more rhetorical and materialist tradition, see McNely, "Lures, Slimes, Time."

76 Ahmed, *Cultural Politics of Emotion*, 214 (emphasis mine).

77 Note that in the previous three sentences I've used the word "affects" to maintain consonance with Ahmed's work, though I would prefer to emphasize "affectivity" instead, so not to conflate feeling, emotion, and affect by implying that certain "affects" can be understood as discrete and representable by a fixed set of qualities.

78 Ahmed, "Happy Objects," 29.

79 Rice, "New 'New,'" 209–10.

80 Rice, "New 'New,'" 210.

81 Thrift, "Intensities of Feeling," 58. Some caution is merited here. Where Thrift sees the leveraging of affect for political or commercial gain as a "whole new" technique of power, I'd urge us to consider that what's new is the theorization of that technique, not the technique itself.

CHAPTER 3: DEMOCRATIZING CREATIVITY, CURATING CULTURE

1   Richard Ellmann tells this story in his biography of James Joyce. Ellmann, *James Joyce*, 649.

2   Dewey, *Art as Experience*, 4, 25.

3   For a more sustained argument about how the ubiquity of digital technologies has made it obsolete to maintain modernist binaries that would separate the "digital" from the "real"—or art from everyday life—see Justin Hodgson's *Post-Digital Rhetoric and the New Aesthetic*.

4   Zolberg, "Happy Few," 100.

5   See Thomas Streeter's explanation of why the word "internet" is not a single thing but a term used metonymically as if it were, giving it "an outsize gravitational force in the description of any emerging social practice that has anything at all to do with computer networks" (Streeter, "Internet," 191).

6   For examples of some who have mentioned just how much this topic has been mentioned, see Lunt and Livingston, "Media Studies' Fascination"; Dahlberg, "Rethinking the Fragmentation"; Dahlgren, "The Internet, Public Spheres"; Goldberg, "Rethinking the Public/Virtual Sphere."

7   Goldberg, "Rethinking the Public/Virtual Sphere," 739.

8   As Hubert Buchstein observed back in 1997, the internet seems so promising because it follows an anti-hierarchical structure; it removes many traditional barriers to access; it accommodates the free expression of anyone; and many of its discursive sites hold autonomy from conventional political institutions. See Buchstein, "Bytes That Bite," 250.

9   Though Tim O'Reilly is widely credited for coining the term "Web 2.0" around 2005, to the best of my knowledge the moniker was first used by web designer Darcy DiNucci in 1999—another unfortunate example of women being elided as important figures in the history of technology.

10 Toffler, *Third Wave*.

11 Beer, "Power through the Algorithm?," 986 (emphasis in original).

12 Hariman and Lucaites, *Public Image*, 1.

13 Bondarenko, "Facebook Quietly Stopped."

14 Massumi, *Parables for the Virtual*, 160.

15 Massumi, *Parables for the Virtual*, 160.

16 See Coyne, *Mood and Mobility*, especially 32. Also see Flatley, *Affective Mapping*, 19. Note that both treat "affect" and "feeling" as effectively synonymous.

17 E. Jenkins, "Modes of Visual Rhetoric," 458.

18 Thanks to Ben Burroughs for this insight. See Lazzaro, "Memes Are Our Generation's Protest Art."

19 Berman, "Coral Gables," 70.

20 Deleuze, *Logic of Sense*.

21 Bourriaud, *Relational Aesthetics*, 70.

22 Bourriaud, *Relational Aesthetics*, 8–9.

23 Bourriaud, *Relational Aesthetics*, 17.

24 For more on the link between participatory art and the rise of new media technologies that make digital participation easier, see Manovich, "New Media from Borges to HTML," and Manovich, "Art after Web 2.0."

25 There's a lot to cite on this topic, but for the critique that started the debate, see Bishop, "Antagonism and Relational Aesthetics." Also see Martin, "Critique of Relational Aesthetics."

26 For more on these two episodes in the "Dada Season" of spring 1921, see Demos, "Dada's Event."

27 Bishop, "Introduction: Viewers as Producers," 10.

28 Bishop, "Introduction: Viewers as Producers," 10.

29 Cicero, *De oratore*, 1.108.

30 Cicero, *Orator and Brutus*, 24.

31 In this paragraph, I'm drawing from a talk called "You Start It" that Nick Tandavanitj, a founding member of Blast Theory, gave at North Carolina State University on March 27, 2018.

32 The art historian Grant Kester makes a strong case for regarding "the work of art as a process—a locus of discursive exchange and negotiation" (Kester, *Conversation Pieces*, 12). Tweaking Bourriaud's relational aesthetics in favor of "dialogical aesthetics," Kester sees the most socially powerful artworks as conversation pieces: both things to discuss and the "discussion" itself. In the cases he explores, the artwork literally involves dialogue: actual people talking or socializing together. Though Kester acknowledges that "it is clearly not sufficient to say that any collaborative or conversational encounter constitutes a work of art," he also observes that "what is at stake in these projects is not dialogue per se but the extent to which the artist is able to catalyze emancipatory insights through dialogue" (Kester, *Conversation Pieces*, 69). In other words, art that takes a dialogical form, often analogous to the discursive participation of citizens in public affairs, can itself become a communicative practice that builds community and actuates social change. For a fascinating collection of interviews about the different ways art works as social cooperation—and often as a gesture—see Finkelpearl, *What We Made*.

33 Dewey, "Creative Democracy."

34 This is the thesis that Richard Lanham advances in *The Economics of Attention*, where he also suggests that art of exceptional wonder is capable of arresting attention long enough so that we pause and look *at* it, instead of merely *through* it while passing by. His best example is the ambitious, site-specific installations of Christo and Jeanne-Claude.

35 Dewey, *The Public and Its Problems*, 184.

36 For more on the relationship Dewey charts between democracy, rhetoric, and aesthetics, see Crick, *Democracy and Rhetoric*, especially chap. 3.

37 For more, see Crick, *Democracy and Rhetoric*, 27, 35, 126.

38 As Scott Stroud explains, "The insight of Dewey's work on art is that what makes art *aesthetic* is not any particular property of that particular human practice, but rather its tendency to encourage the sort of absorptive, engaged attention to the

rich present that is so often lost in today's fragmented world." Stroud, *John Dewey and the Artful Life*, 11.

39 A. Williams, "On the Tip of Creative Tongues."

40 For further exploration of how the ordinary citizen's acts of curation can operate as critical and rhetorical practices—and be useful pedagogically—see Finnegan, "Critic as Curator"; Geraths and Kennerly, "Pinvention"; Kennedy, *Textual Curation*.

41 Burton, "The Curator Rei Publicae."

42 Fagan, *Bathing in Public in the Roman World*, 148–52.

43 *Oxford Classical Dictionary*, s.v. "Curator rei publicae."

44 Fagan, *Bathing in Public in the Roman World*, 165.

45 Kolbet, *Augustine and the Cure of Souls*.

46 Plato, *Phaedrus*, 261a, 271c.

47 Kolbet, *Augustine and the Cure of Souls*, 8.

48 Foucault, "Subject and Power," 782.

49 Hooke's appointment fits well in our history: his father, John Hooke, was the curate at All Saints' Church on the Isle of Wight. See Chapman, "England's Leonardo."

50 Thanks to John Jackson for drawing my closer attention to this phenomenon, particularly as it played out in arguments about the function of natural history museums as they became more professionalized in the nineteenth century. See Jackson and Depew, *Darwinism, Democracy, and Race*, 32–58. For more on the "cabinet of curiosities" and the advent of modern museums, see Daston and Park, *Wonders and the Order of Nature*; and Greenhill, *Museums and the Shaping of Knowledge*.

51 For instance, when the vaunted British Museum was established in 1753, it was stocked with items from the naturalist Sir Hans Sloane's large collection of curiosities. From these, the museum's collection grew in direct correlation with the spread of British colonial power. In consequence, countries worldwide are now calling for the British Museum to repatriate works of cultural heritage plundered by British conquest, including the Elgin Marbles of Greece's Parthenon, Egypt's Rosetta Stone, and human remains from Tasmania, among others.

52 See Klinge, *David Teniers and the Theatre of Painting*.

53 See Gaehtgens and Marchesano, *Display and Art History*, 3.

54 Gaehtgens and Marchesano, *Display and Art History*, 3.

55 Gaehtgens and Marchesano, *Display and Art History*, 37.

56 Émile Zola captured this shift in his novelistic homage to the department store, *The Ladies' Paradise* (*Au bonheur des dames*, 1883), in which he writes that the department store "was producing a new religion; churches . . . were being replaced by [the] bazaar." Zola, *Ladies' Paradise*, 427.

57 America in particular, Steven Rosenbaum wrote in 2011, has become a "curation nation. . . . Not long down the road, curation is going to change the way we buy and sell things, the way we recommend and review things, and the way we're able to mobilize groups of like-minded individuals to share, gather, and purchase as groups." These predictions seem to have already come true. Rosenbaum, *Curation Nation*, 4.

58 There are undoubtedly benefits of this logic. But there are also problems too large to discuss here. The reliance on user data is a form of unremunerated labor; it poses a breach in user privacy. Big data favors a lowest common denominator majority; it misses out on the motives and situational nuances in human behavior. Algorithmic recommendations entrench gendered and racialized subject formations; they expose people mostly to what they already like and believe; and they end up evading the serendipitous encounters that can be so important for individual and social advancement.

CHAPTER 4: CITIZEN ARTISTS, CITIZEN CRITICS

1 Transparency and Accountability: Hearings before the House Judiciary Committee, House of Representatives, 115th Congress (Testimony of Sundar Pichai), December 11, 2018, https://www.c-span.org/video/?455607-1/google-ceo-sundar-pichai-testifies-data-privacy-bias-concerns.
2 Herndl and Licona, "Shifting Agency," 134.
3 See Stormer and McGreavy, "Thinking Ecologically," 5–10; Stormer, "Rhetoric's Diverse Materiality," 309–13.
4 Stormer and McGreavy, "Thinking Ecologically," 5.
5 Thanks to Nathan Stormer for this lovely formulation.
6 Unsurprisingly, there is no shortage of scholarly attempts to understand citizenship in both its actual and ideal variations. One that I have found especially useful is Grant Bollmer's work to emphasize citizenship's nodal configuration in the context of globally networked technoculture. Like Bollmer, I take citizenship, generally, to be an active, fluctuating relationship between an individual and a larger governing body (*Inhuman Networks*, 230). Part of that relationship involves the conferral on citizens of certain rights and abilities, but part also involves the enactment of those liberties in the context of both personal and public affairs. Among other things, Bollmer observes that "in dividing a subject into public citizen and private individual, [citizenship] makes some behaviors worthy of political attention and others beyond the recognition of the state" (112). Today, as social media and other networked technologies blur the line between public and private, we have reason to reexamine how an individual's relationship with larger governing bodies can (and can best) be expressed.
7 Eberly, *Citizen Critics*, 1.
8 For more on the emergence of platform studies, particularly its relation to infrastructure studies, see Plantin et al., "Infrastructure Studies Meet Platform Studies." Each is a relatively new field interested in how media technologies both enable and curb creative ways of participating in social and cultural life.
9 Bowker and Star, *Sorting Things Out*.
10 For more on how algorithms operate on a "premise of objectivity," see Gillespie, "Relevance of Algorithms," 179–83; Gillespie, "Algorithm," 23–25.
11 See, e.g., Galloway, *Gaming*; Kushner, "Freelance Translation Machine"; Striphas, "How to Have Culture."
12 Kushner, "Freelance Translation Machine," 3.

13 Striphas, "How to Have Culture." Elsewhere, Striphas describes algorithmic culture as "the enfolding of human thought, conduct, organization and expression into the logic of big data and large-scale computation, a move that alters how the category culture has long been practiced, experienced and understood" (Striphas, "Algorithmic Culture," 396).

14 See, e.g., Bourdieu, "Production of Belief"; DiMaggio, "Classification in Art"; Janssen, Kuipers, and Verboord, "Cultural Globalization"; Verboord, "Legitimacy of Book Critics."

15 Striphas, "How to Have Culture" (emphasis in original).

16 Striphas, "How to Have Culture."

17 He's not alone in this concern. Many others have been bothered by the concealed and unknown nature of algorithms. For a start, see Beer, "Power through the Algorithm?"; Hallsby, "Rhetorical Algorithm"; Pasquale, *Black Box Society*; Thrift, *Knowing Capitalism*.

18 Gehl, "Archive and the Processor," 1229.

19 See Beninger, *Control Revolution*.

20 Michael Hardt coined the term "affective labor" in 1999. See Hardt, "Affective Labor"; Hardt and Negri, *Empire*, 292–93. Unlike Gehl, Hardt does not address affective labor's algorithmic aspects through affective processing.

21 Kittler, "Spooky Electricity," 67.

22 Marwick, *Status Update*, 75.

23 Dean, *Blog Theory*, 96.

24 Dean, *Blog Theory*, 95. For a similar argument, see Dean, "Affect and Drive."

25 Shouse, "Feeling, Emotion, Affect," para. 14.

26 See M. E. Williams, "Did a Writer Get Bullied on Goodreads?"

27 See Ranie, Anderson, and Albright, "Future of Free Speech."

28 Quoted in Victoria, "Learning to Love by Lauren Howard."

29 Bensinger and Trachtenberg, "Amazon's Goodreads Acquisition Triggers Backlash."

30 For more on the exploitative nature of networked technologies, see Galloway and Thacker, *Exploit*. The literature on digital labor is broad, but readers could do worse than starting with Andrejevic, "Estranged Free Labor."

31 These encoded policies of allowing or disallowing, and of encouraging or discouraging, certain online behaviors and content are a focus of the emergent subfield of platform studies. For what may be the domain's most indispensable book, see Gillespie, *Custodians of the Internet*.

32 The quoted phrase alludes to what is probably Habermas's most succinct statement about the political public sphere. See Habermas, "Public Sphere," 49.

33 I will not discuss *sensus communis* or the lifeworld at any length. On the former, see Schaeffer, *Sensus Communis*, and Schaeffer, "Commonplaces." Schaeffer describes *sensus communis*, via Vico, as "the affective, pre-reflective and somatic quality of language, created when both language and human institutions were formed," adding, "it is what makes eloquence possible" (*Sensus Communis*, 151). Lifeworld, meanwhile, at least as expounded by Habermas, shares some overlap with my notion of an affective commonwealth. Here's a snippet from Habermas to indicate some of

that overlap: "The lifeworld forms both the horizon for speech situations and the source of interpretations, while it in turn reproduces itself only through ongoing communicative actions" (*Between Facts and Norms,* 22).

34 Eberly, *Citizen Critics,* 9.

35 See E. Jenkins, "Modes of Visual Rhetoric," especially 452.

36 Herrick, *History and Theory of Rhetoric,* 6.

37 Many of those who write in multiple languages don't translate the term at all in their non-German writing, Giorgio Agamben and Hans Gumbrecht among them. For an essential overview of the *Stimmung* concept, see Wellbery, "Stimmung." For a history of the word, charting its origins, its "death," and its recent resurgence, particularly vis-à-vis music, see Wallrup, *Being Musically Attuned.* For an older account, see Spitzer, "Classical and Christian Ideas of World Harmony."

38 Heidegger, *Fundamental Concepts of Metaphysics,* 67.

39 See Ahmed, "Not in the Mood."

40 For some key passages where Burke addresses identification, see Burke, *Rhetoric of Motives,* 20–23.

41 The quotable phrase "equipment for living" comes from Burke, *Philosophy of Literary Form,* 293–304.

42 For more on the affective force of the GIF, see Ash, "Sensation, Affect and the GIF."

43 rivka, "How Do Likes Affect Which Reviews Non-Friends See?"

44 For more on algorithmic rhetoric, see Ingraham, "Toward an Algorithmic Rhetoric."

45 Hohendahl, *Institution of Criticism.*

46 This is also true outside the English language. As Hohendahl points out, since the institutionalization of literary studies in German universities in the 1850s, a "rift between academic and public criticism" has demoted the nonexpert criticism of lay readers in the general public to a position of diminished cultural authority (*Institution,* 15). When Hohendahl writes about literary criticism, he uses the German word *Literaturkritik,* which carries different connotations from what English speakers call literary criticism. "In this country," he explains, referring to America, "'literary criticism' is used to describe the work of academic writers, but the German term includes both the academic and popular modes" (*Institution,* 13).

47 In an essay on reviewing, Virginia Woolf observes that by the end of the eighteenth century what in English had once been called "criticism" instead became two distinct types of book evaluating. As she explains it, "The critic dealt with the past and with principles; the reviewer took the measure of new books as they fell from the press" ("Reviewing," 205).

48 In a way, the contentious members of the Goodreads community were doing what Wendy Chun calls "queering homophily," that is, challenging "the axiom that similarity breeds connection," which underlies nearly all network science—and particularly curatorial media. See Chun, "Queering Homophily," 60.

49 See, for instance, Eaton, "Integrating the Aesthetic and the Moral," and Gaut, "Ethical Criticism of Art."

50 Booth, *Rhetoric of Fiction,* 428–29. See also Robinson, "Style and Personality in the Literary Work." Plato, in his disparagement of writing in the *Phaedrus,* similarly

laments that writing is dangerous precisely because it allows for no dialectic interaction between writer and reader: the writer of texts *cannot* be known.

51 For more on the difference between autonomous and attributed ethos, particularly in models of expertise, see Johanna Hartelius's indispensable *Rhetoric of Expertise*, 4–6.

52 Quoted in M. E. Williams, "Did a Writer Get Bullied on Goodreads?" Howard's blog has since been taken down.

53 Pippa, "Learning to Love."

54 See, for instance, Dreyer, "Stop Letting Abuse Continue," and Enchanted Endpaper, "Goodreads Policy on Abuse to Authors."

55 See Stop the Goodreads Bullies, "Why It's Time to Stop the Goodreads Bullies," and Losowsky, "Stop the GR Bullies."

56 Goodreads has since removed this comment, first posted on August 23, 2013, by a user with the moniker "Litchick (is stuck in the 19th Century)."

57 Kara, "Important Note Regarding Reviews."

58 See, for instance, Hoffelder, "Goodreads Announces New Content Policy."

59 Butler, "For a Careful Reading," 129. Thanks to Jodi Dean for turning me on to Butler's work on this topic by quoting it in Dean, "Cybersalons and Civil Society," 250.

60 Agamben, *Means without Ends*, 56.

61 It can, however, be understood to affirm one of the insights that Elisabeth Noelle-Neumann had when she developed her model of the spiral of silence in 1974: namely, that our *perceptions* of regnant social attitudes and public opinions do have an impact on the ways people express their own attitudes and opinions. See Noelle-Neumann, "Spiral of Silence," especially 49.

62 Dean, "Cybersalons and Civil Society."

63 Hale, "'Am I Being Catfished?'"

64 On rhetoric's adaptability, see Hauser, *Vernacular Voices*, 64.

65 Among the many such norms are Habermas's norm of critical rationality and Hauser's norm of reasonableness. Others include, for John Dewey, social cooperation; for Seyla Benhabib, impartiality; for Donald Davidson, charity. There are undoubtedly others. See Bernstein, *Pragmatic Turn*, 83–87; Benhabib, "Deliberative Rationality," 30–35; Davidson, *Inquiries into Truth and Interpretation*.

66 For more on the omnivore model of aesthetic taste, see Peterson, "Understanding Audience Segmentation."

CHAPTER 5: UNCOMMONWEALTH

1 Readers interested in the ways these shelves are used in practice should see Brian McNely's "Circulatory Intensities," a fascinating autoethnography of a free public bookcase in Lexington, Kentucky, in which he tracks the appearance and disappearance of books from its shelves.

2 For more on "wikinomics" and collaboration at scale, see Tapscott and Williams, *Wikinomics*.

3 For more of Locke's thinking about property and the common, see Locke, *Second Treatise*, chap. 5 (especially sec. 27).

4 For more on Locke's theory of language and communication, see Locke, *Essay*, Book III. Also see Peters, "John Locke, the Individual, and the Origin of Communication."

5 Agamben, *Means without End*, 59.

6 Agamben, *Means without End*, 58 (emphasis in original).

7 Berlant, *Cruel Optimism*, 199.

8 Buschman, "Libraries and the Decline of Public Purposes," 2.

9 Ingraham, "Libraries and Their Publics."

10 On this last charge in particular, see Greene, "Rhetoric (Dis)Appearing," 262–63.

11 I have reviewed the literature on vernacular rhetoric elsewhere, arguing that vernacular rhetoric is a language of the masses, of those whose exclusion from elite privilege vests them with a special desire to foster communities in which it's possible not just to speak but to be heard. Though I hadn't conceived of it this way at the time, the vernacular is an "idiot rhetoric" through and through. See Ingraham, "Talking (about) the Elite and Mass," especially 11–16.

12 Doubleday, "A Year's Development."

13 Minto and Hutt, *History of the Public Library Movement*.

14 Barker, "Kensal Rise Library."

15 Barker, "Kensal Rise Library."

16 *Public Libraries and Museums Act of 1964*, chap. 75, sec. 7(1).

17 Brent Council, "Proposals for Consultation."

18 Department for Culture, Media and Sport, *Sixth Report.*

19 Department for Culture, Media and Sport, *Framework for the Future.*

20 Davies, *Taking Stock.*

21 Cooper and Cooper, "Public Library Closures."

22 All figures in this paragraph come from "Brent's Borough Profile," a report compiled by the Brent Council in December 2010. More recent reports indicate improvements in measurable deprivation, perhaps owing to broader trends of urban migration and gentrification, which the LTP can be understood to support.

23 Townsend, *Poverty in the United Kingdom.*

24 Muddiman, "Theories of Social Exclusion," 2. Though he doesn't say so outright, Muddiman implies that the policy model of social exclusion recognizes the preparation necessary for the disenfranchised to be more meaningfully included in society. Libraries, I'm suggesting, are a key site of such preparation.

25 The origins of "social exclusion" as a policy term can be traced at least to a 1980s policy of the French government, which used the new phrase "to refer to a disparate group of people living on the margins of society and, in particular, without access to the system of social insurance" (Percy-Smith, "Introduction," 1). As an idea, it gestated for a while before catching on in the United Kingdom, in 1997, when the British government formed the Social Exclusion Unit in the Cabinet Office and related initiatives soon began in Scotland, Wales, and Northern Ireland. England's Social Exclusion Unit and its counterparts around the British Isles took a more multidimensional approach to poverty and social exclusion, attempting to analyze why progress bringing impoverished communities closer to the main-

stream was so slow in coming. By 2003, "social exclusion" was a common enough policy term around Europe that the World Health Organization published a document detailing "solid facts" about social exclusion and its relation to health. And by the end of that decade, so entrenched was the new term that the EU'S European Commission made 2010 the "European Year for Combating Poverty and Social Exclusion."

26 Commission of the European Communities, *Background Report*, 1.

27 Battles, *Library*, 9.

28 There are striking analogs here to a topos advanced centuries later in notions of "culture" itself. On the Parnassan side is Matthew Arnold's version of culture as "the best which has been thought and said in the world," and on the Universal is Raymond Williams's (early) version of culture as ordinary, "a whole way of life." See Arnold, *Culture and Anarchy*, xi; Williams, "Culture Is Ordinary," 4. For more on "culture" as a keyword, particularly in a digital context, see Striphas, "Culture."

29 Pateman and Vincent, *Public Libraries and Social Justice*, 126–27.

30 Pateman and Vincent, *Public Libraries and Social Justice*, 126.

31 Department for Culture, Media and Sport, "Taking Part," 5.

32 Zickuhr, Rainie, and Purcell, "Library Services in the Digital Age," 4.

33 Davies, *Taking Stock*, 27–30.

34 McMenemy, *Public Library*, 16.

35 See McGee, "The 'Ideograph,'" 7. McGee's project is to think about the terminological condensation of ideology, though the idea of an affective condensation is what interests me.

36 Buschman, "Libraries and the Decline of Public Purposes," 9–10.

37 Buschman, "Libraries and the Decline of Public Purposes," 9.

38 Hauser, *Vernacular Voices*, 61–64.

39 Hardt and Negri have similarly emphasized the necessity of a collective practice "where the state of being-in-common is transformed into a process of making the common." See Hardt and Negri, *Commonwealth*, 125.

40 Brent Council, "Proposals for Consultation."

41 Brent Council, *Library Transformation Plan*.

42 Brent Council, "Consultation Plan."

43 Brent Council, "Detailed Information Requests."

44 Brent Council, "Brent Libraries Petitions."

45 Meeting Notes, "Public Meeting."

46 Meeting Notes, "Willesden Green Open Day."

47 Meeting Notes, "Willesden Green Open Day."

48 Meeting Notes, "Public Meeting."

49 Brent Council, "Correspondence Log."

50 Brent Council, "Proposals for Consultation."

51 Brent Council, "Proposals for Consultation."

52 Brent Council, *Library Transformation Plan*.

53 *Bailey v. Brent*, paras. 4–5.

54 *Bailey v. Brent*, para. 5

55 See Voices for the Library, "Stories."

56 In the same way that I described the queerness of the idiot in the introduction, idiot rhetorics also align with feminist projects committed to the equal and immanent value of all beings. But that alignment should be understood less as a political "position" than as a fundamental commitment to a different, less domineering mode of relation. In the disciplinary study of rhetoric, the notion of "invitational rhetoric" has been productively advanced as one possible alternative. Idiot rhetorics are another. See Foss and Griffin, "Beyond Persuasion."

57 Massumi, *Parables for the Virtual*, 27.

58 Lefebvre, *Critique of Everyday Life*, 97.

59 Leys, "Turn to Affect," 437.

60 By "precondition," I mean something already here, but also something always incomplete and hence both a current condition and one spooling into the not-yet.

61 After the white supremacist protests that killed three people and injured several more in Charlottesville, Virginia, in August 2017, the children's staff of the Charlottesville Public Library created a "Cville Strength" mural that resembled the Wall of Shame in Brent. The mural consisted of popsicle sticks that anyone could color and mark with comments about what made their community strong. The example illustrates another gesture of concern, the force-effect of which was not to change policy, but to contribute to a local affective commonwealth.

62 For more on rhetorics of "display" and demonstration, see Prelli, *Rhetorics of Display*, and Hauser, *Prisoners of Conscience*, chap. 7.

63 For more on coalitional subjects, see Chavez, *Queer Migration Politics*.

64 Across England, and particularly greater London, "pop-ups" of various sorts have lately become an urban phenomenon associated with austerity, precarity, and a craft ethos. Mobile movie theaters, barber shops, housing, clothing boutiques, and other pop-ups have accordingly changed how urban populations understand and navigate commercial and local space. Ella Harris is a cultural geographer doing interesting work on this topic. See, e.g., Harris, "Crafted Places/Places for Craft," and Harris, Nowicki, and Brickell, "On-Edge in the Impasse."

65 Geraghty, "Will Landmark Ruling Rewrite the Book on Library Closures?"

66 See, for example, the British Library Board's report titled "Implications of Brexit for the British Library."

67 Nancy, *Inoperative Community*, 35. Also see Schwartzmantel, "Community as Communication."

CHAPTER 6: AFFECTIVE COMMONWEALTHS

1 Berger, "Understanding a Photograph," 216.

2 Carney, "Leave No Dark Corner."

3 Wagner, "Water and the Commons Imaginary," 619.

4 Haraway, "Situated Knowledges," 581.

5 McClendon, "Explore the World with Street View."

6 In this sense, the work that concerned gestures can do makes them consonant with those projects of prefigurative politics that follow the slogan of the Industrial Workers of the World: "We build the new society in the shell of the old."

7 Chavez, *Queer Migration Politics*, 147.

8 I first came across the idea of a commons imaginary in Wagner, "Water and the Commons Imaginary."

9 Taylor, *Modern Social Imaginaries*, 23.

10 Taylor, *Modernity and the Rise of the Public Sphere*, 227.

11 Taylor, *Modern Social Imaginaries*, 23.

12 Taylor, *Modernity and the Rise of the Public Sphere*, 243.

13 Kittler, *Gramophone*, 4.

14 Raley, *Tactical Media*, 6.

15 Lovink, *Dark Fiber*, 271.

16 This list is likely incomplete, as Google regularly updates its ability to capture different views from ground level around the planet, in public and private spaces alike (to say nothing about the satellite and aircraft photography the company uses for the overhead shots on Google Maps).

17 H. Jenkins, *Convergence Culture*, 291.

18 Though I can't take it on here, this phenomenon articulates nicely with the emergent field of "surface studies." See the 2017 special section on the topic in *Theory, Culture and Society* 34, nos. 7–8. Personal highlights include Coleman and Oakley-Brown, "Visualizing Surfaces, Surfacing Vision," and Ingold, "Surface Visions."

19 Benjamin, "Little History of Photography."

20 See Sontag, *On Photography*, and Sontag, *Regarding the Pain of Others*.

21 Barthes, *Camera Lucida*, 21.

22 Barthes, *Camera Lucida*, 21.

23 Barthes, *Camera Lucida*, 26.

24 Barthes, *Camera Lucida*, 55.

25 Brown and Phu, *Feeling Photography*, 5.

26 Terranova, *Network Culture*, 142. Others approach images in a similar way. See, for instance, Marco Abel's *Violent Affect*.

27 See Dean, *Blog Theory*, 115.

28 The analogy of infection recalls Teresa Brennan's insight that affects are contagious in their social transmission. See Brennan, *Transmission of Affect*, 68–70. Terranova and Brennan, whose books were published in the same year (2004), do not cite each other on this similarity. Incidentally, both books were written at the height of the SARS epidemic across Asia, though a number of scholars have addressed contagion and social theory in step with the rise of networked culture in general. For an exemplary study, see Sampson, *Virality*.

29 See Warner, *Publics and Counterpublics*, 114–24.

30 World Press Photo, "2011 Photo Contest."

31 Quoted in Cooper and Robson, "Do You Really Call This Art?"

32 See, for instance, Doug Rickard and Jon Rafman, both of whom curate photos from the GSV archive. Emilio Varvarella's *The Google Trilogy* (2012) is another fascinating example of artistic efforts to show how Google's visualizing capacities fail at naturalism on account of their encoded biases, blank spots, and glitches. See http://emiliovavarella.com/archive/google-trilogy.

33 Finnegan, "Naturalistic Enthymeme and Visual Argument," 133.

34 Pfister and Woods, "Unnaturalistic Enthymeme," 241.

35 For one helpful theoretical anchor for Wolf's art, consult Doreen Massey's notion that places are events. Massey, *For Space*, 141.

36 Bartholl, "Map. Public Installation."

37 Harold, "Pranking Rhetoric," 192.

38 Hariman and Lucaites, *No Caption Needed*, 40. To some extent, any critique of attempts to overcome cultural hierarchies can be read as a critique of culture jamming, even without naming the practice as such. See, e.g., Stallybrass and White, *Politics and Poetics of Transgression*.

39 Auden, *Age of Anxiety*, 31.

40 See Luke, "Phoneur."

41 Sedgwick, *Touching Feeling*, 13–17.

42 For more, see Carter, "Police Called."

43 For more, see Kinsley, *Street with a View*.

44 For more, see Scott, "Google Ireland's Dublin Staff."

45 Flusser, "Habit," 53.

46 Freud, *Civilization and Its Discontents*, 23.

47 A lot of good scholarship has been done on "habit"—William James and Felix Ravaisson have been particular bellwethers—but for an excellent treatment of habit's relationship to affect, media, and social change, see Carolyn Pedwell's work, especially "Mediated Habits" (2017), "Habit and the Politics of Social Change" (2017), and "Digital Tendencies" (2019).

48 See Braidotti, "Ethics of Becoming Imperceptible," 156. For more on GSV tableaux vivants and the imperceptible, see Ingraham and Rowland, "Performing Imperceptibility."

49 Satz, "Tableaux Vivants," 170.

50 Satz, "Tableaux Vivants," 170.

51 For more on the role of "image events" supplanting signifying argument in public spheres, particularly in the context of social movements, see Kevin DeLuca's classic, *Image Politics*.

52 "El mundo se llenó de sin embargos." Neruda, "The Materials," 55.

53 For instance, in 2007, news of the higher wheat prices afflicting Egypt circulated around the world in ways that gave rise to publics invested in the implications of these rises. These publics no doubt varied in discussing the implications of higher wheat prices from manifold angles: economic, personal, religious, agrarian, and so on. But the opinions that formed from the special interests of these reticulating publics were not made real merely by the experience of people paying attention to the high cost of wheat. Rather, the circulation of that attention *preconditioned* the public opinion that discussion about that topic's implications achieved—a public opinion resulting famously in the broad political uprising that became known as the Arab Spring.

54 This has historically been an American vision. See Boyte, "Building the Commonwealth."

55 Boyte, "Building the Commonwealth," 268–70. The coding wiki GitHub makes a vivid example of what building the commonwealth might involve. The site allows programmers to post their projects and crowdsource their coding problems to others. Even the U.S. government has taken to GitHub by posting hundreds of governmental projects on the site—from internal documents to NASA software—in order to benefit from the kind of "public opinion" an open-source wiki is able to provide as a ballast against what amounts to the government's concession of its limited authority. The major shift here happened in 2012, when, in a historically unprecedented move toward more direct democracy, the American government allowed anyone on GitHub to edit typos in one of the Consumer Financial Protection Bureau's internal documents. For more, see McMillan, "How GitHub Helps You Hack the Government."

56 Self-persuasion or internal rhetorics might seem to be the exception here. We reason with ourselves as much as we reason with others. Yet, as Isocrates observed, our internal self-persuasion trains us for our persuasion with others. Rhetoric cultivates "reflective practitioners" ultimately always in service of social engagement with others.

57 I am indebted to Lauren Berlant for this phrase, as we and others discussed it on July 22, 2014, at Northwestern University's Summer Institute in Rhetoric and Public Culture, the subject of which was rhetoric, politics, and affect.

58 Berlant, *Cruel Optimism*, 198–99.

59 The Greek orator Aeschines, for example, utilized the political advantage of purporting to be a less invested *idiotes*. In competitive speeches against Demosthenes, he frequently referred to his status as an *idiotes*, presumably to differentiate his (earnest) intentions from (cunning) rhetorical ones. Presenting as any other ordinary Joe, Jane, or J'Lyn, Aeschines illustrates one of the earliest cases of someone seeking social purchase from the capital gained by being perceived as disinvested from the political. By taking what amounts to an antirhetorical position, Aeschines sought to separate himself from those whose more invested social commitments and standing might expose them as out of touch with the average person who perhaps operated from a place of greater naivete, but of no less genuine concern. Today, the American politician chomping a corndog at the state fair is just one example of Aeschines's legacy: an attempt to gain the credibility of being ordinary by operating within the people's vernacular. Distancing oneself from "those" politicians in favor of "us" common folk is a standard move in political rhetoric, and has been for some time. The case of Donald Trump—who evidently connected to the average American by calling bullshit on politicians and the news media, despite being a person of incredible wealth and privilege (and bullshit) himself—illustrates with particular poignancy that a modern *idiotes* can leverage a purported distance from the political in disingenuous and dangerous ways. My interest in an "idiot rhetoric," however, has not focused on the dangers of this maneuvering when undertaken by those already vested with some power, so much as the ways we might take seriously the more withdrawn political activities of those whose standing is less secure. See Adams, *Speeches of Aeschines*. For more on Aeschines's antirhetorical argumentation, see Preus, "Art of Aeschines."

60 Nate Stormer calls for a "polythetic ontology" to understand rhetoric's diversity. See Stormer, "Rhetoric's Diverse Materiality."

61 For some smart "early" exceptions, though in a different key, see Muckelbauer, *Future of Invention*, and Vivian, *Being Made Strange*.

62 Dean, *Blog Theory*, 124.

EPILOGUE: THE POET AND THE ANTHROPOCENE

1 Though "Weltanschauung" never once appears in Habermas's original German, the changes Auden notes are roughly analogous to the "structural transformations" that Habermas was charting contemporaneously.

2 Auden, "Poet and the City," 78–80.

3 See Sarah Sharma's masterful *In the Meantime*, for a cultural politics of time.

4 For more on this argument, see Peters, *Speaking into the Air*, 4.

5 James, *Principles of Psychology*, 187.

6 Burke, *Rhetoric of Motives*, 130.

7 Flusser, "What Is Communication?," 4.

8 Flusser, "What Is Communication?," 3.

9 See Stengers, "Cosmopolitical Proposal," 995.

10 Deleuze and Guattari, *What Is Philosophy?*, 62.

11 For more on complete and incomplete gestures, albeit in a different key, see Mead, *Mind, Self, and, Society*, especially 144–49.

12 Raley, *Tactical Media*, 151.

BIBLIOGRAPHY

Abel, Marco. *Violent Affect: Literature, Cinema, and Critique after Representation*. Lincoln: University of Nebraska Press, 2007.

Adams, Charles Darwin, trans. and ed. *The Speeches of Aeschines*. Cambridge, MA: Harvard University Press, 1919.

Agamben, Giorgio. *Means without Ends: Notes on Politics*. Translated by Cesare Casarino and Vincenzo Binetti. Minneapolis: University of Minnesota Press, 2000.

Ahmed, Sara. *The Cultural Politics of Emotion*. 2nd ed. Edinburgh: Edinburgh University Press, 2014.

Ahmed, Sara. "Happy Objects." In *The Affect Theory Reader*, edited by Melissa Gregg and Gregory J. Seigworth, 29–51. Durham, NC: Duke University Press, 2010.

Ahmed, Sara. "Not in the Mood." *New Formations* 82 (2014): 13–28.

Ahmed, Sara. *The Promise of Happiness*. Durham, NC: Duke University Press, 2010.

Ahmed, Sara. *Queer Phenomenology*. Durham, NC: Duke University Press, 2006.

Amazon Kindle. "Frequently Asked Questions: What Are Popular Highlights?" *Kindle .amazon.com*. Amazon.com n.d. Web. January 16, 2015.

Anderson, Chris. Interview by Charlie Rose. *Charlie Rose* (PBS). February 18, 2008.

Andrejevic, Mark. "Estranged Free Labor." In *Digital Labor: The Internet as Playground and Factory*, edited by Trebor Sholz, 149–64. New York: Routledge, 2013.

Arnold, Matthew. *Culture and Anarchy: An Essay in Political and Social Criticism*. 1869. Reprint, New York: Macmillan Company, 1908.

Ash, James. "Sensation, Affect and the GIF: Towards an Allotropic Account of Networks." In *Networked Affect*, edited by Ken Hillis, Susanna Paasonen, and Michael Petit, 119–34. Cambridge, MA: MIT Press, 2015.

Auden, W. J. *The Age of Anxiety: A Baroque Eclogue*. Princeton, NJ: Princeton University Press, 2011.

Auden, W. H. "In Memory of W. B. Yeats." In *Collected Poems of W. H. Auden*, 247–48. New York: Vintage, 1991.

Auden, W. H. "The Poet and the City." In *The Dyer's Hand*, 72–89. New York: Random House, 1962.

Aune, James. *Selling the Free Market: The Rhetoric of Economic Correctness*. New York: Guilford Press, 2002.

Austin, Gilbert. *Chironomia or, A Treatise on Rhetorical Delivery*. 1806. Edited by Mary Margaret Robb and Lester Thonssen. Carbondale: Southern Illinois University Press, 1966.

Bailey and Others v. London Borough of Brent Council. May 27, 2011, EWCA Civ 1586.

Baker, Whitney. "The Populist Conservator: A Sticky Case Study." *Book and Paper Group Annual* 31 (2012): 25–28.

Bakhtin, Mikhail. *Problems of Dostoevsky's Poetics*. Edited and translated by Caryl Emerson. Minneapolis: University of Minnesota Press, 1984.

Barad, Karen. "On Touching—the Inhuman That Therefore I Am." *differences* 25, no. 3 (2012): 206–23.

Barker, Robert. "Kensal Rise Library." Brent Heritage Museum and Archive occasional papers, no. 3 (September 2000). https://brent.gov.uk/media/387413/Barker_Kensal _Rise_Library.pdf. Accessed January 16, 2015.

Barthes, Roland. *Camera Lucida: Reflections on Photography*. Translated by Richard Howard. New York: Hill and Wang, 1981.

Bartholl, Aram. "Map. Public Installation." https://arambartholl.com/de/map. Accessed January 16, 2015.

Battles, Matthew. *Library: An Unquiet History*. New York: W. W. Norton, 2003.

Batuman, Elif. "Ottomania." *New Yorker*, February 17 and 24, 2014. https://newyorker .com/magazine/2014/02/17/ottomania.

Beer, David. "Power through the Algorithm? Participatory Web Cultures and the Technological Unconscious." *New Media and Society* 11, no. 6 (2009): 985–1002.

Benhabib, Seyla. "Deliberative Rationality and Models of Democratic Legitimacy." *Constellations* 1, no. 1 (1994): 26–52.

Beninger, James. *The Control Revolution: Technological and Economic Origins of the Information Society*. Cambridge, MA: Harvard University Press, 1989.

Benjamin, Walter. "A Little History of Photography." In *1927–1934*, vol. 2 of *Walter Benjamin: Selected Writings*, translated by Rodney Livingstone, 507–31. Cambridge, MA: Harvard University Press, 1999.

Benjamin, Walter. "The Work of Art in the Age of Mechanical Reproduction." In *Illuminations*, edited by Hannah Arendt, translated by Harry Zohn, 217–51. New York: Schocken Books, 1968.

Bensinger, Greg, and Jeffrey A. Trachtenberg. "Amazon's Goodreads Acquisition Triggers Backlash." *Wall Street Journal*, April 3, 2013. https://blogs.wsj.com/digits/2013/04 /03/amazons-goodreads-acquisition-triggers-backlash/.

Berger, John. "Understanding a Photograph." In *Selected Essays*, edited by Geoff Dyer, 215–18. New York: Pantheon, 2001.

Berlant, Lauren. "The Commons: Infrastructure for Troubling Times." *Environment and Planning D: Society and Space* 34, no. 3 (2016): 393–419.

Berlant, Lauren. *Cruel Optimism*. Durham, NC: Duke University Press, 2011.

Berlant, Lauren, and Jordan Greenwald. "Affect in the End Times: A Conversation with Lauren Berlant." *Qui Parle: Critical Humanities and Social Sciences* 20, no. 2 (2012): 71–89.

Berlant, Lauren, and Kathleen Stewart. *The Hundreds*. Durham, NC: Duke University Press, 2019.

Berman, David. "Coral Gables." In *Actual Air*, 69–70. New York: Open City Books, 1999.

Bernstein, Richard. *The Pragmatic Turn*. Cambridge, UK: Polity Press, 2010.

Biesecker, Barbara A. "Rethinking the Rhetorical Situation from within the Thematic of *Différance*." *Philosophy and Rhetoric* 22, no. 2 (1989): 110–30.

Bishop, Claire. "Antagonism and Relational Aesthetics." *OCTOBER* 110 (2004): 51–79.

Bishop, Claire. "Introduction: Viewers as Producers." In *Participation*, edited by Claire Bishop, 10–17. Cambridge, MA: MIT Press, 2006.

Bitzer, Lloyd. "A Re-evaluation of Campbell's Doctrine of Evidence." *Quarterly Journal of Speech* 46, no. 2 (April 1960): 135–40.

Bitzer, Lloyd, and Edwin Black (eds.). *The Prospect of Rhetoric*. Englewood Cliffs, NJ: Prentice-Hall, 1971.

Blair, Carole. "Contemporary U.S. Memorial Sites as Exemplars of Rhetoric's Materiality." In *Rhetorical Bodies*, edited by Jack Selzer and Sharon Crowley, 16–57. Madison: University of Wisconsin Press, 1999.

Blair, Carole. "'We Are All Just Prisoners Here of Our Own Device': Rhetoric in Speech Communication after Wingspread." In *Making and Unmaking the Prospects for Rhetoric*, edited by Theresa Enos, Richard McNabb, Carolyn Miller, and Roxanne Mountford, 29–36. New York: Lawrence Erlbaum, 1997.

Blankenship, Lisa. *Changing the Subject: A Theory of Rhetorical Empathy*. Louisville, CO: Utah State University Press, 2019.

Bodie, Graham D., and Nathan Crick. "Listening, Hearing, Sensing: Three Modes of Being and the Phenomenology of Charles Sanders Peirce." *Communication Theory* 24 (2014): 105–23.

Bollmer, Grant. *Inhuman Networks*. New York: Bloomsbury, 2016.

Bolter, Jay David. *The Digital Plenitude: The Decline of Elite Culture and the Rise of New Media*. Cambridge, MA: MIT Press, 2019.

Bondarenko, Veronika. "Facebook Quietly Stopped Offering Flag Profile-Picture Filters after Terrorist Attacks." *Business Insider*, June 10, 2017. https://www.businessinsider.com/facebook-stops-offering-flag-profile-picture-filters-after-terrorist-attacks-2017-5.

Booth, Wayne. *The Rhetoric of Fiction*. 2nd ed. Chicago: University of Chicago Press, 1983.

Booth, Wayne. *The Rhetoric of Rhetoric: The Quest for Effective Communication*. Malden, MA: Blackwell, 2004.

Bourdieu, Pierre. "The Production of Belief: Contribution to an Economy of Symbolic Goods." *Media, Culture and Society* 2 (1980): 261–93.

Bourriaud, Nicolas. *Relational Aesthetics*. Translated by Simon Pleasance and Fronza Woods. Paris: Les Presses du réel, 2002.

Bowker, Geoffrey C., and Susan Leigh Star. *Sorting Things Out: Classification and Its Consequences*. Cambridge, MA: MIT Press, 2000.

Boyle, Casey. *Rhetoric as a Posthuman Practice*. Columbus: Ohio State University Press, 2018.

Boyte, Harry C. "Building the Commonwealth: Citizenship as Public Work." In *Citizen Competence and Democratic Institutions*, edited by Stephen L. Elkin and Karol Edward Sottan, 259–78. University Park: Pennsylvania State University Press, 1989.

Braidotti, Rosi. "The Ethics of Becoming Imperceptible." In *Deleuze and Philosophy*, edited by Constantin V. Boundas, 133–59. Edinburgh: University of Edinburgh Press, 2006.

Braidotti, Rosi. *Nomadic Theory: The Portable Rosi Braidotti*. New York: Columbia University Press, 2011.

Braidotti, Rosi. "On Putting the Active Back into Activism." *New Formations* 68 (2010): 42–57.

Bratton, Benjamin. "We Need to Talk about TED." Opinion. *The Guardian*, December 30, 2013. https://www.theguardian.com/commentisfree/2013/dec/30/we-need-to-talk-about-ted.

Bratton, Benjamin. "What's Wrong with TED Talks?" Presented at TEDxSanDiego, 2013.

Brennan, Geoffrey, and Loren Lomasky. *Democracy and Decision*. Cambridge, UK: Cambridge University Press, 1993.

Brennan, Teresa. *The Transmission of Affect*. Ithaca, NY: Cornell University Press, 2004.

Brent Council. "Brent Libraries Petitions." In *Library Transformation Plan, Executive Report from the Director of Environment and Neighborhood Services*. April 11, 2011.

Brent Council. "Brent's Borough Profile." December 2010. https://www.brent.gov.uk/media/323958/Brent%20Borough%20Profile,%20summary%202010.pdf.

Brent Council. "Consultation Plan." In *Library Transformation Plan, Executive Report from the Director of Environment and Neighborhood Services*, Annexe 3.2. April 11, 2011.

Brent Council. "Correspondence Log." In *Library Transformation Plan, Executive Report from the Director of Environment and Neighborhood Services*. April 11, 2011.

Brent Council. "Detailed Information Requests." In *Library Transformation Plan, Executive Report from the Director of Environment and Neighborhood Services*. April 11, 2011.

Brent Council. *Library Transformation Plan, Executive Report from the Director of Environment and Neighborhood Services*. April 11, 2011.

Brent Council. "Proposals for Consultation." *London Borough of Brent Libraries, Arts and Heritage Libraries Transformation Project*. 2010.

Brinkema, Eugenie. *The Forms of the Affects*. Durham, NC: Duke University Press, 2014.

Brown, Elspeth H., and Thy Phu. *Feeling Photography*. Durham, NC: Duke University Press, 2014.

Brown, Wendy. *Undoing the Demos: Neoliberalism's Stealth Revolution*. Brooklyn: Zone Books, 2015.

Buber, Martin. *I and Thou*. Translated by Ronald Gregor Smith. 1937. Reprint, London: Bloomsbury Academic, 2013.

Buchstein, Hubertus. "Bytes That Bite: The Internet and Deliberative Democracy." *Constellations* 4, no. 2 (1997): 248–63.

Burke, Kenneth. *Language as Symbolic Action*. Berkeley: University of California Press, 1968.

Burke, Kenneth. "(Nonsymbolic) Motion / (Symbolic) Action." *Critical Inquiry* 4, no. 1 (1978): 809–38.

Burke, Kenneth. *The Philosophy of Literary Form*. 3rd ed. Berkeley: University of California Press, 1973.

Burke, Kenneth. *A Rhetoric of Motives*. Berkeley: University of California Press, 1969.

Burton, Graham P. "The Curator Rei Publicae: Towards a Reappraisal." *Chiron* 9 (1979): 465–87.

Buschman, John. "Libraries and the Decline of Public Purposes." *Public Library Quarterly* 24, no. 1 (2006): 1–12.

Butler, Judith. "For a Careful Reading." In *Feminist Contentions: A Philosophical Exchange*, edited by Seyla Benhabib, Judith Butler, Drucilla Cornell, and Nancy Fraser, 127–44. New York: Routledge, 1995.

Butler, Judith. *Notes toward a Performative Theory of Assembly*. Cambridge, MA: Harvard University Press, 2015.

Campbell, George. *The Philosophy of Rhetoric*. Carbondale: Southern Illinois University Press, 2008.

Carey, James W. *Communication as Culture*. New York: Routledge, 2009.

Carney, Matthew. "Leave No Dark Corner." *Foreign Correspondent* (Australian Broadcasting Corporation), September 17, 2018. https://www.abc.net.au/news /2018-09-18/china-social-credit-a-model-citizen-in-a-digital-dictatorship /10200278?nw=0.

Carter, Claire. "Police Called after Google Street View Captures 'Fake' Murder." *The Telegraph*, June 2, 2014. https://www.telegraph.co.uk/technology/google/10869951 /Police-called-after-Google-Street-View-captures-fake-murder.html.

Chapman, Allan. "England's Leonardo: Robert Hooke (1635–1703) and the Art of Experiment in Restoration England." *Proceedings of the Royal Institution of Great Britain* 67 (1996): 239–75.

Chavez, Karma. *Queer Migration Politics: Activist Rhetoric and Coalitional Possibilities*. Urbana: University of Illinois Press, 2013.

Chen, Mel. *Animacies*. Durham, NC: Duke University Press, 2012.

Chun, Wendy Hui Kyong. "Queering Homophily." In *Pattern Discrimination*, edited by Clemens Apprich, Wendy Hui Kyong Chun, Florian Cramer, and Hito Steyerl, 59–97. Minneapolis: University of Minnesota Press, 2018.

Cicero. *Brutus, Orator*. Translated by Harry Mortimer Hubbell. Cambridge, MA: Harvard University Press, 1939.

Cicero. *De oratore*. Translated by Edward William Sutton and Harris Hackham. Cambridge, MA: Harvard University Press, 1942.

Coleman, Rebecca, and Liz Oakley-Brown. "Visualizing Surfaces, Surfacing Vision: Introduction." *Theory, Culture and Society* 34, nos. 7–8 (2017): 5–27.

Commission of the European Communities. *Background Report: Social Exclusion: Poverty and Other Social Problems in the European Community*. ISEC/B11/93. Luxembourg: Office for Official Publications of the European Communities, 1993.

Commoner, Barry. *The Closing Circle: Nature, Man, and Technology*. New York: Alfred A. Knopf, 1971.

Cooper, Gill, and Genevieve Cooper. "Public Library Closures." *House of Commons Parliamentary Briefing Paper*, February 18, 2011. SN/HA/5875.

Cooper, Rob, and Steve Robson. "Do You Really Call This Art? Images of Google Streetview Prostitutes (That You Might Have Seen All over the Web) Now Displayed in Gallery and Nominated for Top Award." *Daily Mail*, April 19, 2013. http://www.dailymail.co.uk/news/article-2311727/Mishka-Henner-puts-images-Google-Streetview-prostitutes-display-gallery.html.

Copeland, Cassandra, and David N. Laband. "Expressiveness and Voting." *Public Choice* 110 (2002): 351–63.

Coyne, Richard. *Mood and Mobility: Navigating the Emotional Spaces of Digital Social Networks*. Cambridge, MA: MIT Press, 2016.

Crick, Nathan. *Democracy and Rhetoric: John Dewey on the Arts of Becoming*. Columbia: University of South Carolina Press, 2010.

Crowley, Sharon, and Debora Hawhee. *Ancient Rhetorics for Contemporary Students*. 3rd ed. New York: Pearson, 2004.

Cusa, Nicholas of. *Idiota*. In *Complete Philosophical and Theological Treatises of Nicholas of Cusa, vol. 1*. Translated by Jasper Hopkins, 493–630. Minneapolis: Arthur J. Banning Press, 2001.

Dahlberg, Lincoln. "Rethinking the Fragmentation of the Cyberpublic: From Consensus to Contestation." *New Media and Society* 9, no. 5 (2007): 827–47.

Dahlgren, Peter. "The Internet, Public Spheres, and Political Communication: Dispersion and Deliberation." *Political Communication* 22 (2005): 147–62.

Daston, Lorraine, and Katharine Park. *Wonders and the Order of Nature: 1150–1750*. Cambridge, MA: MIT Press, 1998.

Davidson, Donald. *Inquiries into Truth and Interpretation*. Oxford: Oxford University Press, 1991.

Davies, Steve. *Taking Stock: The Future of Our Public Library Service*. Cardiff, Wales: UNISON (Cardiff University), 2008.

Davis, Diane. *Inessential Solidarity: Rhetoric and Foreigner Relations*. Pittsburgh, PA: University of Pittsburgh Press, 2010.

Dean, Jodi. "Affect and Drive." In *Networked Affect*, edited by K. Hillis, S. Paasonen, and M. Petit, 89–101. Cambridge, MA: MIT Press, 2015.

Dean, Jodi. *Blog Theory*. Cambridge, UK: Polity, 2010.

Dean, Jodi. "Cybersalons and Civil Society: Rethinking the Public Sphere in Transnational Technoculture." *Public Culture* 13, no. 2 (2001): 243–65.

Dean, Jodi. *Democracy and Other Neoliberal Fantasies: Communicative Capitalism and Left Politics*. Durham, NC: Duke University Press, 2009.

Dean, Jodi. *Publicity's Secret: How Technoculture Capitalizes on Democracy*. Ithaca, NY: Cornell University Press, 2002.

Dean, Jodi. "Why the Net Is Not a Public Sphere." *Constellations* 10, no. 1 (2003): 95–112.

DeLanda, Manuel. *Intensive Science and Virtual Philosophy*. London: Continuum, 2002.

Deleuze, Gilles. *The Logic of Sense*. Translated by Mark Lester with Charles Stivale. London: Athlone Press, 1990.

Deleuze, Gilles. "Postscript on the Societies of Control." *October* 59 (1992): 3–7.

Deleuze, Gilles. "Sur Spinoza." Translated by Timothy S. Murphy. *Cours Vincennes* (January 24, 1978). https://www.webdeleuze.com/texts/14.

Deleuze, Gilles, and Félix Guattari. *What Is Philosophy?* Translated by Hugh Tomlinson and Graham Burchell. New York: Columbia University Press, 1994.

DeLuca, Kevin Michael. *Image Politics: The New Rhetoric of Environmental Activism.* New York: Guilford Press, 1999.

DeLuca, Kevin Michael, and Jennifer Peeples. "From Public Sphere to Public Screen: Democracy, Activism, and the 'Violence' of Seattle." *Critical Studies in Media Communication* 19, no. 2 (2002): 125–51.

Demos, T. J. "Dada's Event." In *Communities of Sense*, edited by Beth Hinderliter, Vered Maimon, Jaleh Mansoor, and Seth McCormick, 135–52. Durham, NC: Duke University Press, 2010.

Department for Culture, Media and Sport. *Framework for the Future: Libraries, Learning and Information in the Next Decade.* London. DCMS, 2003. https://dera.ioe.ac.uk//4709/.

Department for Culture, Media and Sport. *Sixth Report, Session 1999–2000, HC 241.* Culture, Media and Sport Committee Publications. https://publications.parliament.uk/pa/cm199900/cmselect/cmcumeds/241/24102.htm.

Department for Culture, Media and Sport. "Taking Part: 2013/14 Quarter 1 Statistical Release." London: DCMS, September 2013. https://www.gov.uk/government/statistics/taking-part-201314-quarter-1-statistical-release.

Dewey, John. *Art as Experience.* 1934. Reprint, New York: Perigee, 2005.

Dewey, John. 1939. "Creative Democracy—the Task before Us." In *John Dewey: The Later Works, 1925–1953, Volume 14*, edited by Jo Ann Boydston, 224–30. Carbondale: Southern Illinois University Press, 2008.

Dewey, John. *The Public and Its Problems.* New York: Swallow Press, 1927.

Dewey, John. "The Reflex Arc Concept in Psychology." *Psychological Review* 3, no. 4 (1896): 357–70.

Dillon, Elizabeth Maddock. *The Gender of Freedom: Fictions of Liberalism and the Literary Public Sphere.* Stanford, CA: Stanford University Press, 2004.

DiMaggio, Paul. "Classification in Art." *American Sociological Review* 52, no. 4 (1987): 440–55.

Doubleday, William Elliott. "A Year's Development of the Public Library Movement in Greater London." *Library* 1 (1892): 141–46.

Dreyer, Victoria. "Stop Letting Abuse Continue under the Disguise of Freedom of Speech." Change.org, August 22, 2013. https://www.change.org/p/goodreads-com-amazon-com-stop-letting-abuse-continue-under-the-disguise-of-freedom-of-speech.

Eaton, Marcia. "Integrating the Aesthetic and the Moral." *Philosophical Studies: An International Journal for Philosophy in the Analytic Tradition* 67, no. 3 (1992): 219–40.

Eberly, Rosa. *Citizen Critics.* Urbana: University of Illinois Press, 2000.

Edbauer, Jenny. "Unframing Models of Public Distribution: From Rhetorical Situation to Rhetorical Ecologies." *Rhetoric Society Quarterly* 35, no. 4 (2005): 5–24.

Edelman, Lee. *No Future: Queer Theory and the Death Drive.* Durham, NC: Duke University Press, 2004.

Eliasoph, Nina. *Avoiding Politics: How Americans Produce Apathy in Everyday Life.* Cambridge: Cambridge University Press, 1998.

Ellmann, Richard. *James Joyce.* Oxford: Oxford University Press, 1982.

Elster, Charles Harrington. *There's a Word for It! A Grandiloquent Guide to Life*. New York: Scribner, 1996.

Enchanted Endpaper. "Goodreads Policy on Abuse to Authors: Not to Allow Comments to Be Abusive in Nature." Change.org, August 25, 2013. https://www.change.org/p/goodreads-policy-on-abuse-to-authors-not-to-allow-comments-to-be-abusive-in-nature.

Fagan, Garret G. *Bathing in Public in the Roman World*. Ann Arbor: University of Michigan Press, 2005.

Fairey, Shepard. "Manifesto." Obey, April 18, 1990. http://www.obeygiant.com/articles/manifesto.

Fairey, Shepard. "Sticker Art." Obey, April 18, 2003. https://obeygiant.com/essays/sticker-art/.

Finkelpearl, Tom. *What We Made: Conversations on Art and Social Cooperation*. Durham, NC: Duke University Press, 2013.

Finnegan, Cara. "The Critic as Curator." *Rhetoric Society Quarterly* 48, no. 4 (2018): 405–10.

Finnegan, Cara. "The Naturalistic Enthymeme and Visual Argument: Photographic Representation in the 'Skull Controversy.'" *Argumentation and Advocacy* 37, no. 3 (2001): 133–49.

Finnegan, Cara A., and Jiyeon Kang. "'Sighting' the Public: Iconoclasm and Public Sphere Theory." *Quarterly Journal of Speech* 90, no. 4 (2004): 377–402.

Flatley, Jonathan. *Affective Mapping: Melancholia and the Politics of Modernism*. Cambridge, MA: Harvard University Press, 2008.

Flusser, Vilém. *Gestures*. Translated by Nancy Ann Roth. Minneapolis: University of Minnesota Press, 2014.

Flusser, Vilém. "Habit: The True Aesthetic Criterion." In *Writings*, edited by Andreas Ströhl, translated by Erik Eisel, 51–57. Minneapolis: University of Minnesota Press, 2002.

Flusser, Vilém. "What Is Communication?" In *Writings*, edited by Andreas Ströhl, translated by Erik Eisel, 3–7. Minneapolis: University of Minnesota Press, 2002.

Foley, Megan. "Sound Bites: Rethinking the Circulation of Speech from Fragment to Fetish." *Rhetoric and Public Affairs* 15, no. 4 (2012): 613–22.

Foss, Sonja K., and Cindy L. Griffin. "Beyond Persuasion: A Proposal for an Invitational Rhetoric." *Communication Monographs* 62 (March 1995): 2–18.

Foucault, Michel. "The Subject and Power." *Critical Inquiry* 8, no. 4 (1982): 777–95.

Freud, Sigmund. *Civilization and Its Discontents*. Edited and translated by James Strachey. New York: Norton, 1962.

Freud, Sigmund. "Fetishism." In *The Complete Psychological Works of Sigmund Freud*, translated by James Strachey, 21:147–57. London: Hogarth and the Institute of Psychoanalysis, 1927.

Fuehrer, M. L. "Wisdom and Eloquence in Nicholas of Cusa's 'Idiota de Sapientia and de Mente.'" *Vivarium* 16, no. 2 (1978): 142–55.

Gaehtgens, Thomas W., and Louis Marchesano. *Display and Art History: The Düsseldorf Gallery and Its Catalogue*. Los Angeles: Getty Publications, 2011.

Galloway, Alexander R. *Gaming: Essays on Algorithmic Culture.* Minneapolis: University of Minnesota Press, 2006.

Galloway, Alexander R., and Eugene Thacker. *The Exploit: A Theory of Networks.* Minneapolis: University of Minnesota Press, 2007.

Gaut, Berys. "The Ethical Criticism of Art." In *Aesthetics and Ethics,* edited by Jerrold Levinson, 182–203. Cambridge: Cambridge University Press, 1998.

Gehl, Robert W. "The Archive and the Processor: The Internal Logic of Web 2.0." *New Media and Society* 13, no. 8 (2011): 1228–44.

Geraghty, Liam. "Will Landmark Ruling Rewrite the Book on Library Closures?" *The Big Issue,* August 24, 2018. https://www.bigissue.com/latest/will-landmark-ruling-rewrite-the-book-on-library-closures/.

Geraths, Cory, and Michele Kennerly. "Pinvention: Updating Commonplace Books for the Digital Age." *Communication Teacher* 29, no. 3 (2015): 166–72.

Gerdes, Kendall. "Trauma, Trigger Warnings, and the Rhetoric of Sensitivity." *Rhetoric Society Quarterly* 49, no. 1 (2019): 3–24.

Gerdes, Kendall. "What Rhetoricity Can Do." Paper presented at the Rhetoric Society of America's 17th Biennial Conference. Atlanta, GA, May 2016.

Gillespie, Tarleton. "Algorithm." In *Digital Keywords*, edited by Benjamin Peters, 18–30. Princeton, NJ: Princeton University Press, 2016.

Gillespie, Tarleton. *Custodians of the Internet: Platforms, Content Moderation, and the Hidden Decisions That Shape Social Media.* New Haven: Yale University Press, 2018.

Gillespie, Tarleton. "The Relevance of Algorithms." In *Media Technologies*, edited by Tarleton Gillespie, Pablo J. Boczkowski, and Kirsten A. Foot, 167–93. Cambridge, MA: MIT Press, 2014.

Glenn, Cheryl, and Krista Ratcliffe. *Silence and Listening as Rhetorical Acts.* Carbondale: Southern Illinois University Press, 2011.

Goldberg, Greg. "Rethinking the Public/Virtual Sphere: The Problem with Participation." *New Media and Society* 13, no. 5 (2010): 739–54.

Goldblatt, Mark. *Bumper Sticker Liberalism: Peeling Back the Idiocies of the Political Left.* New York: Broadside Books, 2012.

Greene, Ronald Walter. "Rhetoric (Dis)Appearing." *Communication and Critical/Cultural Studies* 10, nos. 2–3 (2013): 259–64.

Greenhill, Eileen Hooper. *Museums and the Shaping of Knowledge.* New York: Routledge, 1992.

Gries, Laurie E. *Still Life with Rhetoric: A New Materialist Approach to Visual Rhetorics.* Logan: Utah State University Press, 2015.

Gross, Daniel. "The Art of Listening." *International Journal of Listening* 21, no. 1 (2007): 72–79.

Guattari, Felix. "The Place of the Signifier in the Institution." In *The Guattari Reader*, edited by Gary Genosko, 148–57. Cambridge, MA: Blackwell, 1996.

Güler, Emrah. "Vandalina: Ankara's New Street Art Collective." *Hurriyet Daily News*, January 28, 2013.

Gumbrecht, Hans Ulrich. "A Farewell to Interpretation." In *Materialities of Communication*, edited by Hans Ulrich Gumbrecht and K. Ludwig Pfeiffer, 389–402. Stanford, CA: Stanford University Press, 1994.

Gumbrecht, Hans Ulrich. *Production of Presence: What Meaning Cannot Convey*. Stanford, CA: Stanford University Press, 2004.

Habermas, Jürgen. *Between Facts and Norms*. Translated by William Rehg. Cambridge, MA: MIT Press, 1996.

Habermas, Jürgen. "The Public Sphere: An Encyclopedia Article (1964)." Translated by Sarah Lennox and Frank Lennox. *New German Critique* 3 (Autumn 1974): 49–55.

Habermas, Jürgen. *The Structural Transformation of the Public Sphere: An Inquiry into a Category of Bourgeois Society*. Translated by T. Burger. Cambridge, MA: MIT Press, 1989.

Halberstam, Judith [Jack]. *The Queer Art of Failure*. Durham, NC: Duke University Press, 2011.

Hale, Kathleen. "'Am I Being Catfished?' An Author Confronts Her Number One Online Critic." *The Guardian*, October 18, 2014. https://www.theguardian.com/books/2014/oct/18/am-i-being-catfished-an-author-confronts-her-number-one-online-critic.

Hallsby, Atilla. "The Rhetorical Algorithm: WikiLeaks and the Elliptical Secrets of Donald J. Trump." *Secrecy and Society* 1, no. 2 (2018).

Hansen, Mogens Herman. "The Athenian 'Politicians', 403–322 B.C." *GRBS* 24 (1983): 33–55.

Haraway, Donna. *The Companion Species Manifesto*. Chicago: Prickly Paradigm Press, 2003.

Haraway, Donna. "Situated Knowledges: The Science Question in Feminism and the Privilege of Partial Perspective." *Feminist Studies* 14, no. 3 (1988): 575–99.

Hardt, Michael. "Affective Labor." *boundary 2* 26, no. 2 (1999): 89–100.

Hardt, Michael, and Antonio Negri. *Commonwealth*. Cambridge, MA: Harvard University Press, 2009.

Hardt, Michael, and Antonio Negri. *Empire*. Cambridge, MA: Harvard University Press, 2000.

Hariman, Robert, and John Louis Lucaites. *No Caption Needed: Iconic Photographs, Public Culture, and Liberal Democracy*. Chicago: University of Chicago Press, 2011.

Hariman, Robert, and John Louis Lucaites. *The Public Image: Photography and Civic Spectatorship*. Chicago: University of Chicago Press, 2016.

Harney, Stefano, and Fred Moten. *The Undercommons: Fugitive Planning and Black Study*. New York: Minor Compositions, 2013.

Harold, Christine. "Pranking Rhetoric: 'Culture Jamming' as Media Activism." *Critical Studies in Media Communication* 21, no. 3 (2004): 189–211.

Harris, Ella. "Crafted Places/Places for Craft: Pop-Up and the Politics of the 'Crafted' City." In *Craft Economies*, edited by Susan Luckman and Nicola Thomas, 173–83. London: Bloomsbury Academic, 2019.

Harris, Ella, Mel Nowicki, and Katherine Brickell. "On-Edge in the Impasse: Inhabiting the Housing Crisis as Structure-of-Feeling." *Geoforum* 101 (May 2019): 156–64.

Hartelius, E. Johanna. *The Rhetoric of Expertise*. New York: Lexington Books, 2011.

Hauser, Gerard. "Incongruous Bodies: Arguments for Personal Sufficiency and Public Insufficiency." *Argumentation and Advocacy* 36, no. 1 (1999): 1–9.

Hauser, Gerard. *Prisoners of Conscience*. Columbia: University of South Carolina Press, 2013.

Hauser, Gerard. *Vernacular Voices: The Rhetoric of Publics and Public Spheres*. Columbia: University of South Carolina Press, 1999.

Hawhee, Debra. *Bodily Arts: Rhetoric and Athletics in Ancient Greece*. Austin: University of Texas Press, 2004.

Hawhee, Debra. *Moving Bodies: Kenneth Burke at the Edges of Language*. Columbia: University of South Carolina Press, 2009.

Heidegger, Martin. *Being and Time*. Translated by John Macquarrie and Edward Robinson. New York: Harper Perennial, 2008.

Heidegger, Martin. *The Fundamental Concepts of Metaphysics*. Translated by William McNeill and Nicholas Walker. Bloomington: Indiana University Press, 1995.

Heidegger, Martin. "The Origin of the Work of Art." In *Poetry, Language, Thought*. Translated by Albert Hofstadter, 15–86. New York: Harper Perennial, 2001.

Heller, Nathan. "Listen and Learn." *New Yorker*, July 9 and 16, 2012.

Herndl, Carl G., and Adela C. Licona. "Shifting Agency: Agency, Kairos, and the Possibilities of Social Action." In *Communicative Practices in Workplaces and the Professions*, edited by Mark Zachry and Charlotte Thralls, 133–53. Amityville, NY: Baywood Publishing, 2007.

Herrick, James. *The History and Theory of Rhetoric: An Introduction*. 5th ed. New York: Routledge, 2016.

Hinck, Ashley. *Politics for the Love of Fandom: Fan-Based Citizenship in a Digital World*. Baton Rouge: Louisiana State University Press, 2019.

Hodgson, Justin. *Post-Digital Rhetoric and the New Aesthetic*. Columbus: Ohio State University Press, 2019.

Hoffelder, Nate. "Goodreads Announces New Content Policy—Now Deletes Reviews Which Mention Author Behavior." *The Digital Reader,* September 20, 2013. https:// the-digital-reader.com/2013/09/20/goodreads-announces-new-content-policy-now -deletes-reviews-mention-author-behavior/

Hohendahl, Peter Uwe. *The Institution of Criticism*. Ithaca, NY: Cornell University Press, 1982.

Holding, Cory. "Rhetorical Gestures in British Elocutionism." PhD diss., University of Illinois at Urbana-Champaign, 2012.

Holding, Cory. "The Rhetoric of the Open Fist." *Rhetoric Society Quarterly* 45, no. 5 (2015): 399–419.

Hoyt, Kate Drazner. "Protest beyond Representation: The Vitalism of Digital Protest Art's Political Aesthetics." PhD diss., University of Denver, 2017.

Ikegami, Eiko. *Bonds of Civility: Aesthetic Networks and the Political Origins of Japanese Culture*. Cambridge: Cambridge University Press, 2005.

Ingold, Tim. "Surface Visions." *Theory, Culture and Society* 34, nos. 7–8 (2017): 99–108.

Ingold, Tim. "'Tools for the Hand, Language for the Face': An Appreciation of Leroi-Gourhan's *Gesture and Speech*." *Studies in History and Philosophy of Biological and Biomedical Sciences* 40, no. 4 (1999): 411–53.

Ingraham, Chris. "Libraries and Their Publics: Rhetorics of the Public Library." *Rhetoric Review* 34, no. 2 (2015): 147–63.

Ingraham, Chris. "Talking (about) the Elite and Mass: Vernacular Rhetoric and Discursive Status." *Philosophy and Rhetoric* 46, no. 1 (2013): 1–21.

Ingraham, Chris. "Toward an Algorithmic Rhetoric." In *Digital Rhetoric and Global Literacies: Communication Modes and Digital Practices in the Networked World*, edited by Gustav Verhulsdonck and Marohang Limbu, 62–79. Hershey, PA: IGI Global, 2014.

Ingraham, Chris, and Allison Rowland. "Performing Imperceptibility: Google Street View and the *Tableau Vivant*." *Surveillance and Society* 14, no. 2 (2016): 211–26.

Jackson, John, and David Depew. *Darwinism, Democracy, and Race: American Anthropology and Evolutionary Biology in the Twentieth Century*. New York: Routledge, 2017.

James, William. "Is Life Worth Living?" In *The Will to Believe and Other Essays in Popular Philosophy*, 32–62. 1896. Reprint, New York: Dover, 1960.

James, William. *Pragmatism*. 1907. Reprint, New York: Dover, 1995.

James, William. *Principles of Psychology*. 1890. Reprint, Great Books of the Western World, edited by Robert Maynard Hutchins, vol. 53. Chicago: Encyclopedia Britannica, 1952.

James, William. *The Varieties of Religious Experience*. 1902. Reprint, New York: Routledge, 2002.

Janssen, Susanne, Giselinde Kuipers, and Marc Verboord. "Cultural Globalization and Arts Journalism: The International Orientation of Arts and Culture Coverage in Dutch, French, German, and U.S. Newspapers, 1955 to 2005." *American Sociological Review* 73 (2008): 719–40.

Jenkins, Eric. "The Modes of Visual Rhetoric: Circulating Memes as Expressions." *Quarterly Journal of Speech* 100, no. 4 (2014): 442–66.

Jenkins, Eric. *Special Affects: Cinema, Animation, and the Translation of Consumer Culture*. Edinburgh: Edinburgh University Press, 2014.

Jenkins, Henry. *Convergence Culture: Where Old and New Media Collide*. New York: New York University Press, 2006.

John, Nicholas. *The Age of Sharing*. Cambridge, UK: Polity, 2017.

Kara. "Important Note Regarding Reviews." Goodreads Feedback Discussion, Goodreads.com, November 18, 2013. Accessed January 16, 2015. No URL for the Goodreads Feedback Discussion group remains.

Karpf, David. *Analytic Activism: Digital Listening and the New Political Strategy*. Oxford: Oxford University Press, 2017.

Keane, John. *The Life and Death of Democracy*. New York: W. W. Norton, 2009.

Kelty, Christopher. "Participation." In *Digital Keywords*, edited by Benjamin Peters, 227–41. Princeton, NJ: Princeton University Press, 2016.

Kendon, Adam. "Language and Gesture: Unity or Duality?" In *Language and Gesture*, edited by David McNeill, 47–63. Cambridge: Cambridge University Press, 2000.

Kennedy, Krista. *Textual Curation: Authorship, Agency, and Technology in Wikipedia and Chambers' Cyclopaedia*. Columbia: University of South Carolina Press, 2016.

Kester, Grant. *Conversation Pieces: Community and Communication in Modern Art*. Berkeley: University of California Press, 2013.

Kierkegaard, Søren. *The Sickness unto Death*. Translated by Howard V. Hong and Edna H. Hong. Princeton, NJ: Princeton University Press, 1941.

Kinsley, Ben. *Street with a View* (2008). http://benkinsley.com/street-with-a-view/. Accessed January 17, 2015.

Kittler, Friedrich. *Gramophone, Film, Typewriter*. Translated by Geoffrey Winthrop Young and Michael Wutz. Stanford, CA: Stanford University Press, 1999.

Kittler, Friedrich. "Spooky Electricity." *Artforum* (December 1992): 66–70.

Klinge, Margret. *David Teniers and the Theatre of Painting*. London: Paul Holberton, 2006.

Kolbet, Paul. *Augustine and the Cure of Souls*. Notre Dame, IN: University of Notre Dame Press, 2010.

Kristeva, Julia. *Revolution in Poetic Language*. Translated by Margaret Waller. New York: Columbia University Press, 1984.

Kushner, Scott. "The Freelance Translation Machine: Algorithmic Culture and the Invisible Industry." *New Media and Society* 15, no. 8 (2013): 1–18.

Lacey, Kate. *Listening Publics: The Politics and Experience of Listening in the Media Age*. Cambridge, UK: Polity, 2013.

Lanham, Richard A. *The Economics of Attention: Style and Substance in the Age of Information*. Chicago: University of Chicago Press, 2007.

Latour, Bruno. "From Realpolitik to Dingpolitik, or How to Make Things Public." In *Making Things Public: Atmospheres of Democracy*, edited by Bruno Latour and Peter Weibel, 4–31. Cambridge, MA: MIT Press, 2005.

Latour, Bruno. *What Is the Style of Matters of Concern?* Amsterdam: Van Gorcum, 2005.

Latour, Bruno. "Why Has Critique Run Out of Steam? From Matters of Fact to Matters of Concern." *Critical Inquiry* 30, no. 2 (2004): 225–48.

Lazzaro, Sage. "Memes Are Our Generation's Protest Art." *Vice,* March 1, 2019. https://www.vice.com/en_us/article/mbzxa3/memes-are-our-generations-protest-art.

Lefebvre, Henri. *Critique of Everyday Life*. Vol. 1. Translated by John Moore and Gregory Elliott. London: Verso, 1991.

Lerner, Ben. *The Hatred of Poetry*. New York: Farrar, Straus and Giroux, 2016.

Leroi-Gourhan, André. *Gesture and Speech*. Translated by Anna Bostock Berger. Cambridge, MA: MIT Press, 1993.

Leys, Ruth. "'Both of Us Disgusted in *My* Insula': Mirror-Neuron Theory and Emotional Empathy." In *Science and Emotions after 1945*, edited by Frank Biess and Daniel M. Gross, 67–95. Chicago: University of Chicago Press, 2014.

Leys, Ruth. "The Turn to Affect: A Critique." *Critical Inquiry* 37 (2011): 434–72.

Lipari, Lisbeth. "Listening, Thinking, Being." *Communication Theory* 20 (2010): 348–62.

Locke, Alain. *The New Negro: Voices of the Harlem Renaissance*. 1925. New York: Touchstone, 1997.

Locke, John. *An Essay Concerning Human Understanding*. Indianapolis, IN: Hackett, 1996.

Locke, John. *Second Treatise of Government*. Indianapolis, IN: Hackett, 1980.

Losowsky, Andrew. "Stop the GR Bullies: An Explanation." *Huffington Post,* July 20, 2012. https://www.huffpost.com/entry/stop-the-gr-bullies-an-ap_b_1690134.

Love, Harry (DJHarryLove). "KENSAL RISE POP UP LIBRARY HAS BEEN TORN DOWN
    IN THE MIDDLE OF THE NIGHT BY HIRED HEAVIES—KENSAL RESIDENTS WE HAVE
    TO RESPOND!!" January 31, 2014. Tweet.

Lovink, Geert. *Dark Fiber: Tracking Internet Culture*. Cambridge, MA: MIT Press, 2002.

Luke, Robert. "The Phoneur: Mobile Commerce and the Digital Pedagogies of the
    Wireless Web." In *Communities of Difference: Culture, Language, Technology*, edited by
    Peter Trifonas, 185–204. London: Palgrave, 2006.

Lunt, Peter, and Sonia Livingstone. "Media Studies' Fascination with the Concept of
    the Public Sphere: Reflections and Emerging Debates." *Media, Culture and Society* 25,
    no. 1 (2013): 87–96.

MacNeice, Louis. "Snow." In *Contemporary Irish Poetry: An Anthology*, edited by
    Anthony Bradley, 116. Berkeley: University of California Press, 1980.

Maddalena, Giovanni. *The Philosophy of Gesture: Completing Pragmatists' Incomplete Revo-
    lution*. London: McGill-Queens University Press, 2015.

Malinowski, Bronisław. "The Problem of Meaning in Primitive Languages." In *The
    Meaning of Meaning: A Study of the Influence of Language upon Thought and the Science of
    Symbolism*, edited by C. K. Ogden and I. A. Richards, 296–336. New York: Harcourt,
    Brace and World, 1923.

Manning, Erin. *The Minor Gesture*. Durham, NC: Duke University Press, 2016.

Manovich, Lev. "Art after Web 2.0." In *The Art of Participation: 1950 to Now*, edited by
    Rudolf Frieling, Boris Groys, Robert Atkins, and Lev Manovich, 66–78. San Fran-
    cisco: San Francisco Museum of Modern Art, 2008.

Manovich, Lev. "New Media from Borges to HTML." In *The New Media Reader*, edited by
    Noah Wardrip-Fruin and Nick Montfort, 13–25. Cambridge, MA: MIT Press, 2003.

Marshall, David L. "Warburgian Maxims for Visual Rhetoric." *Rhetoric Society Quarterly*
    48, no. 4 (2018): 352–79.

Martin, Stewart. "Critique of Relational Aesthetics." *Third Text* 21, no. 4 (2007): 369–86.

Marwick, Alice. *Status Update: Celebrity, Publicity, and Branding in the Social Media Age*.
    New Haven, CT: Yale University Press, 2015.

Massey, Doreen. *For Space*. London: Sage, 2005.

Massumi, Brian. "The Autonomy of Affect." *Cultural Critique* 31 (1995): 83–109.

Massumi, Brian. "Envisioning the Virtual." In *The Oxford Handbook of Virtuality*, edited
    by Mark Grimshaw, 55–70. Oxford: Oxford University Press, 2014.

Massumi, Brian. *Parables for the Virtual: Movement, Affect, Sensation*. Durham, NC: Duke
    University Press, 2002.

Massumi, Brian. *Semblance and Event*. Cambridge, MA: MIT Press, 2011.

Mattelart, Armond. *The Invention of Communication*. Translated by Susan Emanuel.
    Minneapolis: University of Minnesota Press, 1996.

McClendon, Brian. "Explore the World with Street View, Now on All Seven Conti-
    nents." Google Maps blog, September 30, 2010. https://maps.googleblog.com/2010
    /09/explore-world-with-street-view-now-on.html.

McCullough, Malcolm. *Ambient Commons: Attention in the Age of Embodied Information*.
    Cambridge, MA: MIT Press.

McGee, Michael Calvin. "The 'Ideograph': A Link between Rhetoric and Ideology." *Quarterly Journal of Speech* 66, no. 2 (1980): 1–16.

McGuigan, Jim. *Cultural Analysis*. London: Sage, 2010.

McLuhan, Marshall. *Understanding Media: The Extensions of Man*. London: Routledge, 1964.

McMenemy, David. *The Public Library*. London: Facet, 2009.

McMillan, Robert. "How GitHub Helps You Hack the Government." *Wired*, January 9, 2013. https://www.wired.com/2013/01/hack-the-government/.

McNely, Brian J. "Circulatory Intensities: Take a Book, Return a Book." In *Rhetoric through Everyday Things*, edited by Scot Barnett and Casey Boyle, 139–54. Tuscaloosa: University of Alabama Press, 2016.

McNely, Brian. "Lures, Slime, Time: Viscosity and the Nearness of Distance." *Philosophy and Rhetoric* 52, no. 3 (2019): 203–26.

Mead, George Herbert. *Mind, Self, and Society*. Chicago: University of Chicago Press, 1934.

Meeting Notes. "Public Meeting." Libraries Transformation Project Consultation, Questions and Answers Session, Brent Council, London, December 1, 2010.

Meeting Notes. "Willesden Green Open Day." Libraries Transformation Project Consultation, Brent Council, London, January 12, 2011.

Milosz, Czeslaw. *The Captive Mind*. New York: Vintage Books, 1990.

Minto, John, and James Hutt. *A History of the Public Library Movement in Great Britain and Ireland*. London: G. Allen and Unwin, 1932.

Morton, Timothy. *Humankind: Solidarity with Nonhuman People*. New York: Verso, 2017.

Muckelbauer, John. *The Future of Invention: Rhetoric, Postmodernism, and the Problem of Change*. Albany: State University of New York Press, 2008.

Muddiman, Dave. "Theories of Social Exclusion and the Public Library." In *Open to All? The Public Library and Social Exclusion*, edited by Dave Muddiman, Shiraz Durrani, Martin Dutch, Rebecca Linley, John Pateman, and John Vincent, 1–15. London: The Council for Museums, Archives and Libraries, 2000.

Nancy, Jean-Luc. *After Fukushima: The Equivalence of Catastrophes*. Translated by Charlotte Mandell. New York: Fordham University Press, 2014.

Nancy, Jean-Luc. "Art Today." *Journal of Visual Culture* 9, no. 1 (2010): 91–99.

Nancy, Jean-Luc. *The Inoperative Community*. Minneapolis: University of Minnesota Press, 1991.

Neruda, Pablo, "The Materials," In 2000, translated by Richard Schaaf, 55. Falls Church, VA: Azul Editions, 1997.

Noelle-Neumann, Elisabeth. "The Spiral of Silence: A Theory of Public Opinion." *Journal of Communication* 24, no. 2 (1974): 43–51.

Norretranders, Tor. *The User Illusion: Cutting Consciousness Down to Size*. New York: Viking, 1998.

Ober, Josiah. *Mass and Elite in Democratic Athens: Rhetoric, Ideology, and the Power of the People*. Princeton, NJ: Princeton University Press, 1991.

Ong, Walter. "Review of *Classical and Christian Ideas of World Harmony*." *Journal of Religion* 44, no. 3 (July 1964): 245–46.

Osborne, Robin. *The World of Athens: An Introduction to Classical Athenian Culture*. 2nd ed. Cambridge: Cambridge University Press, 2008.

O'Sullivan, Simon. "The Aesthetics of Affect: Thinking Art beyond Representation." *Angelaki: Journal of the Theoretical Humanities* 6, no. 3 (2001): 125–35.

Ott, Brian L., and Diane Marie Keeling. "Cinema and Choric Connection: Lost in Translation as Sensual Experience." *Quarterly Journal of Speech* 97, no. 4 (2011): 363–86.

Oxford Classical Dictionary. 4th ed. s.v. "Curator rei publicae." https://oxfordre.com /classics. Accessed January 16, 2015.

Packer, Jeremy. "Epistemology Not Ideology OR Why We Need New Germans." *Communication and Critical/Cultural Studies* 10, nos. 2–3 (2013): 295–300.

Papacharissi, Zizi. *Affective Publics: Sentiment, Technology, and Politics*. Oxford: Oxford University Press, 2014.

Pasquale, Frank. *The Black Box Society*. Cambridge, MA: Harvard University Press, 2015.

Pateman, John, and John Vincent. *Public Libraries and Social Justice*. Surrey, UK: Ashgate, 2010.

Pedwell, Carolyn. "Digital Tendencies: Intuition, Algorithmic Thought and New Social Movements." *Culture, Theory and Critique* 60, no. 2 (2019): 123–38.

Pedwell, Carolyn. "Habit and the Politics of Social Change: A Comparison of Nudge Theory and Pragmatist Philosophy." *Body and Society* 23, no. 4 (2017): 59–94.

Pedwell, Carolyn. "Mediated Habits: Images, Networked Affect and Social Change." *Subjectivity* 10, no. 2 (2017): 147–69.

Pedwell, Carolyn. *Transforming Habit: Affect, Assemblage and Change in a Minor Key*. Montreal: McGill-Queens University Press, forthcoming.

Percy-Smith, Janie. "Introduction: The Contours of Social Exclusion." In *Policy Responses to Social Exclusion: Towards Inclusion?,* edited by Janie Percy-Smith, 1–21. Buckingham, UK: Open University Press, 2000.

Peters, John Durham. "John Locke, the Individual, and the Origin of Communication." *Quarterly Journal of Speech* 75, no. 4 (1989): 387–99.

Peters, John Durham. *The Marvelous Clouds*. Chicago: University of Chicago Press, 2015.

Peters, John Durham. *Speaking into the Air: A History of the Idea of Communication*. Chicago: University of Chicago Press, 1999.

Peters, John Durham. "The Ten Commandments as Media Theory." In *Communication and Social Life: Studies in Honor of Professor Esteban López-Escobar*, edited by Maxwell McCombs and Manuel Martín Algarra, 275–84. Pamplona: Ediciones Universidad de Navarra, 2012.

Peterson, Richard A. "Understanding Audience Segmentation: From Elite and Mass to Omnivore and Univore." *Poetics* 21 (1992): 243–58.

Pfister, Damien Smith. *Networked Media, Networked Rhetorics: Attention and Deliberation in the Early Blogosphere.* University Park: Pennsylvania State University Press, 2014.

Pfister, Damien Smith, and Carly S. Woods. "The Unnaturalistic Enthymeme: Figuration, Interpretation, and Critique after Digital Mediation." *Argumentation and Advocacy* 52 (Spring 2016): 236–53.

Pippa, Lauren. "Learning to Love." *Goodreads.com*. Goodreads, November 14, 2013.

Plantin, Jean-Christophe, Carl Lagoze, Paul N. Edwards, and Christian Sandvig. "Infrastructure Studies Meet Platform Studies in the Age of Google and Facebook." *New Media and Society* 20, no. 1 (2018): 293–310.

Plato. *Phaedrus*. Translated by Christopher Rowe. New York: Penguin Classics, 2005.

Plato. *Timaeus and Critias*. Translated by Desmond Lee. New York: Penguin Classics, 2008.

Prelli, Lawrence J., ed. *Rhetorics of Display*. Columbia: University of South Carolina Press, 2006.

Preus, Christian Abraham. "The Art of Aeschines: Anti-Rhetorical Argumentation in the Speeches of Aeschines." PhD diss., University of Iowa, 2012.

Public Libraries and Museums Act of 1964. Chapter 75, section 7(1). United Kingdom House of Commons.

Raley, Rita. *Tactical Media*. Minneapolis: University of Minnesota Press, 2009.

Ranie, Lee, Janna Anderson, and Jonathan Albright. "The Future of Free Speech, Trolls, Anonymity and Fake News Online." Pew Research Center, March 29, 2017. https://www.pewresearch.org/internet/2017/03/29/the-future-of-free-speech-trolls-anonymity-and-fake-news-online/

Ratcliffe, Krista. *Rhetorical Listening: Identification, Gender, Whiteness*. Carbondale: Southern Illinois University Press, 2005.

Resmini, Andrea, and Luca Rosati. "A Brief History of Information Architecture." *Journal of Information Architecture* 3, no. 2 (2011): 33–45.

Rice, Jenny. *Distant Publics: Development Rhetoric and the Subject of Crisis*. Pittsburgh, PA: University of Pittsburgh Press, 2012.

Rice, Jenny. "The New 'New': Making a Case for Critical Affect Studies." *Quarterly Journal of Speech* 94, no. 2 (2008): 200–212.

Rickert, Thomas. *Ambient Rhetoric: The Attunements of Rhetorical Being*. Pittsburgh, PA: University of Pittsburgh Press, 2013.

Ritchie, Marnie. "Spectacular Resilience: Visualizations of Endurance in TIME Magazine's 'Beyond 9/11.'" *Visual Communication Quarterly* 25, no 3 (2018): 168–80.

rivka. "How Do Likes Affect Which Reviews Non-Friends See?" Goodreads Feedback Discussion, Goodreads.com, February 22, 2013. Accessed January 16, 2015. No URL for the Goodreads Feedback Discussion group remains.

Robinson, Jenefer M. "Style and Personality in the Literary Work." *Philosophical Review* 94, no. 2 (1985): 227–47.

Rood, Craig. "'Understanding' Again: Listening with Kenneth Burke and Wayne Booth." *Rhetoric Society Quarterly* 44, no. 5 (2014): 449–69.

Rosenbaum, Steven. *Curation Nation*. New York: McGraw-Hill, 2011.

Sampson, Tony D. *Virality: Contagion Theory in the Age of Networks*. Minneapolis: University of Minnesota Press, 2012.

Satz, Aura. "Tableaux Vivants: Inside the Statue." In *Articulate Objects: Voice, Sculpture and Performance*, edited by Aura Satz and Jon Wood, 157–81. Oxford, UK: Peter Lang.

Schaeffer, John. "Commonplaces: Sensus Communis." In *A Companion to Rhetoric and Rhetorical Criticism*, edited by Walter Jost Wendy Olmstead, 278–93. Oxford, UK: Blackwell Publishing, 2004.

Schaeffer, John. *Sensus Communis: Vico, Rhetoric, and the Limits of Relativism.* Durham, NC: Duke University Press, 1990.

Schwartzmantel, John. "Community as Communication: Jean-Luc Nancy and 'Being-in-Common.'" *Political Studies* 55 (2007): 459–76.

Schwarz, Astrid, and Kurt Jax. "Etymology and Original Sources of the Term 'Ecology.'" In *Ecology Revisited: Reflecting on Concepts, Advancing Science*, edited by Astrid Schwartz and Kurt Jax, 144–47. New York: Springer, 2011.

Scott, Piers Dillon. "Google Ireland's Dublin Staff Put on a Performance for the Google Street View Cameras." *The Sociable,* August 10, 2011. https://sociable.co /meme/google-irelands-dublin-staff-put-on-a-performance-for-the-google-street -view-cameras/.

Sedgwick, Eve Kosofsky. *Touching Feeling: Affect, Pedagogy, Performativity.* Durham, NC: Duke University Press, 2003.

Seigworth, Gregory J., and Melissa Gregg. "An Inventory of Shimmers." In *The Affect Theory Reader*, edited by Melissa Gregg and Gregory J. Seigworth, 1–25. Durham, NC: Duke University Press, 2010.

Sennett, Richard. *Together: The Rituals, Pleasures, and Politics of Cooperation.* New Haven, CT: Yale University Press, 2012.

Shannon, Claude E. "A Mathematical Theory of Communication." *The Bell System Technical Journal* 27, no. 3 (1948): 379–423.

Sharma, Sarah. *In the Meantime: Temporality and Cultural Politics.* Durham, NC: Duke University Press, 2014.

Shaviro, Steven. *The Universe of Things: On Speculative Realism.* Minneapolis: University of Minnesota Press, 2014.

Shouse, Eric. "Feeling, Emotion, Affect." *M/C Journal* 8, no. 6 (2005). http://journal .media-culture.org.au/0512/03-shouse.php/.

Shusterman, Richard. *Pragmatist Aesthetics: Living Beauty, Rethinking Art.* 2nd ed. Lanham, MD: Rowman and Littlefield, 2000.

Shusterman, Richard. "Pragmatist Aesthetics: Roots and Radicalism." In *The Critical Pragmatism of Alain Locke*, edited by Leonard Harris, 97–110. Lanham, MD: Rowman and Littlefield, 1999.

Siegert, Bernhard. *Cultural Techniques: Grids, Filters, Doors, and Other Articulations of the Real.* Translated by Geoffrey Winthrop-Young. New York: Fordham University Press, 2015.

Simonson, Peter. "Varieties of Pragmatism and Communication: Visions and Revisions from Peirce to Peters." In *American Pragmatism and Communication Research*, edited by David K. Perry, 1–26. Mahwah, NJ: Lawrence Erlbaum Associates, 2001.

Simonson, Peter, Janice Peck, Robert T. Craig, and John P. Jackson Jr. "The History of Communication History." In *The Handbook of Communication History*, edited by Peter Simonson, Janice Peck, Robert T. Craig, and John P. Jackson Jr., 13–57. New York: Routledge, 2013.

Sontag, Susan. *On Photography.* New York: Anchor Books, 1977.

Sontag, Susan. *Regarding the Pain of Others.* New York: Farrar, Straus and Giroux, 2003.

Spatz, Ben. *What a Body Can Do: Technique as Knowledge, Practice as Research.* New York: Routledge, 2015.

Spinoza, Baruch. *Ethics*. 1677. In *Complete Works*. Translated by Samuel Shirley. Edited by Michael L. Morgan. Indianapolis, IN: Hackett, 2002.

Spitzer, Leo. "Classical and Christian Ideas of World Harmony: Prolegomena to an Interpretation of the Word 'Stimmung': Part 1." *Traditio* 2 (1944): 409–64.

Stallybrass, Peter, and Allon White. *The Politics and Poetics of Transgression*. Ithaca, NY: Cornell University Press, 1986.

"State of the X." TEDx Blog, October 12, 2012. https://blog.ted.com/state-of-the-x-stats -on-tedx-and-tedxtalks-in-january/.

Stengers, Isabelle. "The Cosmopolitical Proposal." In *Making Things Public: Atmospheres of Democracy*, edited by Bruno Latour and Peter Weibel, 994–1003. Cambridge, MA: MIT Press, 2005.

Stewart, Kathleen. *Ordinary Affects*. Durham, NC: Duke University Press, 2007.

Stop the Goodreads Bullies. "Why It's Time to Stop the Goodreads Bullies." *Huffington Post*, July 20, 2012. https://www.huffpost.com/entry/stop-goodreads-bullies_b _1689661.

Stormer, Nathan. "Rhetoric's Diverse Materiality: Polythetic Ontology and Genealogy." *Review of Communication* 16, no. 4 (2016): 299–316.

Stormer, Nathan. "Vibrant Matter: A Political Ecology of Things." *Quarterly Journal of Speech* 101, no. 1 (2015): 317–20.

Stormer, Nathan, and Bridie McGreavy. "Thinking Ecologically about Rhetoric's Ontology: Capacity, Vulnerability, and Resilience." *Philosophy and Rhetoric* 50, no. 1 (2017): 1–25.

Streeter, Thomas. "Internet." In *Digital Keywords*, edited by Benjamin Peters, 184–96. Princeton, NJ: Princeton University Press, 2016.

Striphas, Ted. "Algorithmic Culture." *European Journal of Cultural Studies* 18, nos. 4–5 (2015): 395–412.

Striphas, Ted. "Culture." In *Digital Keywords*, edited by Benjamin Peters, 70–80. Princeton, NJ: Princeton University Press, 2016.

Striphas, Ted. "How to Have Culture in an Algorithmic Age." *Late Age of Print*, June 14, 2010. https://www.thelateageofprint.org/2010/06/14/how-to-have-culture-in-an -algorithmic-age/.

Stroud, Scott. *John Dewey and the Artful Life*. University Park: Pennsylvania State University Press, 2011.

Tandavanitj, Nick. "You Start It." Talk delivered at Communication, Rhetoric, and Digital Media Symposium, North Carolina State University, March 27, 2018.

Tapscott, Don, and Anthony D. Williams. *Wikinomics: How Mass Collaboration Changes Everything*. New York: Portfolio, 2008.

Taylor, Charles. *Modernity and the Rise of the Public Sphere*. The Tanner Lectures on Human Values, vol. 14. Salt Lake City: University of Utah Press, 1992.

Taylor, Charles. *Modern Social Imaginaries*. Durham, NC: Duke University Press, 2004.

"TED Reaches Its Billionth Video View!" TED Blog, November 13, 2012. https://blog.ted. com/ted-reaches-its-billionth-video-view/.

Terranova, Tiziana. *Network Culture: Politics for the Information Age*. London: Pluto, 2004.

Thrift, Nigel. "Intensities of Feeling: Toward a Spatial Politics of Affect." *Geografiska Annaler*, series B, Human Geography, 86, no. 1 (2004): 57–78.

Thrift, Nigel. *Knowing Capitalism*. London: Sage, 2005.

Thrift, Nigel. "Still Life in Nearly Present Time: The Object of Nature." *Body and Society* 6, nos. 3–4 (2000): 34–57.

Toffler, Alvin. *The Third Wave*. New York: Morrow, 1980.

Townsend, Peter. *Poverty in the United Kingdom*. London: Penguin, 1979.

Tuan, Yi-Fu. *Space and Place: The Perspective of Experience*. Minneapolis: University of Minnesota Press, 1977.

Verboord, Marc. "The Legitimacy of Book Critics in the Age of the Internet and Omnivorousness: Expert Critics, Internet Critics and Peer Critics in Flanders and the Netherlands." *European Sociological Review* 26, no. 6 (2010): 623–37.

Victoria. "Learning to Love by Lauren Howard." *Victorialovesbooks*, August 10, 2013. https://victorialovesbooks.wordpress.com/2013/08/19/learning-to-love-by-lauren -howard/.

Vivian, Bradford. *Being Made Strange: Rhetoric Beyond Representation*. Albany: State University of New York Press, 2004.

Wagner, John R. "Water and the Commons Imaginary." *Current Anthropology* 53, no. 5 (2012): 617–41.

Wallace, Benjamin. "Those Fabulous Confabs." *New York*, February 26, 2012.

Wallrup, Erik. *Being Musically Attuned: The Act of Listening to Music*. Surrey, UK: Ashgate, 2015.

Warner, Michael. *Publics and Counterpublics*. Brooklyn, NY: Zone Books, 2002.

Waxman, Olivia B. "This Is the Story behind Your 'I Voted' Sticker." *Time*, November 7, 2016. https://time.com/4541760/i-voted-sticker-history-origins/.

Wellbery, David. Foreword to *Discourse Networks 1800/1900*, by Friedrich Kittler. Translated by Michael Metteer, with Chris Cullens. Stanford, CA: Stanford University Press, 1990.

Wellbery, David. "Stimmung." Translated by Rebecca Pohl. *new formations: a journal of culture/theory/politics* 93 (2018): 6–45.

Wetherell, Margaret. *Affect and Emotion: A New Social Science Understanding*. London: Sage, 2012.

Whitehead, Alfred North. *Adventures of Ideas*. 1933. Reprint, New York: Free Press, 1961.

Whitehead, Alfred North. *Modes of Thought*. 1938. Reprint, New York: Free Press, 1966.

Williams, Alex. "On the Tip of Creative Tongues." *New York Times*, October 2, 2009. https://www.nytimes.com/2009/10/04/fashion/04curate.html ?searchResultPosition=1.

Williams, Mary Elizabeth. "Did a Writer Get Bullied on Goodreads?" *Salon.com*. Salon, August 21, 2013. https://www.salon.com/2013/08/21/debut_author_allegedly_got _rape_threats_on_goodreads/.

Williams, Raymond. "Culture Is Ordinary" (1958). In Raymond Williams, *Resources of Hope: Culture, Democracy, Socialism*, edited by Robin Gable, 3–18. London: Verso, 1989.

Williams, Raymond. *The Long Revolution*. 1961. Reprint, Peterborough, Ont.: Broadview Press, 2001.

Williams, Raymond. *Marxism and Literature*. Oxford, UK: Oxford University Press, 1977.

Winthrop-Young, Geoffrey. "Cultural Techniques: Preliminary Remarks." *Theory, Culture & Society* 30, no. 6 (2013): 3–19.

Wolf, Gary. "The Wurmanizer." *Wired* 8.02, February 2000. Available from https://www.wurman.com/publishedarticles/tag/Gary+Wolf. Accessed October 21, 2019.

Woolf, Virginia. "Reviewing" (1939). In *Collected Essays Volume 2*, 204–17. London: The Hogarth Press, 1966.

World Press Photo. "2011 Photo Contest." Worldpressphoto.org, n.d. Accessed January 16, 2015.

Yeats, William Butler. "The Scholars." In *The Collected Poems of W. B. Yeats*, edited by Richard J. Finneran, 140–41. New York: Scribner, 1996.

Zickuhr, Kathryn, Lee Rainie, and Kristen Purcell. "Library Services in the Digital Age." Internet and American Life Project. Washington, DC: Pew Research Center, 2013. https://www.pewresearch.org/internet/2013/01/22/library-services/.

Zola, Émile. *The Ladies' Paradise*. 1883. Translated by Brian Nelson. Oxford: Oxford University Press, 2008.

Zolberg, Vera L. "The Happy Few: En Masse Franco-American Comparisons in Cultural Democratization." In *The Arts of Democracy: Art, Public Culture, and the State*, edited by Casey Nelson Blake, 97–122. Washington, DC: Woodrow Wilson Center Press, 2007.

Zuboff, Shoshana. *The Age of Surveillance Capitalism: The Fight for a Human Future at the New Frontier of Power*. New York: PublicAffairs, 2019.

Amazon, 111, 116–18, 131

ambience, 6, 17, 24, 26, 41, 50, 65, 77, 120, 133, 162, 181, 183–84

argument: ad hominem, 124–27; vs. assertion, 60; body as, 72; character assassination, 127; *dissoi logoi*, 142–45; enthymemes, 172–73; in public spheres, 70, 76, 118–19; stasis theory and, 84–85; visual, 172–73

art: commodification of, 67, 86; encounters with, 118, 184; ethics and, 126; and experience, 78–80, 87–88, 92–95; gestures as, 64–68; habit and, 178; history of, 87–88; and life boundary, 78–80, 94, 96, 190; and participation, 12–13; as political, 68, 86; as process, 13; understandings of, 12–13, 96, 199n32. *See also* the aesthetic

asignification, 19, 40–42, 50, 66, 85, 119–20, 150–52, 163

atmosphere, 8, 41, 44, 50, 120, 162

attunement: to concerned gestures, 20, 53, 64, 164, 193, 195; to concerned-ness, 29, 188; idiot rhetoric and, 50; to others, 119, 133, 158, 192; and TED, 32, 38

Auden, W. H., 13, 19, 175, 187–92

Barthes, Roland, 168–69, 180

Bartholl, Aram, 175–78, 181

Berlant, Lauren, 4–5, 18, 26, 62, 136, 184–85, 198n13, 200n48, 201n7, 207n26, 222n57

Black Lives Matter, 73–74, 209n66

Blast Theory, 88–89, 93, 211n31

bodies: affect and, 39–41, 64, 74–75, 150, 185; autonomic processes of, 28; biological status, 72; entanglement with, 193; as extrasymbolic, 73–74; field of, 9; hearing and, 31–32; hunger strikes and, 72, 154–55; limits of, 6, 31; movement of, 53, 59–60; parts of, 92–93; politic, 26; proxemics of, 18; race and, 74; rhetoric of, 72–74; sense and, 189–90; technicity of, 56; threat and, 3. *See also*

argument: body as; gestures: bodily; representation: bodies and

bookshelves, 114–116, 120–21, 126–28, 134–35, 153, 216n1

Braidotti, Rosi, 3, 179, 200n52

Burke, Kenneth, 16, 60–61, 106, 121, 192

capacity: and affect, 2, 40; of art, 66; to mean, 72; political, 52, 109; public spheres and, 70; rhetorical force and, 109–10; vs. agency, 109–10

change: background for, 165, 193; as constant; form of concern and, 28; gestures and, 52, 106, 194; hope and, 3–5, 198n3; as ongoing, 145, 154, 162, 184, 189; spurred by speech, 27, 37–38, 47, 51, 88, 109; taking hold, 20–21, 185, 193; and the unfamiliar, 195, 209n66

circulation: of affect, 75–76, 85, 97, 106; of contributions, 62–65; of ideas, 38, 47; and images, 181–82, 207n42; and media, 82, 112, 119, 167; of rhetoric 70–71

citizen: as consumer, 143–44; as nodal, 213n6; types of, 191

citizen artists and critics: affect and, 181–82; conflict between, 109, 125–32, 134; creative democracy and, 96, 107; curatorial media and, 111; defined, 110–11; democratization and, 19, 79–80, 86–88, 94–95; ethos and, 116, 125; gestures of, 109–10, 119, 170; replenishment and, 134, 160

Clegg and Guttman, 134–35, 153

commons: as affective, 198n13; citing a, 178–81; as elsewhere, 176; and private property, 135, 216n3; as public, 99; and shared concern, 119; sighting a, 170–74, 181; siting a, 175–78, 181; as temporary, 85; varieties of, 162

commons imaginary: and affective com-monwealth, 181; vs. social imaginary, 164–66; virtuality of, 176–78 commonwealth: public work and, 6, 182–83, 222n55; public spaces of, 182; shared resources of, 5–6; under construction, 6, 37, 133, 145, 157, 191

communication: aestheticized, 82–83; C-B-S model of, 36, 45–46, 49; constraints on, 111–12, 129, 136–37; content of, 8–9, 50, 63–64, 135; corruptible, 169–70; definition of, 24; digitality of, 8–10; distilled into gesture, 8; emotion as, 39; histories of, 24, 201n4; idea of, 24, 135; materiality of, 56, 72–74, 135, 184; mathematical model of, 46, 205n56; paradoxes of, 192–93; as ritual transmission, 48–49, 64, 67–68, 169; ritual view of, 47; transmission view of, 47

communicative capitalism: and digital culture, 7, 65, 130; and experience, 50; fantasy of, 4, 143; glorifying talk, 36–37, 50; and idiot, 37; messages replaced by contributions, 62–65, 68, 169; reductive politics and, 36, 203n36. See also Dean, Jodi

community: art and, 5–6, 199n37; building of, 48, 92, 154–59, 183, 211n32; and curation, 97–98, 106; Goodreads as, 115–16, 121, 125–28; 133–35; as incomplete, 159; libraries and, 138–42, 145–48; vs. public spheres, 172; without community, 113–14

concern: activity of, 28, 187–88; and affective commonwealths, 11, 166; as chorography, 28; and emotion, 15; etymology of, 193; as existential, 27, 52, 193; experience and, 27–30, 187; expression of, 1, 13, 15, 25, 30–31, 53–54, 60, 85, 140, 193–95; form and content of, 1, 28; identification of, 28–29, 62; as ideologically conditioned, 37; and idiot, 26–27, 31, 49, 79, 195; of lifeworld, 15, 118; as mood, 32; multiple inflections of, 27; and public affairs, 25, 79, 144, 163, 180–81; Quaker sense of, 29–30; as

unknown, 28–29; as vigorous, 145; for Whitehead, 29–30

consensus, 70, 85, 113, 124, 144, 146, 166, 170, 182

content: adjacency of affect to, 4, 20, 85, 114, 152; of concern, 28; contributions to, 11, 62–63, 81–82, 106, 113, 135, 170; curation of, 95, 105; and form, 75; talk itself as, 64; technology and, 19, 106–8, 198n21; TED and, 30–31, 38, 43–50

contingency (rhetoric's), 16, 24–25, 39–40, 60, 112, 118, 130, 181

countability. See quantification

creative democracy, 10–13, 37, 95–96, 107, 199

cultural politics, 10, 48, 187, 223n3

cultural public spheres: and affective experience 14–15, 66; curation in, 97, 111–14, 125–26; gestural engagement in, 15; historical basis of, 14–15, 163, 181–82; the political and, 186; texts-and-talk model, 117–20, 180–81, 183

cultural techniques, 9, 51, 55–59, 71, 120–21, 127, 175

curation: art and, 102–3; as commercial, 103–5; conflict with democratization, 108–9, 125–26, 185–86; culture of, 12, 96; of culture, 79–80, 82, 95–97, 102–3; Google and, 108–9, 170; history of, 97–107; of images, 170–75, 181; pedagogical use of, 103, 212n40; as public, 97–99; as rhetorical, 39, 97, 121, 212n40; as scientific, 100–102; as social practice, 80, 97; as spiritual, 99–100; as technological, 105–7; and TED, 34, 39; as vernacular, 80, 96–99, 114; Web 2.0 and, 81–82

data, 8–9, 48, 106–7, 111–12, 116, 118, 123, 142, 197n8, 198n21, 213n58, 214n13

Dean, Jodi, 4, 36–38, 62–64, 68, 113–14, 130, 169, 186, 197n8, 203nn36–37

Deleuze, Gilles, 47, 85, 194, 198n17, 207n41

deliberation, 36, 64, 83, 113, 137, 145

democratization: of creativity, 12, 19, 79–82, 86–87, 94–96, 107–9, 182, 186, 191; defined, 81

Dewey, John, 11–13, 79, 95–96, 107, 190, 199n32, 200n51, 204n41

discursive norms, 16, 24, 81, 115–17, 124–31, 201n8, 216n65

disposition: as affective, 6, 7, 62, 71, 76, 114, 120, 159, 163, 181, 183; public, 18, 80, 161; and gesture, 26, 83–84; and TED, 32, 36, 38, 43, 50

ecclesia, 24, 27, 47, 50, 99, 164, 201, 201n11

ecologies: as affective, 68, 71, 106, 111, 123, 125, 128, 152, 185; of affective and symbolic orders, 66; collapse of, 193; communicative, 70–71, 77, 117–18; disconnections in, 74; etymology of, 208n55; rhetorical, 17, 208n56; vs. situation 71

efficiency, 8, 18, 45–48, 63, 102, 138–39, 149

emotion: artists and, 95; atmosphere of, 41; elicitation of, 83, 152–53; expression of, 40, 151–53; investments of, 15, 26; non-neutrality of, 30; precarity and, 136–37; semanticized, 7, 39, 150, 159; TED and, 44–46. *See also* affect: vs. emotion and feeling

encounter: affective, 20, 30, 40, 44, 119, 165, 166; agency and, 110; atmosphere of, 41, 44, 50, 120; capacities of, 31; enmeshed in, 25, 28; memes and, 85, 119; with others, 74, 97; as sensuous, 31, 61, 192. *See also* the aesthetic: encounters with; affectability: of encounters; art: encounters with

environments, 10, 64, 67, 70, 74, 105, 123, 178, 184

epistemology, 7–10, 81, 198n21

ethos: of citizenship, 111; conundrum, 114–17, 125, 131; gesture and, 129; parameters of, 125–27; paradoxes of, 128,

participatory, 123; rhetorical, 122–23, 216n51

the everyday: and the aesthetic, 78–80, 82, 87, 94–96, 110; residual space of, 151; and vernacularity, 159

exclusion, 3, 17, 125, 134, 168, 182, 188, 201n8. *See also* social exclusion

experience: communication and, 192; everyday, 3, 50, 70, 94, 137, 189–190; gestures and, 56; impervious to capture, 18, 20; in-process, 5, 7, 10–11, 13, 19, 27–28, 131; new, 179; private, 135, 178; public, 70, 115, 178; rhetoric and, 71; shared, 110; voting and, 69. *See also* the aesthetic: experience and; affect: experience and; art: and experience

expression: affectivity of, 41, 155; defined, 85; as expression, 54; gestures of concern and, 84–85; of ideas, 38–39; phatic, 169; self-, 12, 77, 109, 111, 126–27; of taste, 97, 116, 121; voting and, 68–70, 208n50. *See also* the aesthetic: expression of; gestures: expressivity of

Fairey, Shepard, 66–67, 67, 75, 207n42; 208n43

fetishization, 37, 63

Flusser, Vilém, 59, 178, 192–93, 199n26, 206n17

force: affective, 17, 40, 52, 54, 68, 94, 130; as force-effects, 84; of memes, 85–86; of photo filters, 83; of rhetoric, 46; of stickers, 65, 67; of togetherness, 41

freedom: and the aesthetic, 65; discursive, 81, 117, 127; and gestures, 20; legal, 94

fungibility, 9, 46, 48, 62, 65, 185

gestures: the aesthetic and, 64–68, 83–86, 92–94, 188; bodily, 1, 10, 15, 52, 54, 206nn1–2, 206n19; as commons, 7, 162–64; communicability and, 10, 75, 135, 153, 164; content of, 113; definitions of, 10, 206n1, 206n17; as discursive acts, 122; emotion and, 15; ethos and, 129; examples of, 1–2; expressivity of, 2, 6, 84, 164; force of, 37, 59, 64, 74, 86, 122, 164, 193–194; vs. gestures of concern, 52–53, 206n19; "Get Well" cards as, 1–2, 10, 52, 194; as means and ends, 11, 13, 164, 184–85; mediated nature of, 10, 60, 135–36; as micro-activist, 136; as minor, 62, 113–14, 194, 199n34; as mood-inducing, 63, 65; reconfiguring the social, 7–8, 166; of refusal, 25, 129–30, 194–95; sensibility of, 61, 68; tools and, 56; types of, 52–54

Goodreads, 20, 110–32, 157

Guattari, Felix, 47, 73, 194, 207n41

Haraway, Donna, 5, 162

Hauser, Jerry, 16–17, 70, 72

Henner, Mishka, 171–75, 181

Hooke, Robert, 100–101; 212n49

hope, 3, 5, 7, 37, 44, 49, 63, 66, 76, 143, 155, 170, 184, 198n3

Howard, Lauren, 115–16, 125, 128–32, 195

identification: affect and, 73; rhetoric and, 106, 121, 215n40; books and, 126–27

ideology, 8–9, 31, 37, 54, 67, 77, 114, 151, 167, 170, 175, 198n21, 218n35

the idiot: ambivalence of, 25–26, 52; capacity of, 52; and Cusa, 46, 205n59; and Dostoevsky, 47; figure of, 46–47, 50; listening and, 27, 32, 49–52, 61, 164, 193; queerness of, 25, 201n8, 219n56; Trump as, 108–9; as withdrawn/drawnwith, 24–25, 201n6

idiotes: concern of, 25, 29, 31, 61; historical meaning of, 201n11; as nonengaged, 24, 26, 88; as private, 23, 47, 192–93; vs. *rhetores*, 23–26, 29, 31–32, 37, 49, 88, 130. *See also* idiot rhetoric: in antiquity

idiot rhetoric: affect and, 47; in antiquity, 185, 222n59; building affective commonwealths, 185; commons and, 164; feminism of, 219n56; gestures of concern and, 26, 50–51, 161, 164, 185, 194; as invitational rhetoric, 219n56; not circumscribed, 130–31; passive appearance of, 130, 150; refusal as, 25, 48 129–31, 158, 194–95; slowing down of, 50, 129, 158, 179, 184–85, 195; unfinished character of, 145, 195

inclusivity, 2, 34–37, 81, 117, 130, 137, 141, 148, 162, 168

infrastructure, 7, 111, 134, 213n8

instrumentality, 1–2, 26, 54, 64, 72, 84, 134, 157, 159, 193

interpretation: of the impalpable, 83–84; inadequacy of, 165–66; lost zest from, 4; prefabricated, 184; refusal to be subjected to, 159; regime of, 67–68; of talk, 118–20. *See also* nonhermeneutics

James, William, 75, 192, 197n6

judgment: of the aesthetic, 116, 124–28; as affective, 64, 120, 159; civic context of, 137, 152, 183; as rhetorical, 16–17, 23, 47, 63, 69–70, 121, 125, 155

Kittler, Friedrich, 7–9, 56, 113

labor, 104, 113, 213n58, 214n20, 214n30

Latour, Bruno, 27, 53, 206n3, 209n59

libraries: closure of, 137, 140; crisis of, 136, 139–40, 157; cultural policy and, 136–37, 140, 145; *dissoi logoi* and, 142–45; DIY, 136, 159, 163; history of Brent libraries, 137–39; Kensal Rise, 137–39, 147, 149, 152–58, 195; Library Transformation Project, 139–40, 145–46, 148, 217n22; Open Library Project, 134–35; Pop-Up, 153–58; protest and, 145–49, 152–60; public spheres and, 139–40, 144, 152; rhetoric and, 136, 142–45; stickers and, 51; Willesden Green, 137–39, 146–49 listening: as social practice, 31–32. *See also* the idiot: listening and; TED: listening and

literary public sphere, 14, 118–19, 124–25, 129, 163, 182, 199n36–37

literature, 119, 121, 124–26, 159, 163

matters of concern, 14, 27, 53, 71, 181–84

Massumi, Brian, 39, 84, 150, 197n5, 202n19, 204n42, 204n46

meaning: affect's independence from, 40, 66, 151; constitution of, 9; eclipse of, 168–69; as epiphenomena of communication, 4; interpretive quests for, 20; meaning-full vs. meaning-able, 9, 161, 198n23; possibility of, 183–84; sense preferred over, 31, 67, 82, 85–86, 163, 197n7; symbolicity and, 17, 41, 80, 114; transformation into, 68; without, 2, 4, 47, 68, 73, 192; zest and, 4, 197

meaning-effects, 31, 61, 75, 180

media: curatorial, 106, 111, 116, 131–32, 191, 215n48; digital, 8, 106, 112, 166; and the senses, 189–91; social, 8, 14, 52, 54, 63, 69, 106, 110–11, 114, 121, 213; tactical, 166, 195

memes, 63–54, 85–86, 119

messages: communication of, 26, 47, 51; as contributions, 62–65, 68, 169; gesture and 83; ideological, 167; indifference to, 198; intentional, 60; message board, 115–16, 125; propositional, 86, 114, 163; representation and, 10, 59; symbolic basis of, 43, 50, 67, 97. *See also* communicative capitalism: messages replaced by contributions

Milner, Adam, 92–93

mood: affectability as, 75–76; as ambient, 6, 50, 65, 133; as background, 188, 193; lacking objects, 84; vs. meaning, 43, 49, 65, 82; and orientation, 71, 75, 166, 185; setting a tone, 6, 83, 120, 145, 150, 163; as shared, 6, 26, 84, 145; as social, 71, 85

nonhermeneutics: vs. hermeneutics, 9, 119; interpretability and, 46, 61; interpretation and, 9, 20, 31, 54–55; materiality of communication and, 56; method of, 20, 30–32, 117–20, 165

ontology: as flat, 72–73, 209n59; as polythetic, 223n60

optimism, 3–5, 157

Pedwell, Carolyn, 197n1, 209n66, 221n47

persuadability: and affect, 71–74, 120, 158; and change, 165; cultural public spheres and, 19; and gestures, 20; and rhetoric, 19, 158–59

Peters, John Durham, 7, 9, 24, 43, 198, 206n8

photography: affect and, 169; communication through, 82, 106; digital affordances of, 65, 80–85, 95, 190; emotional power of, 168; Google Street View and, 163, 167–68, *171*, 171–74, 178; punctum and, 168–69, 173, 180; street, 166–68; studium and, 168–69, 173; ubiquity of, 161, 184

Piper, Adrian, 89–92

Pippa, Lauren. *See* Howard, Lauren

pragmatism, 33, 79, 96, 190, 204n41, 208n57; and communication, 10–11, 199n29

preconditions, 6, 20, 30, 42, 120, 137, 151, 219n60, 221n53

presence-effects, 4, 31, 61, 180, 197n7

provisional affinity, 18–21, 64, 85, 194, 201n54

public opinion, 64, 113–14, 117, 145, 160, 170, 181–82, 184, 222n55

public spheres: and civil society, 70, 130, 144, 181; historical basis of, 165, 181–83; and internet, 81–82; as intimate, 62; normative theory of, 130–31, 144, 169–70, 172; rhetorical constitution of, 15–18, 70, 76–77. *See also* cultural public spheres; literary public sphere

pure persuasion, 60–61, 65, 106, 206n19

quantification: and affective remainder, 40, 48; as countability 7–8, 69; and hierarchies, 122–23; and transmission 47–48; and voting, 68–70

relational aesthetics, 20, 86–89, 211n25, 211n32

replenishment, 5–6, 134, 156–60, 162, 184

representation: art and 13, 66, 92, 102; and becoming imperceptible, 178–80; bodies and, 72–74; conditions for, 55; gestures and, 59–60; images and, 169–70, 174, 178; of imaginaries, 164–65; matter and 72–73; meaning and, 55, 75, 85–86; and media, 7, 190; and mediality, 10; and Pop-Up library, 153–55; and public associations, 19, 200n50; rhetoric and, 48, 72, 75, 85, 119–20; stickers as, 60

Rhetores: historical role of, 23, 201n11; as politically active, 31–32, 37, 88; as public subjects, 26, 29, 31; and speech, 23, 26, 29, 32, 37

rhetoric: and affect, 18, 73, 75, 185–86; as ambient, 17, 181; in antiquity, 15–16, 23–27, 49, 88, 222n56, 222n59; art of, 16; of display and demonstration, 219n62; form and content of, 59; making things matter, 185; nonsymbolicity of, 17–18, 46, 71–74; and public life, 71, 76; democracy and, 15–16, 23–24, 207n21, 211nn36–37; as discursive, 72–73; gesture and, 15, 206n2; influence and, 46, 60, 75, 185; materiality of, 72–74, 209n75; practice of, 16, 197n1; as a relational art, 88; and salience, 16–17, 60, 70, 72–73, 106, 118, 137, 142, 144, 150–52, 159, 181; symbolic basis of, 16–18, 66,

185, 200nn43–44; as visual, 209n65; *See also* vernacular rhetoric

rhetorical sociality, 17, 73, 85, 88, 94–95, 119, 183–86

rhetoricity: as always-here, 73, 183; ecology of, 17; as para-symbolic, 17; radical passivity of, 25–26. *See also* persuadability

Rice, Jenny, 61–64, 71, 76, 208n56

Rickert, Thomas, 17, 73, 200n45, 202n18

ritual transmission. *See* communication: as ritual transmission

self-sufficiency, 65, 81, 121, 151, 153–55, 182, 184, 193–94

sense: of concern, 188; -experience, 163; as sensation, 206n19; of something, 26–27, 31, 36, 52, 54, 58, 63, 74, 164; of togetherness, 69

signification, 20, 30–31, 36, 60, 64–68, 72–73, 113, 150, 169

social contract, 88, 93–95, 191

social exclusion, 139–41, 148, 217nn24–25. *See also* libraries: cultural policy and

social imaginary, 24–25, 164–66, 191

sociality: as aestheticized, 82–86. *See also* rhetorical sociality

speech: free, 126; gesture and 15, 53; oratorical, 11, 23, 35–36, 32–39, 43–46, 49, 62, 88, 99, 149, 163. *See also* talk

Spinoza, Baruch, 40–41, 198n17, 206n17

stasis: as affective, 84–85, 194; in rhetoric, 84

status signals, 2, 106, 113–14, 122, 189

stickers: as art, 64–68; bumper, 57–59, 62–63, 71, 162; as cultural technique, 55–59; digital, 64–65, 82; as gestures, 52–54, 59, 64–68; history of, 56–59; prevalence of, 51; rhetorical function of, 60; voting and, 69, 69–70. *See also* Fairey, Shepard; Vandalina

stimmung, *See* attunement

Stormer, Nathan, 46, 110, 205n57, 213nn3–5, 223n60
Striphas, Ted, 112, 214n13, 218n28
structures of feeling. *See* affective commonwealth
the subject: citizenship as formation of, 13, 107; as coalitional, 154, 164, 219n63; as dividuated, 8–9, 198n22; as perceiving, 31, 96; as precarious, 150; as predetermined, 40; as unified, 48, 50; rhetoric's dependence upon, 48
subjectivity: algorithmic culture and, 112; as private, 124; as public, 24–26, 61–62, 109, 125, 181, 191; conditions for, 30
surveillance, 2, 3, 6, 173, 207n26
symbolic orders, 41–42, 47–50, 66, 70–71, 76, 119–20, 125–26, 152, 166, 181, 193, 205n48
symbolicity, 17, 41, 54, 70, 72, 114, 119, 151, 181, 200nn43–44

talk: concern and, 28; as content, 64; as political action, 37–39, 50–51; public, 23, 182; rhetoric and, 49, 183; texts and, 117–19, 181; vs. work, 183
TED: commandments, 42–45; communicative capitalism and, 37–39; history of, 32–36; and ideas, 30–49; inspiring hope, 37; listening and, 30–32, 49–52, 61, 119; rhetoric and, 35, 39, 43–46; TED Talks, 31–39, 51, 54, 119, 165

togetherness, 3, 7, 20, 41, 51, 69, 73, 193–94
touch, 39, 74, 92, 105, 190, 204n44

uncommonwealth, 133, 136, 145, 158, 162, 186. *See also* commonwealth

Vandalina, 53–55, 55, 58, 71, 75, 206n4
vernacular curation. *See* curation: as vernacular
vernacular rhetoric: as affective, 135–36, 150–53, 155, 158–60; and the everyday, 151–52, 159, 191–92; as idiot rhetoric, 217n11; vs. institutional, 136–37; 149, 153; photography and, 166–68; publics and, 15–16, 144; theories of, 136–37, 217n11; voices in Brent protests, 145–49
virality, 12, 38, 63–64, 220n28
the virtual: affect and, 39–41; vs. actual, 64, 79, 88–89; potentiality of, 65, 177, 197n5
voting, 68–69, 201n11, 208n50

Whitehead, Alfred North, 11, 27–30, 49, 202nn19–20, 202n42
withdrawal, 24–25, 31–32, 201n6, 222n59
Wolf, Michael, 170–75, 181, 221n35

zest, 4, 88, 164, 179, 179n6